The Wheel of Time

of

Time

SAND MANDALA

el of Time
ND MANDALA

Visual Scripture of Tibetan Buddhism

FOREWORD BY THE XIV DALAI LAMA

by

BARRY BRYANT

IN COOPERATION WITH
NAMGYAL MONASTERY

HarperSanFrancisco
A Division of HarperCollinsPublishers

FIRST EDITION

Library of Congress Cataloging-in-Publication Data
Bryant, Barry
    The wheel of time sand mandala : visual scripture of Tibetan Buddhism /
Barry Bryant – lst ed.
        p.   cm.
    ISBN 0–06–250089–9
        1. Kalachakra (Tantric rite)—Tibet.   2. Buddhism—Tibet.   I. Title.
BQ7699.K34B73   1992
294.5'37—dc20   91–59044
                                                                                  CIP

92   93   94   95   96   ❖   RRD(H)   10   9   8   7   6   5   4   3   2   1

This edition is printed on acid-free paper that meets the American National Standards Institute Z39.48 Standard.

In Appreciation

For their valued wisdom and time, my deepest gratitude to

Ven. Tenzin Yignyen,

Ven. Lobsang Samten, Ven. Pema Lobsang Chogyen,

Ven. Thondup Lobsang Gyaltsen, Ven. Jamphel Lhundup,

Ven. Tenzin Migyur, Ven. Tenzin Legdan, Ven. Lobsang Gyaltsen,

Very Ven. Kirti Tsenshab Rinpoche,

and

Deborah Moldow and Gregory Durgin

contents

Acknowledgments

THE WHEEL OF TIME SAND MANDALA: *Visual Scripture of Tibetan Buddhism* owes its inspiration to His Holiness the Dalai Lama, who has devoted great energy and commitment to the continuity of these splendid and perfect teachings of the Buddha.

I am deeply indebted to the monks of Namgyal Monastery who participated—in particular Lobsang Samten, the first monk to work on the project, who, with Thondup Lobsang Gyaltsen, Jamphel Lhundup and Pema Lobsang Chogyen, answered countless questions and generously gave of themselves; and to Tenzin Yignyen, who spent one year with me translating sacred Kalachakra literature and explaining the philosophical meanings of Kalachakra, for his steadfast discipline and warmth. Thanks are also owed to Tenzin Migyur, Tenzin Legdan, and Lobsang Gyaltsen.

I would like to pay particular acknowledgment to Sakya Trizen Rinpoche, the 98th Ganden Tripa, Jamgong Kongtrul Rinpoche, Kalu Rinpoche, and Chogay Trichen Rinpoche for their inspiration and devotion to Kalachakra; and to Kirti Tsenshab Rinpoche, whose hours of explanation of the Kalachakra Tantra on beautiful spring days in Dharamsala added substantially to the text. I also want to thank the many translators, including Kalsang Dhondup, Tenzin Sherab, Karma Lekshe Tsomo, and Tenzin Gyatso from the Dialectic School, Philippe Goldin, Ken McLeod, and Namgyal Korkhor. Thanks also to Tenzin Geyche Tethong, Lodi Gyari, Rinchen Dharlo and Michele Bohana.

I would like to express my heart-felt appreciation and thanks to Deborah Moldow, whose long hours and devotion to this book have been invaluable during the lengthy process of writing, rewriting, and editing. My thanks also to William Meyers for his generous support in completing the editorial process. I am also grateful for the research and editorial work done by Norvie Bullock, Karma Lekshe Tsomo, Daia Gerson, Helen Tworkov, Elizabeth Selandia, Ellen Pearlman, Vivian Kurz, and especially Peter Sheene and Maria Dolores Hajosy Benedetti.

Without the able input of the indomitable Gregory Durgin and my brother Stan Bryant, this project simply would not have been possible. I also greatly appreciate the guidance I received from Valrae Reynolds of the Newark Museum concerning the visual materials in the book.

Other valued advisors included Alexander Berzin and Professor Robert A.F. Thurman, holder of the Jey Tsong Khapa Chair of Columbia University. My thanks also to Phuntsok Dorje, Moke Mokotoff, Barbara Lipton of the Jacques Marchais Center of Tibetan Art, Jean and Francis Paone, Christian Lischewski, Perkins + Will, Daniel Maciejczyk, Somi Roy, Dr. Mikhail Khusidman, John Bigelow Taylor, and Dianne Dubler.

I also want to express my special thanks to my parents Carolyn and Frank Bryant, and to Glenn Bryant, Nancy Scheyer, Warner Scheyer, Joe Cobuccio, Kathryn Feldman, Scott Friedman, Elena Konovalova, Brian Adams, Soho Black and White, Ann Wilson (whose introduction to Malcolm Arth at the American Museum of Natural History opened the door), Dr. Peter Keller of the Natural History Museum of Los Angeles County, Dr. Pratapaditya Pal of the Los Angeles County Museum of Art, Beverly Walton and John Denver of Windstar Foundation, and Jean and Francis Paone.

Thanks are due to Helene Silverman with whom long hours of design esthetics were shared to illuminate this book, with the help of Scott Frommer and the inspiration of Tony Smith and Marcel Duchamp.

Further, I would like to express my gratitude to Fred Segal, Joan Brady, LeVar Burton, Barry and Connie Hershey, Chris Sarazen, Maggie Kress, Barbara and Bruce Bordeau, Dennis Konner, Fred Koenig, Marvin Ostroff, Stanley and Elyse Grinstein, Jane Smith, Sally Sachs, David LaFaille, Bruce Bryant, Madelaine Brostrom, Carol Moss, Szajna Kellman, Tom and Margot Pritzker, Bonnie Lundgren, Rita Narang, Francesca Kress, Jack Mayberry, and the New York State Council on the Arts for their enthusiasm, support, and encouragement.

And for their support in bringing this book from concept to publication, my sincere thanks to Mia Grosjean, Barbara Ascher, Jacqueline Onassis, Judy Sandman, Kara Laverte, Patrick Jordan, Kate Coleman, Ani Chamichian, Dick Carter, Dennis Dalrymple, Karen Lotz, Julia Moore, and especially John Loudon and HarperSanFrancisco.

Finally, my special thanks for their diligence and clarity to Tashi Tsering, Ngawang Topgyal, and Thupten Champhel of the Namgyal Monastery Committee, Michael Cohen, Esq. and Ada Clapp, Esq. of Davis, Polk & Wardwell, Sidney Piburn of Snow Lion Publications, Richard Weingarten of the Tibet Fund, Frank Douglas, Esq., Barbara Hoffman, Esq., Reed Wasson, Esq., the staff of Volunteer Lawyers for the Arts, and last, but certainly not least, Robyn Brenano.

The XIV Dalai Lama

FOREWORD

FROM THE VERY BEGINNING, the teachings of the Buddha have been
concerned with fulfilling the wish shared by every living being to find
peace and happiness and avoid suffering. Moreover, because all beings
have an equal right to pursue these goals and because, even among
human beings, there are wide differences of interest, character, and ability, the Buddha taught a vast array of methods.

These mostly deal with the need to develop clarity of mind, purity
of behavior, and a correct view of reality. They involve meditation and a
code of ethics summarized as seeking to avoid harming others, actively
helping them if you can, and a realization of the interdependence, and
hence the lack of an inherent identity, of all phenomena.

Of all the different kinds of teachings the Buddha gave, Tibetan tradition regards the tantras as the highest. Outwardly, the practitioner
maintains a life-style that accords with pure ethics; internally, he or she
cultivates an altruistic intention to attain the state of a Buddha. Then,
secretly, through the practice of deity yoga, concentrating on the inner
channels, essential drops, and energy winds, the practitioner enhances his
or her progress to enlightenment.

The Kalachakra system was one of the last and most complex tantric
systems to be brought to Tibet from India. In recent years many Westerners have become acquainted with this tradition as various lamas have
given the Kalachakra Initiation to large groups of people. I myself have
given it several times in Western countries, as well as in India and
Tibet. Such initiations are given on the basis of a mandala, the sacred
residence with its resident deities, usually depicted in graphic form.
The tradition I follow employs a mandala constructed of colored sand,
which is carefully assembled prior to each initiation and dismantled
once more at the end.

Due to their colorful and intricate nature, mandalas have attracted a great deal of interest. Although some can be openly explained, most are related to tantric doctrines that are normally supposed to be kept secret. Consequently, many speculative and mistaken interpretations have circulated among people who viewed them simply as works of art or had no access to reliable explanations. Because the severe misunderstandings that can arise are more harmful than a partial lifting of secrecy, I have encouraged a greater openness in the display and accurate description of mandalas.

Consequently, Barry Bryant and Samaya Foundation, assisted by monks from Namgyal Monastery here in Dharamsala, have done a great deal of good work to increase appreciation of the Kalachakra Mandala and its larger significance in the context of Buddhist practice. This book, containing material drawn from authentic sources and presented clearly to be easily understood, is a further welcome fruit of their efforts.

Whereas the Buddha initially gave most of the tantras to individual disciples, the Kalachakra was from the outset given to an entire community, the citizens of the Kingdom of Shambala. Subsequently, in Tibet it became customary for the initiation to be granted to great gatherings of people. I feel that introducing such a profound means of enlightenment in this way creates a strong positive bond among all those who are present and so plants fertile seeds of peace.

With this in mind I congratulate the author and all who contributed to this book and offer my prayers that their good intentions be fulfilled.

June 2, 1992

The
Wheel
of
Time

SAND MANDALA

Introduction

IN OCTOBER 1973, I watched the Fourteenth Dalai Lama of Tibet walk down the steps of an Alitalia jet at the airport in Copenhagen, and my life was changed forever.

The Dalai Lama is the exiled spiritual and temporal leader of the occupied nation of Tibet, of both its oppressed inhabitants and its thousands of refugees living in exile. In 1973, at the age of thirty-eight, he was on his first European tour and was arriving from Rome, where he had just met the pope. His message in Denmark was unlike anything I had ever heard. He helped me to understand that each of us has the right to be happy and that there is a path to happiness, which we can freely choose to follow. But more than his words, it was the Dalai Lama's compassionate presence that shook my foundation of beliefs and assumptions, and allowed me to see beyond my own arrogance and self-importance.

A World War II baby, I had grown up in material comfort during the 1950s in Washington State and had become a fervent participant in the revolution of values that took place during the 1960s. In 1970 I traveled to Copenhagen to visit my twin brother and found the atmosphere so friendly toward my work as an artist that I stayed there three years to develop an environmental art project, which included making films and videos for Danish television.

Even though this work was very rewarding, it didn't satisfy my urge to express something more meaningful or profound.

Fifty thousand students assemble to receive the Kalachakra Initiation from the Dalai Lama at Bodhgaya, India in 1973.

Friends led me to a Tibetan meditation center, where I felt instantly at home. I was inspired by what I heard regarding Tibetan Buddhism and particularly by its emphasis on the perfection of the mind.

Having begun to study and meditate there daily, I heard that the Dalai Lama would be visiting soon. As I looked forward to his visit, the focus of my art shifted from concern for the environment to expression of inner vision, using Tibetan Buddhist-inspired images. But it wasn't until I actually met the Dalai Lama that I began to understand the subtle levels of consciousness where my pain and dissatisfaction could be transformed into inner fulfillment.

His heartfelt concern for others was inspiring. He paid particular attention to personal details and always seemed to be genuinely considerate, asking the right question at the right moment. I continually probed him with my '60s-style antiauthoritarian questions. His objective, good-humored responses were always just what I needed to hear. After years of searching, I sensed that I had finally found something that would lead me beyond the limited thinking imposed by my conditioning. I immediately began to film the Dalai Lama as part of the Danish television workshop. When he was teaching I seemed to receive a personal message, as though the Dalai Lama were silently saying to me, "Put your camera down. Just sit and listen." That is how I became a student of Buddhism.

Relatively little public attention was being paid to the Dalai Lama at that time, so I was able to follow him on his speaking itinerary, attend his teachings, and even bring my camera to his private meetings. Twelve years later, I returned to Copenhagen to see that the crowd for his public talk had increased from 100 to more than 10,000.

But my work with the Dalai Lama had only just begun. I requested a private audience, after which my whole life seemed to pass before me like a movie. I saw the deceit, the confusion, the abusive relationships, the struggle with my family, and most of all, the need for gentleness and clarity in my life. My suffering was a result of my own distorted perceptions and ignorance. It became clear that I needed to take full responsibility for my actions.

The following week I went to Germany and Switzerland to video-tape the Dalai Lama as he performed ritual ceremonies and gave teachings, continuing the ancient oral tradition. In Rikon, Switzerland, more than 2,000 Tibetans living in exile in Europe lined up on either side of the road to greet the man they consider to be the living Buddha. Their faces were jubilant as they anticipated receiving the teachings and his blessing.

Before leaving Switzerland, I was invited by one of the Dalai Lama's secretaries to film the Kalachakra (Wheel of Time) Initiation, which he was to confer on 50,000 Tibetans two months later in Bodhgaya, India, the site of the Buddha's enlightenment.

Upon confessing that I had no idea what this initiation was, I was told that it was an empowerment ritual. At the center of the ritual was a sand *mandala,* a complex and colorful design which symbolized the teachings of the Buddha. Through contemplation of this mandala one could attain an enlightened state of mind, free of all obstacles and filled with compassion and wisdom. Just what I had been seeking, I thought.

I had neither been to India nor been part of a Buddhist initiation before, but the thousands of Tibetans around me at Bodhgaya during that Christmas holiday in 1973 made me feel welcome. In spite of the language barrier, I learned much from their ever-present kindness throughout the ten days I was there.

On the night before the final day, the initiation site seemed strangely still under the full moon. Many Tibetans were doing prostrations—bowing down to the ground and then lowering their entire bodies to the earth in a gesture of prayer and homage to the throne of the Dalai Lama. I had never prostrated myself before, but each time I did, I felt as though I were somehow letting go of the accumulated burden of my past misdeeds.

Then I heard someone reciting the mantra (or chant) *OM MANI PADME HUM.* When I recited it myself, I felt heat being generated inside my body, and I began to understand how reciting a mantra could help one to feel and generate compassion toward others.

Tibetans listening to the Dalai Lama during the 1973 Kalachakra Initiation at Bodhgaya, India. The woman in the center foreground is spinning a prayer wheel.

During this profoundly meaningful night, I sat under the brilliant light of the full moon reciting a Buddhist prayer before the enormous bodhi tree where the Buddha had attained enlightenment 2,600 years ago. At about 6:00 A.M., I felt a growing exhilaration as a crowd of thousands of monks began to gather for their full moon morning prayer. The Dalai Lama's attitude of reverence and patience seemed to pervade the entire community. I felt a sense of wholeness within myself that I had been seeking for a lifetime, and I realized

A Tibetan monk prostrates toward the Great Stupa monument at Bodhgaya. In his right hand he holds a *mala*, or rosary, used for counting mantras, prayers, and prostrations.

how such a ritual could engender what the Tibetans call "bliss consciousness."

The only English I remember hearing during the entire initiation was while the Dalai Lama was describing—in Tibetan—the deities of the mandala to the students, who were to imagine or visualize them in their minds. Suddenly, he said clearly in my own language, "Now you enter the mandala."

Those words had the weight of prophecy for me. At that point, which was near the completion of the twelve-day ceremony, the multitude of initiates were lined up to see the Kalachakra Sand Mandala and to receive the blessings of His Holiness the Dalai Lama.

Years later I would learn that each person has a unique spiritual experience upon seeing the mandala for the first time. Some people experience peace; some feel their own suffering; some feel humanity's suffering; others feel bliss; still others see their spiritual teacher. According to my journal entry that night, when I saw the mandala for the first time, "I felt my insides lighting up like a sunburst . . . as if firecrackers were exploding. When they settled, I saw the mandala before me in a large gallery in a North American museum, with thousands of Westerners experiencing the peace and light I felt at that moment."

From that day on, my work was cut out for me. Fifteen years later Samaya Foundation, under my direction, would present the Kalachakra Sand Mandala at the American Museum of Natural History, fulfilling this vision and marking the first time the mandala would be displayed as a cultural offering outside its ritual context.

More than 50,000 museum visitors saw the Kalachakra Sand Mandala at that exhibition, and millions more throughout the world have since had the opportunity to view it in museums and galleries and through its extensive exposure in the electronic and print media.

At the American Museum, visitors marveled at the monks as they went through their rituals—praying and applying sand—and always moving about the gallery explaining the meaning of the mandala. It was as though their every gesture embodied the very essence of their training.

Many visitors had questions: "Are the monks making up the design of the mandala as they go along? Where does the colored sand come from? What are those tools they're using?" I heard repeatedly, "Is there a book we can get about sand mandalas? Or about the

A Namgyal monk uses the tip of a *chakpu*, a metal funnel, to produce a decorative design on the rim of a dharma wheel in the Kalachakra Sand Mandala. The Kalachakra Initiation, Bodhgaya, India, 1973.

Buddha? Or Tibetan Buddhism?" This book was conceived in response to those questions.

The Dalai Lama has said that the practice of the Kalachakra Tantra, an esoteric but profound teaching of the Buddha, ultimately affects everyone. But nothing can communicate the beauty and the power of a Tibetan sand mandala like seeing it in person. My hope is that this book will bring the general reader as close as possible to that experience and serve as an introduction to the tantric path of Tibetan Buddhism.

I have been a student of Kalachakra since 1973, and I feel that I have only just begun to explore its depths. Yet I have come to understand enough to be aware of its potential benefit for the individual, the community, and for all life on the planet. May this book act as a seed for peace through compassion and wisdom, which are the essence of the Kalachakra teachings.

Barry Bryant, 1993

Opposite: At the Kalachakra Initiation,
Bodhgaya, India, 1973.

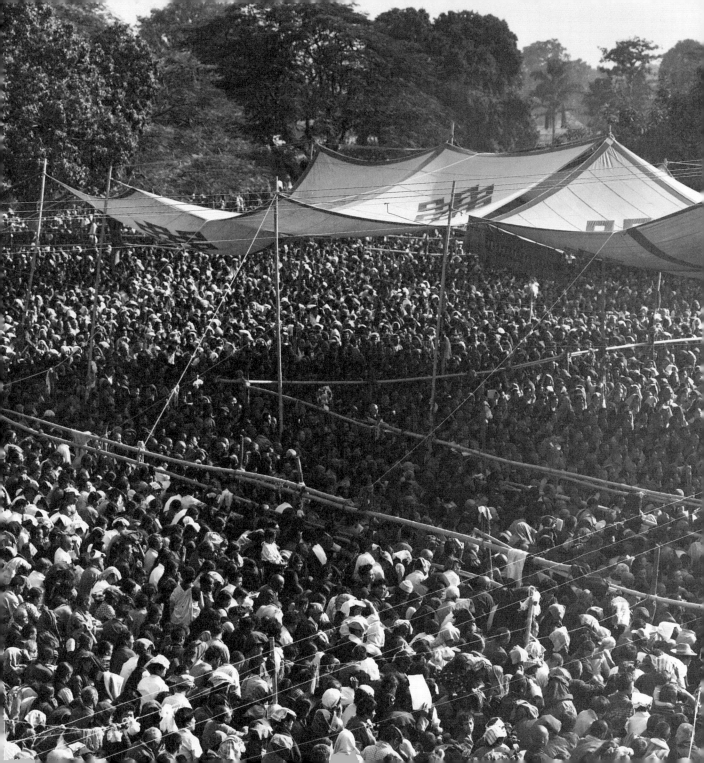

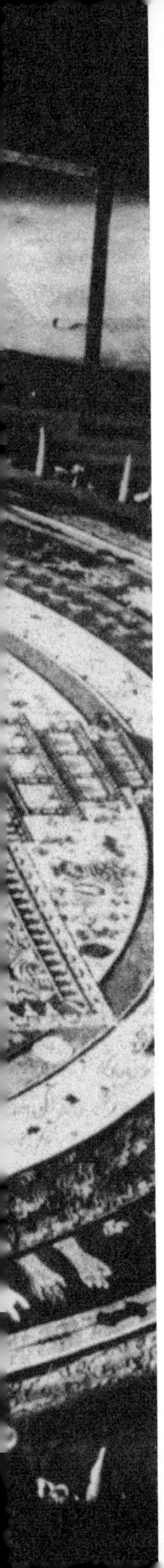

This photograph of a Kalachakra Sand Mandala was taken by Basil Crump, who wrote an article entitled "The Meaning of the Great Peace Mandala" for the *Peking Chronicle* on October 30, 1932. The mandala was constructed for the Kalachakra Initiation conferred by the Panchen Lama on October 21 at the Tai-ho-tien, which Crump called "the most important hall in all Peking." The grand scale of the mandala (approximately 32 feet in diameter) may be determined by the figure in the upper left corner. Surrounding the mandala are ten *purbas*, ten vases, and a circle of *torma* offerings.

Crump wrote, "It was interesting to watch them applying the powdered colors through tapered tubes (somewhat like icing a cake) and the skill with which they executed the intricate drawing of the various symbols."

The Path of Kalachakra

Praise glorious Kalachakra,
conqueror of all fears and disillusionment,
at whose feet I bow in great humility.

sharing the secret path

"KALACHAKRA is a vehicle for world peace," the Fourteenth Dalai Lama of Tibet, recipient of the 1989 Nobel Peace Prize, has stated time and again. What does he mean? Can unlocking the mysteries of a secret doctrine taught by the Buddha over 2,600 years ago help to address present-day concerns for our endangered planet and the very survival of our species?

The Buddha and other enlightened beings return to this life to help others when the world is in need. The

Kalachakra Tantra has been handed down from generation to generation in an unbroken lineage of oral transmission, from teacher to student to the Dalai Lama of our own time. Today it is coming to the West when, for the first time in history, we are beginning to attend to the concerns of our planet as a whole. These include easing international tensions and violence, recognizing and dealing with the threat of global warming, overpopulation, malnutrition, environmental pollution, and epidemic plague—in short, the many physical and psychological challenges of human suffering.

The Kalachakra Tantra is one of the most advanced and complex teachings of the practice of Buddhism. Like all Buddhist teachings, Kalachakra serves as a path to enlightenment.

While he was still living in Tibet, the Fourteenth Dalai Lama conferred the Kalachakra Initiation twice on thousands of followers, many of whom traveled hundreds of miles on foot for this once-in-a-lifetime experience. One of the highlights of the pilgrimage was the opportunity to view the magnificent Kalachakra Mandala, made of colored sand, at the completion of the ritual.

Since he went into exile in 1959, the Dalai Lama has given this twelve-day initiation numerous times throughout the world and has welcomed all who wish to attend. In such empowerment rituals, practitioners must pledge "not to reveal the supreme secrets of the mandala to those who have not entered, nor to those who have no faith." However, the Dalai Lama says, "It's already become an open secret with many misconceptions, and it's my responsibility to correct them. A profound explanation should be available."

In 1988, his commitment to world peace and to sharing the treasures of Kalachakra inspired him to break with tradition. He sent four monks from his Namgyal Monastery in India to construct the Kalachakra Sand Mandala as a cultural offering at the American Museum of Natural History in New York City. The reaction of Westerners to this timeless masterpiece was one of awe, appreciation, and delight.

Like all of Tibetan Buddhism, the precious legacy of Kalachakra is in danger of extinction in Tibet, which has been occupied by the

People's Republic of China since the 1950s. As a result, many Tibetan lamas seeking to preserve these teachings of the Buddha have come to the West, where interest in expanding spiritual awareness has been increasing as faith in material solutions has declined.

the meaning of tantra

The Kalachakra Sand Mandala, like all Tibetan Buddhist mandalas, is part of a tantra imparted by the Buddha. The literal translation of the Sanskrit word *tantra* is "continuity," although an exactly corresponding English word or concept does not exist. "Way of life according to the teaching" is a more comprehensive translation. Tantra is a living expression of the timeless nature of the teaching—its origin, its practice, and its fruits.

The teachings of the Buddha are all classified as *sutras* or *tantras,* both of which exist as written scriptures, recorded centuries after they were taught. Sutras were taught publicly in dialogue form and have always been widely available. There are various types of tantric texts, including medical and astrological tantras, as well as the root texts of Vajrayana meditation practice, such as the Kalachakra Tantra. The Buddha conferred the tantras while assuming the form of various deities. He taught them secretly to individuals or groups because only those who had a certain background and education were prepared to integrate them into their practice. These tantras have until recently been accessible only to scholars and devout practitioners.

Tantra is the core of Vajrayana Buddhism, which has been widely practiced in Tibet and Mongolia for more than 1,300 years. Vajrayana is one of the three *yanas,* or Buddhist paths. The three yanas are *Hinayana,* also known as *Theravada,* which is the path to individual liberation; *Mahayana,* the path of altruism, or the attainment of enlightenment through compassionate dedication to the liberation of all sentient beings; and *Vajrayana* (the "diamond path," also known as *Tantrayana* and *Mantrayana*), which is said to be the most direct path to transformation and enlightenment through tantric practice. "Tibetan Buddhism" refers to the Indo-Tibetan Buddhist tradition which came to Tibet directly from India, and which includes the practice of all three yanas.

the tantric deities

Kalachakra is one of thousands of tantras taught by the Buddha. At the center of each tantra is a deity, which is regarded as a manifestation of a particular aspect of Buddha mind. Rather than gods to be adored, the deities are perceived as personified states of mind, to be attained and mastered as one progresses on the path toward enlightenment. In addition to the central deity Kalachakra (wheel of time), three deities important to the history of Kalachakra are Manjusri (wisdom), Avalokiteshvara (compassion), and Vajrapani (power).

Buddha literally means "awakened one." A Buddha is one who has "gone beyond," beyond the endless cycle of cause and effect, or suf-

Above: Avalokiteshvara, Buddha of Compassion, holds a lotus flower in his left hand. 10^7/$_8$" high, cast gilt copper with jewel inlay, Nepal, 14th century.

Right: Vajrapani, Buddha of Power, wields the ritual implement called the *vajra*. 8" high, cast gilt copper with painted detail, Tibet, 17th century.

fering, to realize the state of complete awareness of all phenomena—both matter and mind—and their essential emptiness. *Buddha mind,*

Manjusri, Buddha of Wisdom, is recognized by the sword which cuts through ignorance. Front and rear view. 4 1/2" high, brass with copper inlay, Kashmir, 10th century.

then, is the state of omniscience, the perfected mind that realizes the union of compassion and wisdom, the state referred to as bliss consciousness or pristine awareness.

Compassion and wisdom, which figure prominently in the teachings of the Buddha, refer to those qualities of mind that are the result of practicing the meditative concentration associated with the tantra or deity. Compassion refers to that altruistic state of being where our actions and their consequences are for the benefit of others. It is the sense of unconditional love and kindness that goes beyond ego in the realization of true selflessness.

Wisdom, from the Buddhist perspective, is the realization of emptiness, the direct knowledge of things as they are. This knowledge is universal in nature and arises spontaneously from pure intention, thought, and action. It is a wisdom of discernment, functioning in accord with the fundamental laws of natural phenomena. Its essence is grounded in altruism.

The realm of the deity of wisdom and compassion known as Kalachakra is one of omniscience—or the knowledge and understanding of all events and perceptions, past, present, and future. His omniscience has been obtained through his practice of abandoning all faults. Kalachakra is not only a deity but a teaching, a tantra. It has its own mandala, its own text, its mantras, prayers, meditation practices, ritual practices, ritual dances, and a long and colorful history. It is through the integration of its many components that one is able to realize and experience the mind of Kalachakra. The more deeply one practices it, the more expansive and profound is its result.

Each Buddhist deity has many forms. In its simplest form, it has one head and two arms, while more elaborate forms have multiple heads or arms. Many principal deities, whether male or female, are in a state of perpetual union with a consort known as *yab-yum,* literally "mother-father," symbolizing the union of wisdom and compassion.

The early exposure of tantric art to Western culture without proper explanation often resulted in yab-yum being misinterpreted as a purely sexual embrace. In the practice of the Kalachakra Tantra, the deities are visualized as being in that state of consciousness where the feminine and masculine principles are in union or balance. Realizing the completion stage of the meditation practice, one is able to master the energies of the right (female) and left (male) channels of the body, to realize the totally awakened and clarified state (Buddha mind) of the central channel, which is represented by this embrace.

The Kalachakra deity has a number of forms, but the one associated with its sand mandala has four faces and twenty-four arms and stands in union with his consort Vishvamata. An example of a complex deity form is the thousand-armed Avalokiteshvara, whose numerous arms represent boundless, infinite compassion.

Opposite: The deity Kalachakra and his consort Vishvamata. Scroll painting (*thangka*), Tibet, 18th century.

14

Every deity has a *mantra,* which is a series of Sanskrit syllables. When recited together, the particular combination of syllables or sounds evokes a specific, desired state of mind.

For example, *OM MANI PADME HUM* literally means "the jewel in the lotus." This mantra is intended to evoke the jewel of enlight-

Above: This visual representation of the Kalachakra mantra is known as the "Power of Ten."

Right: The mantra *OM MANI PADME HUM* carved in stone. These *mani stones* are usually placed in heaps by pilgrims at holy sites as offerings.

enment arising in the purified mind, which is symbolized by a beautiful lotus flower emerging from the mud in which it grows. Reciting this mantra repeatedly with a motivation to be of benefit to others increases the potential to attain such an exalted state. A mantra, like a friend, is always accessible and reliable; association with it deepens the bond. *OM MANI PADME HUM,* the mantra of Avalokiteshvara, is the most widely recited mantra in Tibetan Buddhism.

The principal mantra of Kalachakra is *OM AH HUNG HO HANG KHYA MA LA WA RA YA HUNG PHAT.* This mantra cannot be translated because the syllables, which do not form words, encompass all aspects of the Kalachakra Tantra.

The pantheon includes both benign deities, which embody the gentle nature of the Buddha of compassion, and wrathful deities, which are the seemingly fierce manifestations of a fundamentally compassionate nature. Their wrath corresponds to the righteous anger of a parent scolding a child who plays with fire.

The most peaceful deities are often depicted as white, light blue, or green, whereas the wrathful ones are frequently red, dark blue, or black, with flames spewing from their bodies to dissolve the poisons of the mind and other obstacles on the path. They carry implements to cut through ignorance and delusion and are often shown displaying the trophies of their conquests. Wrathful deities are frequently seen as protectors of the gates who prevent those with bad intentions from entering. They also encourage those with good intentions into the mandala or monastery, etc.

There is no tantra without a deity; likewise, each deity embodies a tantra. With each deity thus representing an aspect of Buddha

The Kalachakra mantra, *OM AH HUNG HO HANG KHYA MA LA WA RA YA HUNG PHAT,* in Tibetan characters. This configuration of the syllables represents the cosmic Mt. Meru with the Kalachakra mantra at its top.

mind, each tantra discloses methods for realizing the awakened state of the deity.

the mind in tantra

In tantra, the mind is seen as the central source of being. It is the stream of consciousness which connects the individual to his or her past and future. This can be observed within the actions of this life alone or, according to the principle of reincarnation, in the actions of past and future lives. The mind is a repository of these actions and the impressions they make, known altogether as *karma,* the law of cause and effect which carries over from lifetime to lifetime.

As the Dalai Lama and other lamas have said, the primary difference between human beings and animals is that human beings have the quality of mind that is able to practice the *dharma,* the law of nature as taught by the Buddha. The dharma includes the natural phenomena of the physical plane and of the mind, as well as their interdependence.

At the center of tantric practice is the subtle mind, which from the Buddhist perspective resides at the heart center (not to be confused with the physical heart) and is the source of our vitality, compassion, and wisdom. This is significantly different from the Western viewpoint, which regards the mind as a function of the brain, with an emphasis on deductive reasoning. The tantric mind holds both the relative truth and the absolute or ultimate truth.

a guide to enlightenment

Each of the tantras contains instructions for entering into the practice, in order to realize the perfected quality of mind represented by the particular deity. Thus the tantra is not only the teaching but also a guide to achieving and abiding within the enlightened state of being. It is also the transmission of its teachings, which are passed from generation to generation by lineage holders who are empowered to do so.

To gain some perspective on the ageless quality of the tantra, we need to understand the Buddhist conception of time. We are presently in the age of the fourth Buddha—the historical Shakyamuni Buddha, known before enlightenment as Siddhartha or Gautama—who lived approximately 600 years before Jesus Christ. The Buddha of the previous (or prehistoric) age, who was called Osung, lived when the average life span was 20,000 years; and the one before, known as Serthup, when the average life span was 40,000 years.

Shakyamuni Buddha, 70 feet high, carved into a mountainside two miles south of Lhasa, Tibet in the 12th century. His right hand touches the earth, indicating that the earth is witness to his enlightenment. The bowl in his left hand may be the begging bowl of a monk or the bowl of healing herbs of the Healing Buddha. Students regularly paint the face, hands, feet, bowl, and lotus flowers at the base as an act of devotion. A pile of mani stones is in the right foreground.

The first Buddha, Khorvajig, appeared at a time when the life span had just been reduced to 60,000 years. The Dalai Lama reminds us gently that we Westerners are very impatient, due to our limited view of time.

The Buddha's teachings spread throughout India until they were threatened, and ultimately driven out, by the foreign invasions which took place from the 10th to 13th centuries. During that time Vajrayana, or tantric, Buddhism spread northward to Tibet, where it was practiced and passed down to our own time through the teachings of eminent lamas, including the preservation of ritual arts. An example is the Kalachakra Sand Mandala, which contains symbols embodying the entire Kalachakra Tantra.

the transmission

The Buddha taught students according to their individual capacity and disposition. Some only understood his words, while others received his teachings on a more profound level. This type of learning is called "mind transmission," a direct transfer of consciousness that can pass from a deity to a human or from one human to another. It requires a qualified sender and a receiver whose mind has been tuned to the frequency of the signal being transmitted. This attunement is achieved through the generation of *bodhicitta,* the awakened state of mind that arises through the practice of compassion.

When the Buddha conferred a tantra, he manifested as the deity of that tantra and imparted the complete teaching through mind transmission. This empowerment by the deity included authorization to practice the tantra, instruction in the philosophy of the tantra, training for the practice of meditative concentration, and directions for the practice of the tantra's rituals and ritual arts.

The practice of ritual arts is a means of invoking the deity in one's mind, awakening the Buddha nature which we already possess. Ritual arts include chanting, music, dance, making *torma* (barley flour and butter) and butter sculpture, as well as sand mandalas, all of which are offerings to the deities. They are an integral part of the practice of tantric Buddhism.

The ritual arts serve as a "visual scripture" in communicating the tantra. They not only provide another dimension of the teachings but also the opportunity to develop devotion through their practice.

It is said that seeing the image of the Buddha or a Buddhist deity can activate the seed of Buddha nature in the mind of the viewer. In the Tibetan Buddhist canon such visual imagery includes *thangkas* (scroll paintings), statues, and mandalas. When properly made and consecrated, these works are believed to contain the same empowering energy as the text, the deity, or even the Buddha himself. They are considered to embody that which they represent.

the mandala

The Tibetan word for mandala is *kyilkhor,* which means "center and surrounding environment." The mandala of a tantric deity includes the deity and his palace, which is also a representation of the mind of the deity. Based on symbols familiar to the people of India during the Buddha's lifetime, each mandala is a pictorial manifestation of a tantra. It may be "read" and studied as a text, memorized for visualization during meditation, and interpreted.

The most commonly known mandalas are depicted in two-dimensional form, showing a floor plan—like a blueprint—of the three-dimensional palace of the deity, including the architectural design and the many decorative details. Every component is a symbol representing an aspect of the teaching.

The purpose of a mandala is to acquaint the student with the tantra and the deity and to allow the student to "enter into the mandala"; that is, to enter into the state of being in which the deity dwells.

The texts state that a mandala can be drawn, painted, made of particles, or constructed by meditative concentration. A two-dimensional mandala may be made of powdered and colored rice or flowers, particles of stone or jewels, or colored sand. There are also three-dimensional mandalas constructed out of wood, metal, or other solid materials.

There are two types of meditation mandalas, which are constructed in the mind. In one, the practitioner visualizes the entire three-dimensional mandala in minute detail. The other, the most advanced tantric practice, known as "actualizing the mandala," requires the reorientation of the subtle energies of the body to conform to those of the deity.

Raktayamari Mandala, a painted meditation mandala of Sakya master Kunga Lekpa, teacher of Tsong Khapa. Central Tibet, circa 1400.

the practice

The student wishing to penetrate these mysteries begins his or her practice by "taking refuge" in the Three Jewels: the Buddha, the dharma, and the *sangha* (the teacher, the teachings, and the community of practitioners). In order to practice tantra, he or she receives an initiation that grants permission or authorization. There is such an initiation for each of the thousands of tantras. The ceremony, also referred to as an empowerment, is given by a ritual master who has received this empowerment from his own teacher

through oral transmission, in an unbroken lineage traceable to the original exponent of this teaching, the Buddha himself. The essence of a tantra is transmitted through the empowerment ritual, so that the student is not only receiving permission to practice but also the actual blessing of the Buddha as embodied by the ritual master.

Monks making a sand mandala on the floor of Drepung Monastery in Tibet. This photograph was taken in 1935 by C. Suydam Cutting, who led the first American expedition to Tibet.

Buddhists see the ritual master as conferring, bestowing, or giving the initiation rather than performing or conducting a ceremony. Similarly, the student does not "undergo" an initiation, but simply receives it.

Preparation for the initiation, including the making of the sand mandala into which the deities of the tantra are invoked by the ritual master, is considered very important, and it often takes longer than the empowerment itself. In the case of the Kalachakra Initiation, it takes nine days of purification and consecration before the students may enter the mandala site, then one day of student preparation and two days of initiation.

the kalachakra tantra

Kalachakra (in Tibetan *Du kyi khorlo*) is a Sanskrit word that can be translated literally as "wheel of time." *Kala,* or "time," is not linear time but the flow of all events, past, present, and future. This is similar to our concept of space, which does not imply a particular direction or limitation. The Kalachakra deity represents omniscience, for he is one with all time and therefore knows all. *Chakra,* meaning "wheel," refers not only to the cycle of time but also to the way in which the enlightened experience of great bliss radiates like the sun from the self to all sentient beings. The wheel, with no beginning and no end, is also the universal symbol of Buddhism, representing the teachings of the Buddha.

The Kalachakra Tantra comprises three unique and simultaneous cycles of instruction: the external Kalachakra teachings on cosmology; the internal Kalachakra teachings on the nature and functioning of the human body; and the alternate Kalachakra, the meditative path toward enlightenment.

The Kalachakra Sand Mandala is a visual representation of the entire Kalachakra Tantra. It is also a two-dimensional representation of the five-story palace of the Kalachakra deity, in which a total of 722 deities reside, with Kalachakra and his consort Vishvamata united in an embrace of perpetual bliss at the very center.

Those who participate in making the sand mandala place themselves within the realm of the deity. While we tend to see the mandala as a work of art in the process of creation, the monks who do this work say they are not creating, but reconstructing a representation of something that already exists. By doing so, they are perfecting or attaining the awakened state of mind. Rather than the emphasis being placed on creating something of material value, the monks are engaging in a process that benefits them and will also serve to benefit others.

a teaching for our time

One of the important features of the Kalachakra Tantra is that it is given for a community. The Buddha offered it for an entire country, the mythical kingdom of Shambala, so historically the initiation has been given to large groups. The Dalai Lama has remarked that in earlier times communities were separated by valleys, rivers, mountains, or oceans, whereas today, with instant communication and transportation, our community includes the entire planet. This is another reason why he feels Kalachakra is a teaching for our time.

Although it is particularly useful for subduing crisis or warfare (both internal and worldwide), the Dalai Lama makes it clear that the Kalachakra Tantra alone is not enough to achieve world peace. We need world leaders in economics, religion, sociology, politics, and, perhaps most importantly, the physical sciences to work together, sharing their different traditions in order to find innovative solutions to the problems ahead of us. He states further that this cooperation must be motivated by a true sense of universal responsibility to all fellow human beings, which, as an expression of the union of wisdom and compassion, is itself the very essence of Kalachakra.

The
Sand Mandala
as a Cultural
Offering

WHAT WE KNOW today as Tibetan ritual art came to Tibet primarily from India between the 8th and 12th centuries A.D., as part of the Buddhist tantra. Stylistic influences also came from Nepal, Kashmir, and China, as well as other neighboring countries.

Over the centuries, Tibetans have developed their ritual arts—including dance, chanting, music, thangka painting, butter sculpture (a uniquely Tibetan art form), and the elaborate and exquisite sand mandalas—to a highly sophisticated degree. But until very recently, the expression of those arts had never been seen outside their intended

The Kalachakra Sand Mandala, the first Tibetan sand mandala in history to be presented as a cultural offering, captivates viewers at the American Museum of Natural History in New York City, 1988.

27

sacred setting. When the Kalachakra Sand Mandala was presented at the American Museum of Natural History, it was extracted from its larger ritual context. The term "cultural offering" evolved as a means to describe this transplant of a sacred art into a cultural and anthropological institution.

In appreciating the Kalachakra Sand Mandala as a work of art, Westerners are challenged to see beyond their own definition of art, which places value on innovation and self-expression. In Tibetan ritual arts collaboration in the execution of the intricate sand mandala is considered to be more valuable than originality, and the ritual artist's single most important objective is to cultivate a pure motivation to benefit others.

In the museum, the art form is demonstrated for a public generally unfamiliar with the larger ritual. In addition to drawing and painting the sand mandala, the monks' very presence in the museum creates a tranquil atmosphere which conveys the essence of the larger ritual. The cultural offering includes the daily recitation of prayers used in the initiation. The monks recite the Kalachakra prayer in which, through a process of visualization, they generate themselves as the deity Kalachakra. The state of mind resulting from this practice remains with them throughout the day while they demonstrate the sand painting and talk with visitors.

the moving sands

In 1988, Samaya Foundation received a grant from the New York State Council on the Arts for a Tibetan monk from Namgyal Monastery to be artist-in-residence at the foundation and to demonstrate the construction of sand mandalas in New York. We discussed an exhibition with Dr. Malcolm Arth of the American Museum of Natural History, who encouraged us with the simple statement, "Just let me know when the monk will arrive."

When Lobsang Samten arrived at JFK Airport with two suitcases filled with colored sand, Samaya Foundation was waiting for his instructions. He thought it best that we make the Guhyasamaja

Namgyal monk Lobsang Samten painting the Guhyasamaja Sand Mandala at Samaya Foundation, 1988.

Sand Mandala first, before tackling the much more complex Kalachakra at the museum. Lobsang explained the belief that if the Guhyasamaja Tantra were preserved, then all tantras would be preserved, so it seemed a good omen to begin with this sand mandala. Also, the Guhyasamaja Mandala is of a size and complexity appropriate for one monk working alone, although it is traditionally made by several monks together. But Lobsang informed us that first of all we would have to build a *thekpu,* or mandala house.

The methods of building the thekpu, which would have to be both strong and portable, were translated into Western engineering concepts by architect Stan Bryant. Our thekpu was designed to

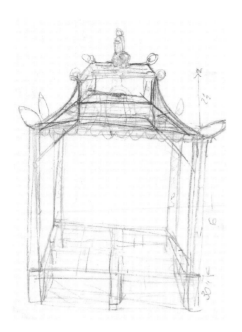

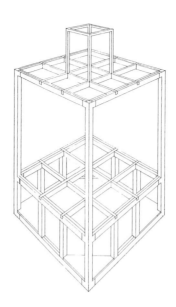

house a video camera directly above the mandala, as well as ceiling lights, all supported by vertical columns made of hollow steel to act as conduits for electrical lines for lighting, audio, and video.

The project became a real community effort, entailing the work of many friends, volunteers, and family members. Samaya Foundation's technical director Greg Durgin designed the base of the thekpu for recorders, circuitry for the lights, and a robotically operated camera, along with other electronics. Since there was no precedent or plan for what we were doing, we had to experiment and improvise. The Samaya thekpu became a beautiful merging of ancient and modern technologies.

Next came the decorative design details. Lotus flowers and other decorations were carved out of wood and painted by Tibetan artist Phuntsok Dorje. Silk brocade valances and banners were sewn and hung.

Lobsang learned English as he taught us philosophical aspects of the Guhyasamaja Tantra. The complex and sometimes obscure

Tibetan explanations of the tantra had to be translated into simple layman's English for the press and the public.

The Guhyasamaja Sand Mandala was constructed at Samaya Foundation during the month of June in 1988, marking the first time a Tibetan sand mandala had ever been presented as a cultural offering. No longer accessible only to Buddhist practitioners, the mandala attracted hundreds of New York artists, as well as eminent lamas and the simply curious.

Lobsang, watching himself create the tiny details of the mandala on a video monitor as he worked, appreciated the capacity of this new tool to help him perfect his skill. And he learned to discuss his work so that we could all understand.

Thus the groundwork was being laid for the American Museum, where the Kalachakra Sand Mandala would be presented during July and August of 1988.

After the Guhyasamaja Sand Mandala was completed, the traditional dismantling ceremony was performed. More than 300 people

The Samaya Foundation *thekpu,* or mandala house, for the American Museum of Natural History exhibition in New York City, 1988. From left to right: artist's sketch; structural drawing; museum installation with silk banners; Phuntsok Dorje painting lotus flowers on the roof detail; the completed thekpu.

came to Samaya Foundation to join Lobsang Samten as he removed the thirty-two deities represented in the mandala and swept up all the delicately applied sand. The sand was then carried to the Hudson River, in a procession that passed by the 110-story World Trade Center, a striking juxtaposition of the ancient and modern worlds.

At the river, Lobsang recited prayers and offered the consecrated sand to the spirits of the water, while cameras recorded the setting sun illuminating New Jersey's industrial landscape across the Hudson. In a shared moment of joy, we poured the colored sand into the water for the benefit of the aquatic life.

John Perrault, an art critic who attended the dismantling ceremony, wrote the first article on the Tibetan sand mandala in the United States, published in the *Village Voice.* He called the demonstration of sand mandalas "performance art of a high order."

living natural history

On July 6, we started work at the Museum of Natural History. We began to learn the Kalachakra Tantra and the museum staff became part of our sand mandala family in this unique, historic event. Lobsang Samten was then joined by three other Namgyal monks: Lobsang Gyaltsen, Pema Lobsang Chogyen, and Jamphal Thundup.

On the day the sand mandala opened at the museum, *New York Times* reporter Dennis Hevesi wrote, "Amid the clamor and clatter of the city, a pinpoint of pure calm—a 'gateway to bliss'—is being created." Other writers and photographers from newspapers, magazines, television, and radio soon followed.

During our six weeks at the museum, at any time one might find up to 100 people totally involved in the exhibit. People contemplated the monks at work with great respect, as if witnessing a ceremony in a church or temple. Each morning at 10 A.M. as many as fifty people might be waiting to join the monks for their morning prayers, which lasted up to forty-five minutes. Then the special Plexiglas protective cover was lifted so that the monks could begin their work.

The Namgyal monks performing their preparatory prayers at the Museum of Natural History , as they did each morning before beginning to paint with sand. New York City, 1988.

More than 50,000 people came to see the exhibition. What they saw in the room was a monk sitting on the waist-high mandala base, applying sand through an elongated funnel to a mandala seven feet in diameter. Viewers walked in a circle around the thekpu, which was surrounded by stanchions because the mandala's fragility made

Above: Live, close-up images of the step-by-step process of constructing the mandala were provided by closed-circuit video feed from the camera located in the ceiling of the thekpu. The detail shown here, actually 3" wide, was magnified 600 per cent on the video monitor.

Left: Museum visitors join the Namgyal monks in contemplating the completed Kalachakra Sand Mandala. New York City, 1988.

it inadvisable for viewers to get too close. What they heard was the sustained rasping of the metal funnel used to apply the tiny stream of colored sand particles.

Painting the Kalachakra Sand Mandala in its ritual context traditionally takes six days, employing as many as sixteen monks. At the museum it was slowed down so that the visitors could experience the entire process in detail over a period of six weeks. Four large TV monitors placed throughout the gallery allowed the visitors to see details of the mandala emerge as they were painted. Accustomed to television, visitors found the enlarged video view provided by the overhead robotic camera both comfortably familiar and educational. This bird's-eye view magnified minuscule details 400 per cent, prompting one woman to say it was "just like being in the monks' shoes."

The exhibition also included a stationary video installation with a twenty-minute film of the Kalachakra Initiation bestowed by the Dalai Lama at Bodhgaya, India, which served to illustrate the sacred context of the mandala.

One of the questions asked most frequently was, "How do the monks feel about doing this sacred work in the museum?" The monks always responded positively: "When we paint a mandala in the monastery, it is usually seen only by our fellow monks. But here

A vase containing the sand from the Kalachakra Sand Mandala is carried in procession through the streets of New York from the American Museum to the Hudson River. 1988.

in the museum, thousands of people are able to see it. Here we are showing the culture of Tibet, and the mandala itself will benefit many people."

The monks learned to describe their work to people who had no knowledge of the culture and its traditions. They were soon able to reduce their detailed explanations of the teachings to succinct phrases, such as one monk's assertion that work on the mandala offered him "peace of mind." Most of New York's television news teams covered the story, interviewing both the monks and the public.

Art writers came from various publications. Kay Larson, in her *New York* magazine column, said, "A sand mandala is an extraordinary thing, collaborative, ephemeral, unsigned, ahistorical—contrary in every way to 'art' as we mean it in the world." This reflected the New York public's fascination with a work of art which, after six weeks of meticulous craftsmanship, would be swept up and offered to the natural spirits of the Hudson River.

We discussed with the museum staff the possibility of preserving the mandala so that more people could benefit from seeing and studying it. We experimented with sprays and other protective coating techniques and received a great deal of advice. Finally, we all

Monks praying at Santa Monica Bay before offering the blessed sand to the marine life of the Pacific Ocean. This followed the dismantling of the Kalachakra Sand Mandala at the Natural History Museum of Los Angeles County in 1989.

agreed that the best way to preserve the mandala would be to follow tradition: sweep it up and pour it into the Hudson.

The dismantling ceremony was witnessed by hundreds of people. The four monks recited prayers requesting the 722 deities which they had invoked during the process of constructing the Kalachakra Mandala to now return to their sacred homes. The monks adroitly removed the colored sands which represented the deities and, within minutes, six weeks of painstaking labor was swept up and put into an urn. The urn was then carried in a ceremonial procession from the museum and the sand was poured into the river.

The dismantling ceremony was as solemn and as important as the construction of the mandala itself. Prayers were said at the

79th Street Boat Basin as television news crews brought the event into millions of homes.

on to the west coast

When Samaya Foundation presented the Kalachakra Sand Mandala at the Natural History Museum of Los Angeles County in 1989, there were several differences in presentation, including a more sophisticated video system and another group of Namgyal monks. Instead of a small, dedicated gallery, the installation was located in the middle of the museum's huge Hall of North American Mammals. Surrounded by dioramas of grizzly bears, buffalo, and other large beasts, the thekpu shone like a radiant jewel. A special area was set apart for children to try their hand at sand painting under the guidance of one of the monks.

Samaya Foundation worked closely with both museum staff and the Tibetan Buddhist meditation center Thupten Dhargye Ling, which organized the Los Angeles Kalachakra Initiation that the Dalai Lama was giving at the same time to 3,000 Buddhist practitioners. Many initiates came to the museum to spend more time studying the mandala; likewise, many museum visitors became interested in learning about Tibet and its spiritual traditions.

The museum staff told us some visitors, attracted by the sand mandala project, had come to the museum for the first time; some had even traveled across the country to see it. Members of the Hollywood film community appeared frequently and treated the monks to tours of Disneyland and the *Star Trek* set at Paramount Studios. Regular visitors became friends of the monks and of Tibetan Buddhism.

The dismantling brought hundreds of spectators to the museum and to the procession (which was by car on the Santa Monica Freeway this time) to the Sand and Sea Club on the Pacific Ocean. There, once more, the blessed sand was offered to the water spirits. It was unique to see the Tibetan monks praying on the beach surrounded by friends, television cameras, roller skaters, beach bunnies, body builders, homeless people, and bikers.

rocky mountain high

From Los Angeles we journeyed to Aspen, Colorado, to be part of Windstar Foundation's CHOICES IV Symposium, attended by 1,700 environmentalists, nutritionists, faith healers, and socially conscious

Namgyal monk Tenzin Yignyen discusses the Kalachakra Fire Offering Sand Mandala with John Denver and the author at Windstar Foundation's CHOICES IV Symposium in Aspen, Colorado, 1989.

promoters of the "New Age." The monks demonstrated the Kalachakra Ritual Fire Offering Sand Mandala, which is traditionally constructed after the completion of a ritual ceremony or a prolonged meditation practice to remove any obstacles on the path.

At the closing ceremonies the monks offered a vase filled with blessed sand from the Fire Offering Sand Mandala to the endangered streams of the Rocky Mountains. Another vase was given to John Denver, a founder of Windstar Foundation, to take to Prince William Sound in Alaska the next day as an offering to the marine life threatened by the Exxon Valdez oil spill. The Wheel of Time was continuing to expand its reach deep into the culture of the 20th century.

The Life
of
The Buddha

In Tibet, the literary form of biography, which is otherwise completely foreign to the culture, is reserved for the highest realized teachers of Tibetan Buddhism. Such a biography is known as *namtar*. Its purpose is to illuminate the deeds of the master and it is used as a teaching aid. Usually written by a disciple, the namtar, like other Tibetan Buddhist texts, is considered to retain the enlightening qualities of the teacher himself. Like the life story of Jesus, the biography of the Buddha is rich with anecdotes of his achievements and brings life to his teachings.

The Conception (of the Buddha). Queen Maya dreams that a tusk of a white king elephant penetrates her rib cage. Gandhara stone carving, India, 2nd–3rd century.

A Buddha is one who has awakened, becoming liberated from the habitual patterns that perpetuate suffering, and has attained enlightenment. Versions of the life of Shakyamuni Buddha vary, from the biography of an exceptional but very human man to legendary deification. His story has inspired innumerable people over the centuries to turn to the dharma as a means to achieve happiness and liberation from suffering.

Shakyamuni, "the sage of the Shakya clan," was born in 527 B.C. The Buddha of "this fortunate era" is regarded as the fourth of one thousand Buddhas, with the others yet to come. After many years of rigorous pursuit of the truth, Shakyamuni Buddha realized his own Buddha nature, or the potential for perfection that is innate within all sentient beings. He spent the last forty-five of his eighty years disseminating his teachings, also known as the *Buddha dharma.*

The Buddha taught in India at a time when Hinduism flourished, with its pantheon of colorful gods and rigid social structure. Defying the strict hierarchical customs that regulated social behavior in the India of his day, the Buddha received outcasts and aristocrats alike, subdued warrior kings and wild beasts, and converted infidels and criminals. His teachings on compassion and his espousal of democratic social views were revolutionary for his day. In defiance of the customs of the times, he allowed women to be ordained.

The Buddha bequeathed to humanity methods for attaining self-realization that could be utilized by individuals according to their differing needs and capacities—by householders and monastics, mystics and pragmatists, scholars and peasants. From this approach, three levels of his teaching and practice evolved: Hinayana (or Theravada), Mahayana, and Vajrayana Buddhism.

The Buddha's basic teaching is that life is suffering, and that this suffering arises from our dualistic view that all things are either desirable or undesirable. This constant state of desiring, or attachment, can never bring us lasting fulfillment. The suffering can only end when we are able to set aside our narrow conceptions of self and gain access to our true, inherently altruistic identity, or pure nature.

The Nativity. To the left of Queen Maya is Indra, king of the gods, holding the infant Siddhartha. To the right is an unidentified goddess. Gray schist, Pala Dynasty, India, 9th–10th century.

the tradition
of oral transmissions

Three months after the Buddha's death, 500 devotees gathered to recount his teachings. A cohesive written canon did not appear until several hundred years later. During that time, a vital oral transmission flourished and it continues to this day.

Although a vast number of commentaries have expounded the Buddha's teachings from the time they first appeared as written texts, the authority of the written word has not suppressed or invalidated the oral teachings. The reason for this is that in ancient India oral transmission alone resanctified religious teachings. The written word was considered helpful to merchants but inappropriate for sacred studies.

Consequently this dual tradition, functioning like counterpoint in music, has resulted in an ongoing, energetic dialogue. And the dialogue process has consistently served to revitalize Buddhism throughout its long history, allowing for its adaptation into a great diversity of cultural environments.

the story of the buddha's birth

Shakyamuni, born Siddhartha Gautama, was the son of King Suddhodana and Queen Maya. Prior to the full-moon night on which Shakyamuni's conception took place, the queen dreamed that a tusk of a multi-tusked white king elephant had entered her rib cage. This indicated that a child of strength and majesty would be born.

Toward the end of her confinement, Queen Maya journeyed to her father's house, stopping at the fragrant gardens of Lumbini in what is today southern Nepal. There, according to legend, in a golden palanquin attended by thousands of court ladies, the queen gave birth from her right side at the very moment that she reached out to pluck the flowering branch of an ashoka tree.

The legend holds that the deities Indra and Brahma immediately descended from the heavens to take the infant in their arms, that the other gods blinked in wonder, the galaxies quivered, the earth shook, the raging fires of hell were consumed, showers of petals cascaded

Infant Buddha. "In keeping with the usual Indian convention, Siddhartha appears as a fully grown figure, simply reduced in scale, rather than as a child." (P. Pal) Detail, gilt bronze, Ming Dynasty, China, 16th–17th century.

The Education of Siddhartha. This silk panel and the one on the opposite page, drawn in ink and colors, are from the Dunghuang Cave Temples in China, 9th century.

from the heavens, prisoners were freed, blind men regained their sight, the mute spoke in praise, and celestial trumpets heralded the child's glory.

Seven days after Siddhartha's birth, Queen Maya died. As was the custom, King Suddhodana then married Queen Maya's sister Prajapati, who raised Siddhartha as her own at the king's palace in Kapilavastu.

The king summoned renowned seers from their mountain abodes to predict the child's destiny. Pointing to auspicious constellations in the skies and to the child's perfect features, they agreed that Siddhartha was destined for immeasurable greatness, that his influence would be boundless and his benevolence unsurpassed.

But his astrological chart also held an ambiguity: If the prince succeeded to the throne, he would become India's greatest king, a universal monarch. On the other hand, if he pursued a spiritual path, his magnificence would be unmatched, for if he looked inward, he would conquer himself. The king was pleased to have fathered a great future king, but he was worried for the kingdom, should his son become a sage.

The eminent hermit and prophet Asita was beckoned to Kapilavastu by the miraculous signs that heralded the birth of a future Buddha. When he arrived at the palace, Asita told the king, "For the welfare and happiness of the world, your son will teach the dharma."

prince siddhartha's life

In response to the prophecies, King Suddhodana embarked upon futile attempts to beguile the prince with worldly pleasures.

The palace was surrounded by exquisite gardens, lotus ponds, pleasure groves, and forests. Within his residence the most beautiful maidens, cultivated in the arts of singing, dancing, making music, and making love, were provided for his pleasure. Splendid banquets, the finest steeds, and all earthly delights were designed to win Siddhartha's heart. He also received an extensive education in mathematics, astronomy, and metaphysics under prestigious Brahman tutors. And, as the future leader of the warrior caste, he became skilled in archery, horsemanship, and the arts of battle. He met his challengers on the tournament grounds and defeated even the most accomplished opponents with precision, strength, and grace.

At the age of sixteen, Prince Siddhartha married Yasodhara, a young woman of great beauty and intelligence. Although his life was rich and full, the prophecies of Siddhartha's spiritual awakening remained unrefuted.

Siddhartha devised a means to leave the palace in order to satisfy his curiosity about life outside. When King Suddhodana heard of this, he ordered that the kingdom be whitewashed and that every sign of suffering, old age, and sickness be removed. But Siddhartha's destiny had to be fulfilled.

Riding out from the eastern gate in his chariot, the prince caught sight of an old man, bent, withered, and toothless. Astonished, he asked his driver to explain the disturbing sight. He learned that all beings are subject to the ravages of old age.

Riding out from the southern gate, Siddhartha saw a man disfigured by bodily rot and covered with sores. Dismayed, he again requested an explanation and learned that all beings fall prey to the calamity of disease.

Riding out from the western gate, he discovered a bloated and maggot-ridden corpse deserted by the roadside. Shaken, he learned that all beings inevitably succumb to the finality of death.

Transformed by these experiences, Siddhartha realized the futility of worldly affairs. "Why pursue that which is doomed to such a fate?" he wondered.

Finally, riding out from the northern gate, he saw a gaunt recluse standing with quiet dignity, staff in one hand and an alms bowl in the other. Impressed, he was told, "That is a holy man—one who seeks to break the bonds of becoming and attain a mind that abides nowhere."

While these encounters were certainly pivotal in the transformation of Siddhartha, he also noted how others on the periphery appeared oblivious to the suffering in their midst. He was determined

The Four Encounters of Prince Siddhartha outside the palace of his father, King Suddhodana.

Palace Scenes. Upper panel: The enthronement of Prince Siddhartha and his wife Yasodhara. Lower panel: Life in the palace of King Suddhodana, father of the Buddha. Gandhara stone carving, Pakistan, 2nd century.

to do differently and to live a life of discipline structured by acute, unflinching awareness.

Leaving the palace once again, Siddhartha requested his driver to take him to the countryside, where he slipped off in search of solitude. His driver later found him seated in deep meditation under a fruit tree. This taste of meditation awakened the young prince to his birthright and destiny.

A new situation opened up for Siddhartha. His wife, Yasodhara, had given him a son, assuring that there would be an heir to the throne. This event accomplished Siddhartha's primary mundane responsibility, enabling him to set his mind free to pursue the life necessary for his liberation. The spiritual goals he set himself led to an ultimate renunciation and provided an example for all those who would follow.

leaving the palace: the great renunciation

Thus, at the age of twenty-nine, forsaking his wife and child, Siddhartha left the palace by chariot and rode into the night. Reaching the edge of the forest, he removed his golden ornaments, cut his long hair, and changed from silks into cotton clothes. His driver attempted to dissuade him, but Siddhartha vowed not to return to the palace until he had attained enlightenment.

Siddhartha's decision, on the one hand, was inevitable. Not only did the laws of karma predetermine his decision, but his own insight took him beyond equivocation. Yet to idealize his determination in ways that diminish the degree of his sacrifice is to miss the point. He left a life of luxury to sleep on the forest floors; he forfeited security to beg for his food; he left the love of family and wife for a solitary life; he gave up a throne to live like a beggar. At the same time, the great renunciation his life continues to exemplify was that of the self.

Miracle Below the Jambu Tree. Upper panel: Siddhartha leaves the palace in search of the cause of suffering. Lower panel: Siddhartha meditates beneath a fruit tree, with his father and stepmother on either side. White limestone carving, India, 3rd century.

siddhartha's life as an ascetic

Living the life of a renunciate, Siddhartha went from house to house asking for alms, then retired to the forest to eat what he had gathered. There he began a search for the renowned Arada-Kalama, a hermit sage who lived in the mountains north of Rajagriha.

Siddhartha's noble demeanor escaped no one's notice, and the news of an aristocratic mendicant soon reached the palace of King Bimbisara, the most powerful sovereign of central India. Curious to know who this might be, King Bimbisara sought out the mendicant and was astonished to discover that he was none other than Siddhartha, royal heir of the Shakyas. The king offered him a kingdom, but Siddhartha rejected it and returned to his spiritual quest.

At last locating the master Arada-Kalama, Siddhartha learned methods for developing concentration through breathing techniques and yogic postures. He was soon able to enter the "sphere of nothingness," but he was still not free of his passions. His questions about the source and cessation of suffering had not been resolved.

The Great Departure and Mara's Assault. Upper panel: Siddhartha is enticed by Mara, Lord of Temptation, and his daughters. Lower panel: Prince Siddhartha's departure from the palace. 56" high stone relief, India, 4th century.

Therefore, since the master had no more to teach him, Siddhartha bowed respectfully and left the hermitage to seek further.

From there he went to study with another hermit sage, Udraka-Ramaputra, a great philosopher whose doctrine guided Siddhartha past the sphere of nothingness to the "sphere of neither perception nor nonperception." Although he quickly mastered this more difficult doctrine, he knew there was more to be learned and again left to continue his search. He determined thereafter not to seek help from teachers but from within himself, and to practice on his own.

One day, as he was meditating on Mt. Gaya, he was joined by five ascetics who so respected his attainments that they were convinced he would become enlightened. They wandered together, living in the forests and subsisting on alms as they pursued their contemplative life.

Siddhartha practiced austerities to the most extreme degree, eventually eating only one grain of rice per day. But he found that this did not lead to liberation; after six years, his body had become so emaciated that he lacked the strength even to meditate. On the verge of collapse, he encountered the maiden Sujata, who recognized how majestic he was despite his appearance and, inspired to help him, offered him a bowl of rice milk. Acknowledging Sujata as a providential presence, Siddhartha accepted the sustenance, at the same time recognizing the futility of his extremist practices.

Taking this as a sign of weakness, Siddhartha's five companions abandoned him. He understood, however, that the nourishment of food and the warmth of compassion were necessary to make him fit for the revelation of the sacred mysteries that had so long eluded him. Now he was able to walk on to the place which would later become known as Bodhgaya, his strength restored and his resolve to attain enlightenment renewed.

enlightenment

Siddhartha was now prepared to meditate until true transformation had been achieved. He seated himself upon some kusha grass, beneath a tree that would be known thenceforward as the bodhi (*bodhi*

Ascetic Shakyamuni. The emaciated Siddhartha during his ascetic period. Bronze with silver inlay, China, 16th century.

is the Sanskrit word for "awake") tree, with the determination not to rise until his goal had been attained.

Now he was beset by passions embodied by the demonic forces of Mara, the Lord of Temptation. It could be said that Mara is only a state of mind and that Siddhartha was at that point engaged in a final challenge to let go of his own internal attachments. If Siddhartha were to slip and fall back into believing that his enemies were outside his own mind, then Mara would win and delusion would reign. However, recognizing the true nature of these forces, he defeated them.

At last, meditating with equanimity, wisdom, and total attentiveness, his enlightenment came in four successive stages, which came to be known as the Four Watches, after a term used by ancient peoples to denote division of time during the night.

the four watches

During the First Watch, the details of all of Siddhartha's past lives came to him with such clarity and presence that he actually relived, rather than recollected, his previous incarnations. Filled with empathy for all creatures, he watched the repeated cycles of creation and dissolution of all forms and states of animate and inanimate existence. Here he saw the suffering caused by our clinging to forms as if they were substantial instead of accepting the fact of impermanence.

During the Second Watch, he turned his attention to the cycle of death and rebirth, or *karma*. He saw how the degree of pleasure or pain a sentient being experiences in each moment is determined by that being's prior actions, whether they be committed in the present lifetime or in one from the past; that is, he recognized the underlying causes of the quality of life. And he saw as well that lifetime after lifetime, because of the ever-present fear of death, there is no end to suffering.

The opening of the wisdom eye occurred during the Third Watch. This allowed Siddhartha the inner vision to penetrate the coarseness of the physical world and to experience the true nature of mind.

The Temptation of Mara. "In this beautiful ivory relief from Kashmir, Shakyamuni sits in meditation with downcast eyes. He remains calm and serene, although two of Mara's attendants blow conchs into his ears and a third beats a drum nearby. Simultaneously, several ferocious-looking demons attack him with weapons. Two handsome figures, each smiling and holding a flower, flank the meditating Shakyamuni. The male figure on the left of the relief may represent Mara, and the figure on the right, who appears to be female, may be one of his daughters. The position of Shakyamuni's right hand touching the earth in the gesture known as *bhumisparsamudra* indicates the moment of his Enlightenment and hence his victory over Mara." (P. Pal)

In the Fourth Watch, he focused on the apparent reality of present time. He saw that people are born, they age, they experience good health and sickness, they die and are reborn—that, fettered by desire and ignorance, they live like moles, scurrying blindly through successive lifetimes, too entrapped by their attachments to find their way to the light.

Shakyamuni Buddha at the moment of enlightenment. Brass with colors, Tibet, 11th-13th century.

Thus, having experienced his own prior incarnations and the cycle of death and rebirth, Siddhartha entered the great emptiness. Now, although he searched from the summit of the world downward, he could find no trace of himself. As the morning star rose, he proclaimed, "How wonderful! How wonderful! All things are enlightened exactly as they are."

What he had so arduously pursued had been there all along—obscured by illusions, but still there, within, and waiting to be discovered. The journey of the Buddha had been completed.

Siddhartha continued to sit under the bodhi tree. He had no desire to take action. For seven days he looked into his own mind. Having fully comprehended the essence of suffering, he now formulated the Four Noble Truths. At last, having achieved his goal, he was motivated to leave his "diamond seat" (the diamond being symbolic of the indestructible mind), and he set out to teach. He became known as the Buddha.

The Buddha's decision to teach after attaining his own enlightenment helped to define Buddhism as a path of compassion. Furthermore, his return to the world, to work helping others, was not a descent from Buddhahood to a less elevated realm but was, in fact, the next stage of enlightenment.

the missed opportunity

As the Buddha made his way from Bodhgaya toward the town of Sarnath, the first person he encountered was the mendicant, Upaka. Awed by the countenance of Shakyamuni and perceiving that his senses had been tamed while those of all others were as restless as wild horses, Upaka asked, "What are you?"

Shakyamuni answered, "I am a Buddha."

Upaka then made a deep bow in recognition of Shakyamuni's attainment and proceeded on his way. By not asking to be instructed, he missed an opportunity to become the Buddha's first disciple and to become enlightened.

the buddha's teaching

When the Buddha arrived in Sarnath, he met his former companions, the five ascetics, in a park full of gentle deer thereafter to be known as Deer Park. Remembering his acceptance of the rice milk given him by Sujata, they planned among themselves to reject him when they saw him approach. Yet as he drew nearer, they were awed by his enlightened presence and rose up in unison to take his robe, receive his bowl, arrange a place for him to sit, and prepare water for bathing his feet. However, they addressed him by his former name, Gautama.

The Buddha explained that this name was no longer appropriate, since he was no longer who he had been. He then drew a parallel between those who are hopelessly attached to satisfying their senses and those who are determined to deny them. Both, he told the astonished ascetics, are equally distant from the path of deathlessness, the perpetually enlightened state of mind that is without beginning or ending.

This was the teaching of the Middle Way.

But, asked the ascetics, what alternatives are there to austerities? The Buddha then elucidated the Four Noble Truths.

Shakyamuni Buddha began his first sermon by analyzing the root symptom of the human predicament: suffering. The First Noble Truth is often stated as "Life is suffering," meaning that suffering and dissatisfaction are symptomatic of the human condition. In truth, life is just life, neither good nor bad, neither pleasurable nor painful. It is our attachment to life—how we relate to it, try to control it, manipulate it, regulate it, and cling to it—that causes suffering. The Buddha thus located the problem of suffering within the human mind, not in the external phenomena of life.

In the Second Noble Truth, the Buddha identified the cause of suffering: desire and attachment. Its source is unreal, impermanent, changeable, and insubstantial. Nonetheless the experience of suffering is concrete and cannot be ignored; that is, the Buddha does not dismiss suffering just because it is manifested by the ephemeral self. Since the cause of suffering does not reside outside the mind, suffering cannot be alleviated with material solutions. ("You can't buy happiness" is a familiar Western expression of this essential insight.)

Constructing his teaching the way a doctor assesses the needs of a patient, Shakyamuni offered his diagnosis in the Third Noble Truth. Suffering can come to an end; its cessation is possible and within the

The Buddha Teaching. His hands are in the gesture of "turning the wheel of the law," or teaching the Buddha dharma. Gandhara, 29", stone carving, Pakistan, 2nd century.

reach of everyone. The debilitating disease of self-interest can be transformed and transcended.

In the Fourth Noble Truth, the Buddha outlined the way to bring about this end, known as the Eightfold Path:

1. *Right View:* that which is directly in line with the teaching, or the dharma.
2. *Right Intention:* the motivation of altruism, or being of benefit to others, rather than selfishness.
3. *Right Speech:* verbalizing things which are related to the teachings or otherwise express Right Intention. Buddhists place great importance on speech, seeing it as a direct reflection of mind.
4. *Right Conduct:* action which directly expresses the heart, exemplary of the teachings of the Buddha.
5. *Right Livelihood:* a vocation which is of service to others, advancing oneself and one's fellow beings along the path of virtuous activity.
6. *Right Effort:* the diligence or energy with which one practices the dharma and engages in activity leading to the realization of the enlightened state of mind.
7. *Right Mindfulness:* being attentive, present, and focused in all one's daily activities of body, speech, and mind.
8. *Right Concentration:* "one-pointed" attention, developed through meditative practice, on the teaching of the Buddha.

The Eightfold Path defines the basis of all Buddhist studies.

Upon listening to the Buddha's teaching, the five ascetics attained liberation and became *Arhats,* which literally means "foe destroyers." Thus began the *sangha,* the community of ordained practitioners. They stayed together in Sarnath for the three months of the summer rainy season. Then the Buddha instructed his many disciples to travel throughout the land and teach for the benefit of all living beings.

The Buddha was thirty-five years old at this time. He spent the rest of his long life walking through northern India and teaching the dharma. Disregarding the conventions of caste, he welcomed anyone

Circumambulating the massive stupa at Sarnath, India, the site where the Buddha first taught. A small stupa within this one contains relics of the Buddha.

to come and converse with him and, if they wished, receive the teachings and enter the order. Almost all who came to the Buddha did not merely receive the teachings but were completely enlightened and became exemplary members of the sangha.

The Buddha emphasized practice and training rather than superstition, ritual, and worship. Part of the significance of the Eightfold Path is that it affirms the capacity of human beings to change and to take responsibility for their own well-being. He rejected dependency on anything other than the mind in attaining enlightenment and advocated verification of truth through personal experience.

He denied the existence of an individual, independently existing self. He did acknowledge that an apparent self exists, but only as a projection of the mind shaped by human convention. It is this mind that experiences suffering, he said, and the mind can be transformed. And he taught a way of viewing the world and of behaving in it that would achieve that aim.

The Buddha was always skillful in presenting the teachings. One day, while meditating under a tree, he was approached by a group of young noblemen. They were chasing a prostitute who had run off with their wives' jewelry as they dozed after a picnic. The Buddha asked, "Which is more important, to seek the woman or to seek yourselves?"

Sensing the profundity of this question, the men gathered around to hear more. And the Buddha, seeing that the men were ready to listen, talked about the nature of human existence, and of the senselessness of seeking outside oneself and of blaming others for one's own unhappiness. The men and their wives thus became students of the Buddha.

On another occasion, a jealous priest with great psychic powers put a poisonous snake in the hut where the Buddha was to spend the night. When the Enlightened One emerged unharmed the next morning, the priest asked him to explain his powers.

"Having tamed myself, there is no difficulty taming others," he replied. In the face of such tranquillity, the snake had curled up beside him in the night.

Overcome with remorse, the priest confessed that he himself was more vicious than the venomous snake. He bowed down at the Buddha's feet and requested instruction in taming the mind. The news of this powerful priest's conversion spread quickly and attracted others to the path.

In another version of the story, the Buddha was pitted against the priest in a four-day competition of supernormal powers. Although he easily beat his opponent, resulting in the priest's initiation into the sangha, the Buddha explained that such powers do not lead to enlightenment and are trivial compared to true wisdom. Nonetheless, tales of the Enlightened One's great powers inevitably spread far and wide.

The defeat of the priest also resulted in the conversion of his thousand disciples. The event was monumental historically, because it marked the end of animal sacrifice and supernormal feats as representing the pinnacle of spiritual practice. In their place the Buddha conceived of a path to the ultimate in spiritual experience—enlightenment—through ethical conduct, meditation, and wisdom.

To disciples who had previously been fire worshipers, he taught that the flames of suffering are fanned by greed, anger, and ignorance, and that the fire within the mind must be controlled. To Bimbisara, king of the realm of Magadha, he dared to challenge the concept of caste. With regard to both society and religion, his views were thoroughly revolutionary.

Philosophical debate and metaphysical abstraction were highly popular in the India of that day. Pragmatic mystic and universal healer, the Buddha asked, "Suppose a man were shot by an arrow. What should he do? Should he ask who shot it, of what clan, what complexion, what caste? Or should he busy himself with the task of removing the arrow?"

With such logic he revealed the profound immediacy of spiritual life. One day, when questioned, he simply held a flower aloft. Kashapa the Great, who understood the significance of the silent gesture, was designated the Buddha's first successor.

In time the Buddha returned to Kapilavastu, to the palace where he had spent his youth. His wife Yasodhara, still grieving for the loss of her former husband, eventually dried her tears and bowed down at his feet. The king, at first shocked to see his son seeking alms with his retinue of monks, was filled with awe upon meeting him. No one was quite prepared for the effect of the great presence of the Buddha. His half-brother Ananda and a number of childhood friends became monks, and the ranks of the ordained swelled. Wherever he went, the Buddha affected people profoundly, and his attainments elicited their devotion.

He later visited Kapilavastu again to see his dying ninety-seven-year-old father. After receiving the comforting words of his son, the king died serenely. Queen Prajapati, recognizing the truth of impermanence and the suffering that follows from desire and attachment, requested admission to the order.

At first the Buddha was reluctant to admit her in view of the prevailing attitudes of the day. But eventually he agreed, and asserted the potential of women for achieving enlightenment, thereby defying social norms by allowing them to abandon household life. Prajapati, along with 500 noblewomen, formed the first order of Buddhist nuns. Eventually Yasodhara herself joined the community. Shakyamuni continued to expound the spiritual equality of the sexes, again contradicting one of the most cherished beliefs of his day.

Not all of the Buddha's disciples became immediately enlightened. One among them, his own cousin Devadatta, slandered him and attempted to kill him out of jealousy. But even when Devadatta rolled a huge boulder down a mountain and released a mad elephant to crush him, the Buddha remained unscathed.

The Lotus Sutra, considered to be the final sermon, proclaims the potential for anyone to attain enlightenment, from any point in his or her life, thus neutralizing any fixed definition of good and evil. Making specific reference to Devadatta, the Buddha implied that even he, after all his "evil deeds," had as good a chance for enlightenment as any upstanding member of the sangha.

Buddhists summarize the accomplishments of the Buddha by presenting them as the Twelve Deeds:

1. Life and teaching in Tushita heaven, a pure land
2. Entering the womb of his mother
3. Taking birth
4. Displaying his skill in the worldly arts—mathematics, fencing, archery, horsemanship
5. Fully experiencing the pleasures of women
6. Renouncing worldly life and ordination as a monk
7. Engaging in arduous ascetic practices
8. Meditating under the bodhi tree
9. Defeating the host of demons
10. Attaining full enlightenment
11. Teaching, or turning the wheel of doctrine
12. Passing into the state of peace.

the death of the buddha

By the age of eighty-one, after more than forty years of traveling the length and breadth of northern India disseminating his teachings, the Buddha's physical body began to fail. Upon completing the annual rainy-season retreat, he began a journey to Kusinagara to prepare for his *parinirvana,* or passing away.

The group stopped in the village of Pava for lunch. The meal caused the Buddha immediate discomfort and he became very sick. Sympathetic to the cook Chundra's despair at the inadvertent result of his meal, the Buddha called Ananda to his side and said, "Tell Chundra that the two meals in my whole life that I am most grateful for are Sujata's and his. One helped me to attain enlightenment, and the other is helping me to enter nirvana. Tell this to Chundra and ease his mind."

At Kusinagara the party entered a grove, and there the Buddha instructed Ananda to prepare a place for him to lie down with the head of his bed facing north. Some interpret this to mean that his teachings would spread to the north—to Tibet, Mongolia, and beyond.

The Buddha lay on his right side, resting his head on his right palm, and put one leg over the other in the posture of parinirvana, also known as the lion's pose. He instructed his grief-stricken disciples to take the dharma as their teacher, relying neither on any person nor on anything else, and to work diligently for enlightenment.

Legend has it that the earth trembled, celestial music filled the air, and the Buddha's golden form was showered with a rain of heavenly flower petals. The Enlightened One had fulfilled his mission. He died an ordinary death, demonstrating the impermanence of life and the suffering of cyclic existence to his followers.

Nehan (paranirvana), the passing of the Buddha. Detail from hanging scroll, color on silk, Japan, Mouromachi Period, 14th century.

The Early History *of* Kalachakra

INDIA AND SHAMBALA

OUT OF HIS GREAT compassion and desire to benefit all beings, the Buddha manifested himself as the Kalachakra deity to confer the initiation at Dhanyakataka in South India. Some say this happened one year after he attained enlightenment, while others say it was one year before he shed his body. However, the Dalai Lama says that logically it must have been at the end of his life, because the Kalachakra Tantra reflects so many of his lifelong accomplishments.

A three-dimensional Kalachakra Mandala of gold, 12 feet in diameter, in the Potala Palace, Lhasa, Tibet. 18th century.

59

The Buddha gave the Kalachakra Initiation at the request of Suchandra, the king of Shambala. Shambala is said to be to the north of India and Tibet, a land where an enlightened society

King of Shambala. King Suchandra, who requested the Kalachakra Initiation from the Buddha. Suchandra is identified by his golden crown and wheel pendant, symbolic of the Kalachakra Tantra. Thangka painting, Tibet, 18th-19th century.

lives in a perpetual state of bliss consciousness. Some say it is as close as northern Tibet while others believe that it is in Siberia or as far north as the North Pole. Others believe it is still farther, as far as North America, or even the stars. Early texts do, however, contain elaborate, graphic descriptions known as guidebooks to Shambala.

During the lifetime of the Buddha, when ordinary communications and travel were extremely limited, a pure land beyond the treacherous northern mountains of India was presented as an almost unattainable goal and only those with the highest realization attempted it. But no matter where the believer lived, Shambala has existed as a goal symbolic of the enlightened state of mind.

the setting

The Buddha taught the Kalachakra Tantra inside the *stupa* known as Sri Dhanyakataka. This sacred place, existing from the time of the third historical Buddha (the incarnation of the Buddha prior to Shakyamuni, the Buddha of our time), is located in a southern Indian village currently known as Amaravati.

During the time of the third Buddha there had been a famine, so the people had prayed to the appropriate deities and were saved by a shower of rice that came down from the sky and formed itself into the stupa at Dhanyakataka. This came to be known as the Rice Pile Shrine, the sacred and miraculous place where Shakyamuni Buddha came to confer the Kalachakra Initiation.

Shakyamuni, although he led the life of a monk, manifested himself as the Kalachakra deity in union with his consort Vishvamata, and the entire mandala of Kalachakra. The palace of Kalachakra, replete with deities, offerings, balconies, and portals, was projected in its fully three-dimensional form resting on the cosmic Mt. Meru.

Placed upon the mountain were several different "seats" for the mandala, such as the seat of the sun and the seat of the moon. And at the top center of the mandala itself stood the Buddha in the form of the deity Kalachakra with his consort, surrounded by the many hundreds of other deities who reside within the mandala, deities who are all manifestations of Kalachakra, or the Buddha's realized mind.

But this was not all. There was a second mandala projected upon the ceiling of the stupa, in a configuration that we might imagine to appear like a canopy of stars and comets. This was called the

Miniature Chorten. A stupa (*chorten* in Tibetan) is a monument composed of a square, a circle, a triangle, a cresent, and a flame, one on top of the other. Consecrated to have the power of the Buddha, a stupa may be a small personal reliquary or as large as several acres. 7⁵/₈" high, cast brass, Tibet, 12th century.

Glorious Constellation Mandala, or Great Integration Mandala, which consisted of ten different mandalas. The initiation took place within the time it takes to snap one's fingers.

Above: *Meru Mandala*. Abstract representation of the universe, including the elements earth, water, fire, and wind, which are depicted by squares, circles, triangles, and cresents. On top of the cosmic Mt. Meru is the palace of Kalachakra. Kalachakra and his consort are symbolized by a crystal on a lotus flower. 12" in diameter, gilt copper, eastern Tibet, 18th century.

Right: The cosmic Mt. Meru as it is traditionally visualized, in the shape of a cone composed of earth and water, and resting on the other elements of the universe. On top of the mountain is the five-story palace of Kalachakra. All of this is depicted in the Kalachakra Sand Mandala.

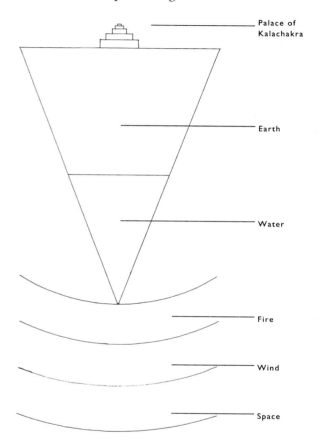

Palace of
Kalachakra

Earth

Water

Fire

Wind

Space

Manjusri, the Buddha of Wisdom, is always present at the transmission of the Kalachakra Tantra. He hovered over the mandala in the stupa, in luminous colors, to assist Shakyamuni.

How could it be that something as great as a mountain could fit inside a mere stupa? We can begin to understand this if we think of what it is like to look through the eye of a needle. If we hold the needle up close to our eye and look through it, we can actually see things that are very large, even something as large as a mountain. It is a matter of perspective, and what is happening in the mind of the person who is having the experience.

king suchandra and the ninety-six generals

King Suchandra, a member of the Shakya clan of which Shakyamuni Buddha was the prince, was king of Shambala. He was more than an ordinary human being—he was an emanation of Vajrapani, the deity who represents the power of all the Buddhas. This is how he knew of the Kalachakra teachings and had the wisdom to request them.

In fact, there were many advanced disciples in Shambala who were particularly suited to this initiation. The people of Shambala already had a strong faith in the Buddha dharma and in spiritual practice in general. They were a peaceful people, unlike the peoples around them and unlike those of today.

Suchandra was accompanied by his retinue of ninety-six generals, governors, and chieftains of provinces, or minor kingdoms within Shambala, most of whom were ready for these highest of teachings. The people were so advanced that they were adept in the practice of the *powa*—that is, at the time of death they could transfer their consciousness at will and with great dexterity from this physical body to the next so that they could be reborn in a pure realm.

They had other powers as well, which is why they were able to make the journey from Shambala to south India to witness the miraculous appearance of the Kalachakra Mandala and of the deities that the Buddha manifested.

the guidebooks

In Tibetan literature there are many guidebooks to Shambala. The most famous was written in 1775 by the Third Panchen Lama, Lobsang Palden Yeshe, and was called *Shambhalai Lamyig* [the Description of the way to shambala]. An older one is found in the *Tengyur,* the commentary section of the Tibetan Canon, which the Panchen Lama's version closely follows. To succeed in the journeys described, one needs to be particularly adept at the path and practice of meditation, and must possess great physical stamina. Many have actually attempted this arduous journey northward, without success.

The Buddha Vajrapani, who represents the power of all the Buddhas. This Sanskrit name literally means, "holder of the vajra." Ink on paper, Nepal, 19th century.

The guidebooks were written to serve those who, in degenerate future times, might wish to seek enlightenment for the benefit of others. Those qualified for the journey would have received an initiation into the Kalachakra Mandala, learned the science of the ritual, and become students of the tantra.

According to Edwin Bernbaum in *The Way to Shambhala,* Shambala "symbolizes the end of a journey into the hidden depths of the mind." The unexplored lands between India (or Tibet) and Shambala represent the subconscious mind, that which lies just beneath the familiar realm of surface consciousness. The pure land of Shambala, on the other hand, is the superconscious mind. The fact that there is such a great distance between Shambala and the known world tells us that the superconscious is "hidden deep in the mind, far from the illusions of the surface consciousness." According to the guidebooks, this subconscious area, which stands between the surface consciousness (or self-conscious mind) and the superconscious mind, contains a mixture of different elements, "bright rays of illuminating awareness" mixed with "dark clouds of delusion."

description of shambala

Shambala is said to lie within a ring of snow-covered mountains, which serves to bar all those not fit to enter. These mountains are forever hidden in mist, so that there is no way the kingdom's presence might be detected. Inside this outer ring lies another ring of even higher mountains. And the area between the two rings is divided into eight regions by rivers and smaller mountain ranges. These regions are shaped like petals symmetrically arrayed around the center of a flower; the entire shape is often compared to a lotus blossom. Each of these regions is in turn divided into twelve principalities, making up the individual domains of the ninety-six chieftains or governors.

Despite its great northerly location, the land of Shambala is lush with parks and meadows, flowers and abundant vegetation. Peace reigns throughout the land, and there is no need for harsh laws. Even the poorest of inhabitants has more material wealth than he or she can use and lives free of sickness. These qualities coincide with those in the description of Shangri-la, the idyllic realm created by James Hilton in his romantic novel *Lost Horizon.* However, the people of Shambala devote their entire lives to the study and practice of the Kalachakra Tantra.

The inner-ring mountains surrounding the central portion of the "lotus blossom" shine brilliantly because they are made entirely of

ice crystals. At the very center of this complex system lies Kalapa, capital of Shambala.

In *The Way to Shambhala,* Bernbaum has translated descriptions of Shambala from Tibetan texts. He writes, "The jeweled palace of the King at the center of Shambhala shines with a glow that lights up the night like day, reducing the moon to a dim spot in the sky. The palace's pagoda roofs gleam with tiles made of the purest gold, and ornaments of pearl and diamond hang from the eaves. Coral molding carved with dancing goddesses decorates the outside walls. Emeralds and sapphires frame the doorways while golden awnings shade windows made of lapis lazuli and diamonds. Pillars and beams of coral, pearl, and zebra stone support the interior of the palace, which is sumptuously furnished with carpets and cushions of fine brocade. Different kinds of crystal embedded in the floors and ceilings control the temperature of the rooms by giving off cold and heat."

At the center of the palace is the king's golden throne, supported by eight carved lions encrusted with jewels. "As long as the King remains on this seat of wisdom and power, a magic jewel given him by the serpent deities who guard hidden treasures enables him to satisfy all his wishes."

The inhabitants of Shambala also possess extraordinary powers. They have developed an advanced science and technology, which has been put to the service of spiritual ends. "Tibetan medical texts believed to have come from the kingdom describe human anatomy and physiology, sophisticated theories and methods of diagnosis, and ways to cure and prevent serious diseases such as smallpox. Other Kalachakra texts from Shambala have provided Tibetans with their systems of astronomy and astrology, as well as one of the calendars they use today." Their "stone horses with the power of wind" sound very much like our modern aircraft. The skylights in the king's palace are fitted with lenses that reveal life in other solar systems, and the king has a mirror that enables him to view whatever is happening in his country. But all of these sciences are only important to the Shambalans to the extent that they aid them in mastering "the highest science of all—the science of mind, or meditation." Through

Opposite: The mythical kingdom of Shambala, with the king at the center surrounded by the domains of the ninety-six governors. Shambala is known for its development of advanced sciences and technologies used in the practice of enlightened activity. Thangka painting, Tibet, 19th century.

the direct awareness and control of their minds and bodies which they have developed, they are able to heal their own bodies. They are also capable of telepathy and clairvoyance and can walk at very high speeds. Despite these marvelous abilities, the people of Shambala are not yet fully enlightened. "They still retain some human failings and illusions, but many fewer than people of the outside world. They all, however, strive to attain enlightenment and bring up their children to do likewise. Theirs is the closest to the ideal society that can be reached in this world."

The Kalachakra Tantra was given to the people of Shambala to help them make that final step to the highest enlightenment.

kalachakra in shambala

Following the empowerment at the Rice Pile Shrine, King Suchandra returned to Shambala and, over the next two years, transcribed all that had been imparted to him by the Buddha in what is known as the *mula,* or root text. It comprised twelve thousand verses, written in an unknown tongue called "twilight language." The Buddha had instructed Suchandra to teach the Kalachakra Tantra and also to build a three-dimensional Kalachakra Mandala in his native land. Some scholars say that certain realized practitioners who went to Shambala in search of these teachings returned to India without the texts in written form, but with an understanding of them. They then wrote the teachings in Sanskrit.

It is, of course, impossible to provide scholarly documentation or irrefutable proof of the history of Kalachakra in Shambala before these written teachings. But Tibetans feel that this kind of concern derives from too linear a way of seeing the world, or of having only one level, or interpretation, of reality. By getting beyond this limited perspective, we are able to see and understand how the world functions on subtler levels. Those who believe in Shambala and practice the Kalachakra Tantra, for example, feel that they have become one with the deity and have been given instant and nonlinear access to a vast resource of knowledge, wisdom, and compassion.

the seven shakya kings
and the twenty-five kalkis

King Suchandra was the first of seven Shakya kings of Shambala, each of whom was an emanation of a different *bodhisattva,* and each of whom reigned for 100 years. The seventh was called Yashas, "the Renowned." King Yashas was an emanation of Manjusri, the Buddha of Wisdom, and predicted the coming of the "barbarian dharma" after 800 years. Through his skill as a teacher, he converted the Brahman sages to Buddhism, combining all the castes of Shambala into one "vajra family" (those who have received the tantric empowerment from the same lama). Henceforth, the rulers were known as *kalki,* meaning governors who hold the lineage.

In this way, Yashas ensured that Shambala would remain outside the range of the barbarian influences and that his descendant, the prophesied twenty-fifth kalki, Raudra Chakri, and his army would perform their role at the end of the *Kali Yuga,* or the current Age of Darkness or Strife. Shakyamuni Buddha prophesied that the twenty-fifth kalki would usher in the Age of Enlightenment, transforming all the ignorance of the barbarians to Buddha mind. This age was prophesied to last for 1,000 years before the cycle returned to a degenerative process.

We are currently in the reign of the twenty-first kalki king, which would place the new Golden Age some 400 years from now; but such calculations are futile, in any case, since we cannot even be sure of what constitutes 100 years of Shambala time. Many scholars think the Golden Age will occur during the twenty-first century.

The first of the kalki was named Manjukirti, again an emanation of Manjusri. He was also the first to put the Kalachakra Tantra into condensed form, called the *Sri Kalachakra,* which became the basic tantra for the Kalachakra system.

At the time the Buddha gave the first initiation, he prophesied that 600 years later Manjusri would take the form of the first of the kalki and would compose a Kalachakra text. Then he said that Manjusri would appear again much later in the form of the twenty-fifth

69

kalki, whose particular task would be to overcome the forces of the barbarians.

Manjusri represents the mind that realizes emptiness. Because the disputes that arise between nations and between individuals come about through wrong views, only Manjusri, emanation of the Wisdom Mind of the Buddha, can truly overcome the "barbarians."

It was King Yashas's son, Pundarika, who wrote the commentary on *Sri Kalachakra* entitled the *Vimalaprabha.* These two texts comprise our basic written sources for the Kalachakra system as a whole.

Of the twenty-five kalkis, the seventeenth, Shripala, is especially important to us because it was through him that the Kalachakra lineage reentered India in A.D. 1027. The kalki system continues even to this day in Shambala.

kalachakra returns to india

The Kalachakra Tantra was nurtured and kept alive in Shambala for at least 1,500 years before it reemerged in India. However, there is evidence that there was at least an aspect of it still known and practiced in India. For example, the Indian yogi Mahasiddha Ghanda had composed a *sadhana* (meditation practice) of Kalachakra.

There are many different accounts of how the transmission of Kalachakra reentered India from Shambala. One commonly accepted version states that the tantra reappeared in India during the 10th century and was first brought to Tibet in 1027 by a Kashmiri scholar named Somanatha. However, others insist that 1027 was the year in which the tantra returned to India through King Shripala and that it was brought to Tibet later.

king shripala

This version of the story comes to us from Buton, a Tibetan scholar, writer, spiritual master, and historian of the early 14th century. He says that the tantra was brought to India by the seventeenth kalki of Shambala, Shripala himself, in 1027.

Opposite: *Kingdom of Shambala,* detail. This painting depicts the defeat of the "barbarians" (those who hold wrong views) through the application of the wisdom mind of the Buddha. Following this conflict, the present Age of Darkness will be transformed into an enlightened society. Kalachakra appears in a colored circle at the top right. 44"x44" thangka, Mongolia, 19th century.

It had become psychically known to Shripala that a young man who had a burning desire to master the profound tantras would attempt to cross the dangerous terrain from India to Shambala. Concerned for the youth's welfare on a journey across a waterless desert that would have taken four months, the king, through an emanation body, went to meet him. He initiated the young man and over the next four months taught him all the highest yoga tantras. The youth remembered all he heard and attained a mastery of the knowledge he received. When he returned to India, he became famous as an emanation of Manjusri and was known as Kalachakrapada.

tsilupa

Another version of the coming of the Kalachakra Tantra from Shambala to India tells of Tsilu, a great 11th-century *pandit* (highly realized scholar) who was born in Orissa, in the eastern part of India. He studied all the available texts on Buddhism at several of the great Buddhist universities of his day, but he did not find what he was seeking. He realized that in order to become self-liberated within a single lifetime, he needed further clarification of the doctrines associated with the Vajrayana, or tantric Buddhism. Hearing that the kings of Shambala had kept the sacred and secret doctrine intact in their distant reaches to the north, Tsilu resolved to visit them.

According to one version, Tsilu's intuitive voice told him to seek the protection of a group of traders who dealt in pearls and other jewels from the sea. However, in his restlessness he could not wait for them, so he set out on his own to traverse the mountains. Luckily, as he was climbing a mountain one day, he met a man who offered to spare him the long and arduous journey by giving him the teachings he sought then and there.

Recognizing the man to be an emanation of Manjusri, Tsilu prostrated himself before him, and Manjusri imparted to Tsilu all the initiations, the tantric commentaries, and the oral instructions of the Kalachakra Tantra through mind transmission. At last, he placed a flower on the top of Tsilu's head, blessed him, and said, "Realize the entire bodhisattva corpus," whereupon Tsilu realized the entirety of

Opposite: A *Mahasiddha*, or great yogi master, most likely sculpted by one of his students. Somanatha of Kashmir, who was such a Mahasiddha, translated the Kalachakra Tantra from Sanskrit and brought it to Tibet in the 11th century. Brass, 12 1/2", Tibet, 11th-12th century.

Naropa, an Indian Mahasiddha of the 11th century
who was instrumental in the transmission of
Kalachakra. Naropa was the abbot of Nalanda
University. Detail from *Virupa, Naropa,
Saraha, and Dombi Heruka,* thangka,
eastern Tibet, 18th century.

the transmission. Henceforth, he was known as Tsilupa, as a title of
respect.

Some think that Tsilupa was in fact Naropa, a well-known master
of Kalachakra and other tantras of the 11th century.

kalachakrapada
the elder and younger

Tsilupa's foremost student, Pindi Acarya, taught the bodhisattva corpus to Kalachakrapada the Elder. He in turn taught it to Kalachakrapada the Younger, who taught it openly at Nalanda University, the great seat of Buddhist learning in northern India.

There Kalachakrapada the Younger, intent on establishing and propagating the Kalachakra Tantra, issued a challenge to the five hundred pandits residing at Nalanda, who immediately engaged with him in a debate. With the knowledge of the highest tantra on his side, Kalachakrapada the Younger proceeded to defeat them all. They became his disciples, and the Kalachakra Tantra was firmly established in India.

Nalanda University, the great Buddhist learning center of northeastern India, had as many as 20,000 students during the 11th century, when Kalachakra became part of its curriculum. It was destroyed by foreign invaders in the 12th century.

Kalachakra Comes *to* Tibet

mountains and mystery

TIBET IS A NATURAL setting for a highly developed spiritual culture. It is ringed by lofty peaks, some the highest on the planet, which have traditionally formed borders with China, Mongolia, Ladakh, Pakistan, India, Nepal, and Myanmar (Burma). Tibet is the size of Texas and Alaska put together, and has an astounding average altitude of more than 12,000 feet. This challenging geography limited outside influences, while the harsh climatic conditions kept the population low and the country sparsely settled. Although the stark magnificence

Padma Sambhava, known to the Tibetans as Guru Rinpoche, or "Precious Teacher," was instrumental in establishing Buddhism in Tibet in the 8th century. Thangka painting, Tibet, 18th century.

of the so-called roof of the world offers little creature comfort, it seems to inspire spiritual pursuit. In fact, the mythologies of both India and China place the mountains of Tibet as home to their gods and immortals.

Archeological excavations date Tibetan civilization back 3,600 years to the Late Stone Age. Tibetan mythology holds that all Tibetans are descended from the union of the deity Avalokiteshvara in the form of an ape and the goddess Tara (who is the Mother of All Buddhas) in the form of an ogress. Their progeny gave birth to the Tibetan people in the Yarlung Valley of central Tibet. Long before the common era, Tibetans developed a particular brand of shamanism that was ideal preparation for the arrival of Buddhism in the 7th century.

the early kings and the bon tradition

As legend tells it, the first nine kings of Tibet descended a rope ladder from the sky onto a mountain top. Other stories suggest that the first king, Nyatri, was fleeing defeat in the Mahabharata war in India when he was seen coming down from the mountains by the peasants who inhabited the Yarlung Valley. The peasants took him for a mountain god and gave him the title of *tsenpo,* meaning "mighty one." Nyatri Tsenpo reigned around 127 B.C., approximately 400 years after the birth of the Buddha, although other accounts place him as far back as 400 B.C. He was the first of what became known as the Yarlung dynasty, whose kings united the many tribes scattered over this wide area.

The shamanic practices of the ancient Tibetans, which may have originated in Iran, were performed to appease local gods and demons. They placed great emphasis on divinations and sacrifices conducted by priests, primarily at burial sites, as well as rites concerning oracles, magical possessions, and healings. The word *Bon,* meaning "priest," was eventually applied to the religion as a whole, which began to take shape about the time of the ninth Yarlung king. The heavenly ladder was said to have been cut during this

The goddess Tara. 28' high, solid cast copper with jewel inlay, Nepal, 17th century.

king's reign, so that he died on earth instead of returning to heaven. The kings, or tsenpos, were worshiped as divine, so the coronation or burial of a tsenpo provided a great occasion for religious ceremonies. The practice of Bon continues in contemporary Tibet, with the strong influence of Buddhist doctrine and monasticism.

the coming of buddhism to tibet

Although Buddhism may have been introduced to Tibet as early as A.D. 173, during the period of the twenty-eighth Yarlung king, Lha Thothori Nyantsen, it was not well known until the reign of the thirty-third king, the great Songtsen Gampo. He began his reign in the year 627 at the age of thirteen and succeeded in unifying Tibet by defeating the armies of Tang China, extending his empire to the trade cities of the Silk Route to the north and into what is now Ladakh, Nepal, and northern India, and to Myanmar to the south. He was introduced to Buddhism through his exposure to the cultures of India and China as his kingdom expanded. He decided it would be useful to incorporate elements of Buddhism into his own culture to establish a greater governmental stability based on its teachings of nonviolence. He introduced several aspects of Indian culture to Tibet, including writing and a legal system.

Songtsen Gampo's conquests brought him two foreign wives, one from the Chinese imperial family and the other from the royal family of Nepal. Both princesses brought Buddhist scholars and artists, as well as dowries which included gifts of great Buddhist art. The king built temples based on Indian architecture, with wooden doorways and pillars adorned with celestial carvings reminiscent of the 5th-century Buddhist cave temples of Ajanta in western India. The temples built by Songtsen Gampo housed images of the Buddha, including one statue, the famous Jowo (or "Precious Lord") Buddha, brought by the Chinese queen, which is said to contain relics of Shakyamuni Buddha. The Jowo Buddha is now housed in the Jokhang temple, also built by Songtsen Gampo, in Lhasa, the capital of Tibet, and it remains the holiest image in Tibet to this day.

King Songtsen Gampo, who unified Tibet in the 7th century. This detail is from the oldest known Tibetan thangka, from the 11th century, which was discovered by Mokotoff Asian Arts.

79

Songtsen Gampo is thought by Tibetans to have been an incarnation of Avalokiteshvara. He was the first to assume the role of "Dharma King," although he continued to support the indigenous religion which assured his theocracy.

During the reign of the thirty-seventh king, Tri Song Deutsen (755-797), Tibet became a very powerful country and Buddhism spread throughout the kingdom. Tri Song Deutsen brought the abbot Shantarakshita, known in Tibet as the "Bodhisattva Abbot," from India to teach and to establish the first monastery at Samye. But there

Above: This sculpture of the Jowo Buddha was part of the dowry of Songtsen Gampo's Chinese wife, Princess Wencheng. It was bejeweled by Tsong Khapa in the early 15th century and contains relics of Shakyamuni Buddha. Housed in the Jokhang Temple in Lhasa, *Jowo Rinpoche* is Tibet's most revered icon.

Right: The roof of the Jokhang Temple in Lhasa, Tibet. The eaves terminate with decorative guardians to ward off evil spirits.

was great resistance from the Bon deities, so Shantarakshita suggested that Tri Song Deutsen call upon a practitioner from the land of Swat (an area of Pakistan) known for his great power, to subdue the warrior deities. This extraordinary man was Padma Sambhava.

Padma Sambhava is revered by Tibetans even today as Guru Rinpoche, or "Precious Master." His success became known far and wide, along with his great strength and vision. Thought to be an incarnation of the Buddha himself, Padma Sambhava was skilled in magic and mysticism; he performed many miracles, such as flying and emanating his presence into several places at once. He buried precious teachings known as "treasures" throughout the country for later generations to discover and put into practice.

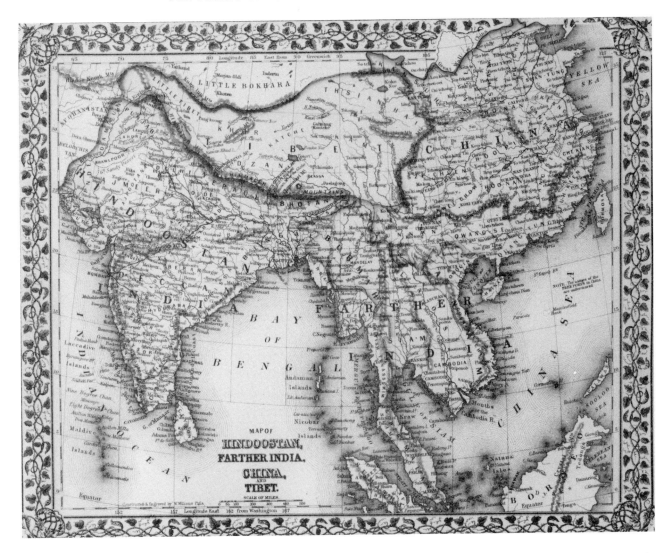

Official map from the United States Library of Congress showing India, China, Southeast Asia, and Tibet, published in 1872.

Samye Monastery was eventually completed based upon a mandala made by Padma Sambhava. A great philosophical debate was held at Samye in about 792 to determine whether Tibetans would follow Indian or Chinese Buddhist practice. The Indian scholars argued the Mahayana position, which held that it was necessary to accumulate merit and knowledge over many lifetimes to attain

Buddhahood. The Chinese position was that any practitioner could achieve Buddhahood by establishing a state of complete repose, regardless of his morality or intellectual endeavor. The Indian view prevailed, and it was determined that Tibetan Buddhist doctrine would thereafter come from India.

Buddhism entered a golden age in Tibet during which it grew in popularity as monasteries appeared throughout the land, along with serious Buddhist practitioners and renowned scholars. The fortieth king of the Yarlung dynasty was Tri Relwajen. Songtsen Gampo, Tri Song Deutsen, and Tri Relwajen are known as the Three Great Religious Kings of Tibet. Tri Relwajen was a great supporter of Buddhism, responsible for the construction of many temples. He issued a decree that every monk should be supported by seven households, which made him highly unpopular with the nobles and the Bon priests. A reaction set in, and Tri Relwajen was assassinated. His brother, Lang Darma, came to power in 836, bringing the golden era and the Yarlung dynasty to an end.

During the violent persecution in the reign of Lang Darma, Buddhist temples and texts were destroyed. Monks who didn't flee to safety in eastern Tibet were forced on pain of death to choose between marriage, the army, and adoption of the Bon religion, which they proclaimed by ringing a bell wherever they went. Bon flourished for a century, acquiring a written canon, and Buddhism went underground. After the death of Lang Darma, the country was split into small kingdoms and many outlying territories were lost.

a new wave of buddhism

In the 10th century, interest in Buddhism was revived by a religious king in western Tibet named Yeshe O, who came from the Guge dynasty, which was descended from the Yarlung kings. Monks began returning from exile in the East, monasteries were rebuilt, and ancient texts reappeared, some of which had been buried by Padma Sambhava. Many important teachers came from India, including the great Atisha in 1042, whose arrival heralded the Buddhist revival in Tibet. A disciple of Atisha's named Drom Tonpa founded the

Samye Monastery, Tibet's first monastery, which was built in the 8th century according to a plan by Padma Sambhava. Thangka painting, Tibet, 18th-19th century.

Kadam school, which is the historical predecessor of today's Gelug order of Tibetan Buddhism.

During this new wave of enthusiasm, many Tibetans traveled to India to study directly with Indian masters, transforming themselves into the embodiment of the teachings. Several of them, in-

The Three Great Religious Kings of Tibet: Songtsen Gampo, Tri Song Deutsen, and Tri Relwajen. These kings implemented the development and practice of Buddhism in Tibet during the 8th and 9th centuries.

cluding Rinchen Sangpo, Drokmi, and Marpa, brought back new Tibetan translations of many sutras and important tantras. Rinchen Sangpo's translations, which included the Kalachakra text, added a new vitality to the science of mind the Tibetan Buddhists were so eager to perfect.

The translator Drokmi is considered to have been among the first to bring the Kalachakra Tantra to Tibet. Drokmi's descendants founded the first Sakya Monastery in 1073. In the 13th century, the high lama of Sakya Monastery, named Kunga Gyaltsen, was invited to visit the camp of the Mongol prince who was threatening to invade the Tibetan states. He impressed the warlord with his spiritual wisdom and he became honored as a teacher of Buddhism. In 1253, the lama's nephew Phagpa became the court priest of Kublai Khan. When he became emperor, Kublai Khan granted Phagpa the administration of all Tibet, establishing a "patron and priest" relationship that would maintain the Sakyas in power for a hundred years.

Another important translator was the famous teacher Marpa, who studied with the Indian master Naropa. Among Marpa's thousands of disciples was the yogi poet Milarepa, who became a legend for having attained Buddhahood, or complete enlightenment, within one lifetime. The teachings of Naropa, Marpa, and Milarepa were responsible for the establishment of the Kagyu lineage of Tibetan Buddhism. In the 12th century, Dusum Kyenpa was the head of one of the twelve sub-orders of the Kagyu lineage, known as the Karma Kagyu. He became known as the Karmapa, the first line of religious leaders to be recognized as reincarnations of their predecessors. This tradition of recognizing incarnations, called *tulkus,* became widespread in Tibetan Buddhism and is the system used to determine the succession of the Dalai Lamas.

kalachakra enters tibet

As many as sixteen translations of the *Sri Kalachakra* from Sanskrit to Tibetan appeared between the 11th and 14th centuries. Because there is no written proof that the Kalachakra Tantra was originally transmitted by the Buddha himself, some scholars speculate that it was invented in invasion-plagued India in the 11th century. But its message of compassion and loving kindness clearly overshadows any debate concerning its origin.

The translations of Rwa and Dro, dating from the latter part of the 11th century, emerged as the primary sources for the Kalachakra Tantra as it exists today. The Tibetan Rwa Lotsawa (*lotsawa* is Tibetan for "translator") was a student of Samantashiri of Nepal, while Dro Lotsawa was a student of Somanatha, the first Indian to travel to Tibet to spread the Kalachakra system. The Rwa translation became the most widespread.

The two lineages of Rwa and Dro continued through successions of teachers and eventually flowed together. Buton (1290-1364) played a key role in the preservation of all the different

The 11th-century yogi master Milarepa, who sang his expressions of enlightenment in verses known as the *100,000 Songs.* He was the foremost student of Marpa, a great scholar who traveled to India and translated many important Buddhist texts into Tibetan, including the Kalachakra. 4 3/8" high, cast brass with inlay, Tibet, 16th century.

types of tantras and produced a close study of the Kalachakra in particular.

Born in the Tsang province of central Tibet, the infant Buton had a very shriveled and ugly appearance. But, according to legend, when Buton was very small he would say to his mother that she

The oldest known image of Kalachakra, this bronze came to the Newark Museum from eastern Tibet, though its style indicates that it probably traveled from Kashmir with the spread of the teachings. The faces of Kalachakra on the front side were decomposed by a blessing substance commonly applied by practitioners in Kashmir; the back face is intact. Front and back. 8¹/₂" high, solid cast bronze with silver inlay, 10th-11th century.

shouldn't be afraid to show her unattractive child to others, since he was prepared to deal with them. In fact, *Bu* means "son" and *ton* means "to show."

Buton became a superior scholar and, unlike other scholars, an expert in all the teachings, from sutra to tantra to poetry, astrology, and grammar—a kind of Renaissance man of Tibet. He became a master of Kalachakra with a powerful personal practice and even saw Kalachakra himself. He wrote about thirty volumes, most of which deal with the Kalachakra Tantra, and he is regarded as the most reputable of all the scholarly sources on the subject.

It was under Buton's hand that the Rwa and Dro traditions became consolidated into one. His translation was incorporated into many different Kalachakra traditions, including the Sakya, Kagyu, and, later, the Gelug.

from tsong khapa to the dalai lamas

The great Tsong Khapa Lo Sang Drakpay (1357-1419) was one of the most eminent of Tibetan meditation masters, scholars, and writers. Although he was ordained as a novice monk by the fourth Karmapa, he studied with Nyingma, Kadam, and Sakya, as well as Kagyu, masters for twenty years. He is believed to have achieved complete enlightenment in 1398.

Concerned with the decline in monastic discipline, Tsong Khapa convened a great council of all of the major orders of Tibetan Buddhism, which resulted in a movement of monastic renewal. The Gelug (meaning "virtue") order arose out of Tsong Khapa's reform of the Kadam tradition originated by Atisha in the 11th century, as well as from his own teachings.

Tsong Khapa's hermitage was built up to become Ganden Monastery, which, with a community of more than 10,000 monks, was one of the largest monasteries in the world until its destruction during the Chinese takeover of Tibet in the 1950s. Drepung and Sera Monasteries were built after Ganden, forming the three major monasteries of the Gelugs. Those who continued to follow the form of Buddhism introduced by Padma Sambhava had become identified as the Nyingma (meaning "ancient") order. Thus the four great orders of Tibetan Buddhism were now fully established: the Nyingma, Kagyu, Sakya, and Gelug.

Buton, a master Kalachakra scholar of the 14th century, consolidated many translations of Kalachakra into one text, which has been used by the major traditions of Tibetan Buddhism since that time. Thangka, central Tibet, 17th century.

Opposite: Tsong Khapa (1357-1419) was an incarnation of Manjusri, the Buddha of Wisdom. A realized master and important reformer of Tibetan Buddhism, he was a pivotal figure in the transmission of Kalachakra. Thangka painting, Tibet, 18th century.

Tsong Khapa had a student named Khe-Drub. Khe-Drub's life work on Kalachakra resulted in the text used by the Dalai Lama today, called *The Mandala Rite of Glorious Kalachakra: Illumination of Thought*.

It is important to note that these lineages, orders, or schools of Tibetan Buddhism share the same teachings of the Buddha and the same goal of attaining liberation from suffering for the benefit of others. The orders distinguish themselves from one another by the

Ganden Monastery, built on the hermitage site of Tsong Khapa, the largest monastic universities in the world. This photograph was taken in 1932 by Sir Hugh Richardson, who served as the representative of British India to Lhasa.

different teachers who are the lineage holders and by the particular teachings they emphasize at various stages of the path.

Tsong Khapa studied Kalachakra under Chokyi Palwa, a disciple of Buton. He conducted an extensive meditation retreat on the completion stage of Kalachakra. At the conclusion of the retreat, he received a vision of Kalachakra who, laying his hands on Tsong Khapa's head, said he would do the same work as King Suchandra of Shambala in propagating the teachings of Kalachakra.

Near the end of his life, Tsong Khapa transmitted the entire Kalachakra teachings to Khe-Drub, who, as a result of extensive meditation practice, wrote a comprehensive text and commentaries on Kalachakra.

A successive lineage of eminent lamas transmitted the Kalachakra Tantra directly from Khe-Drub to the Seventh Dalai Lama, who in-

troduced it to Namgyal Monastery in the early 1700s. By the middle of the 14th century, the *Sri Kalachakra* had been translated into Tibetan at least fifteen times, and the *Vimalaprabha* commentary more than ten times, which represents the most attention given any Buddhist text by the great Tibetan translators. Even though the Kalachakra Tantra was widely practiced throughout Tibet in hundreds of monasteries, it was Khe-Drub's text which was retained by Namgyal Monastery over the centuries and which is followed by the Dalai Lama of today.

Ganden Monastery after its destruction in 1959. The buildings that were still relatively intact were reconstructed after 1981.

The Dalai Lamas *and* Namgyal Monastery

TENZIN GYATSO, the warm and charismatic man we know today as the Fourteenth Dalai Lama, has been a major influence in the preservation and practice of Tibetan Buddhism throughout the world. The attention he has placed on the Kalachakra Tantra is appreciated by the thousands of students who have entered into its practice, and the tens of thousands of museum visitors who have been drawn to demonstrations of the Kalachakra Sand Mandala and other ritual arts. The Dalai Lama, with his great energy and devotion to the

The mystical lake, Lhamo Lhatso (Lake of Visions), located in central Tibet at an altitude of 12,000 feet. Since the early 15th century, auspicious signs have been seen in its waters, such as clues to the birthplace of a newly reincarnated Dalai Lama.

teachings of the Buddha, is the holder of a lineage that is part of a rich tradition unique to Tibet.

The Dalai Lama is believed to be an emanation of Avalokiteshvara, the Buddha of Compassion. Since 1642, the Dalai Lamas

Shadakshari Avalokiteshvara. The Dalai Lamas are said to be manifestations of this four-armed form of the Buddha of Compassion. Detail from a huge 11th-century wall fresco in Alchi Monastery, Lhadak.

have been both the political and spiritual leaders of their country, a situation that was complicated by the Chinese takeover of Tibet in the 1950s.

Buddhists believe that all sentient beings are reborn again and again. However, until we have achieved liberation (sometimes referred to as *nirvana*) from this cyclic existence, we are automatically reborn as a result of our actions in previous lives. This is an aspect of the law of karma. "Incarnations" such as the Dalai Lama are beings who have achieved a level of realization where they can choose rebirth at any time or place, or in any form, in order to help or liberate all sentient beings.

When a Dalai Lama dies, a committee is formed to find his reincarnation. Search parties go out into the countryside, following the prophecies of the State Oracle, predictions of high lamas, visions from the sacred lake Lhamo Lhatso, and mystical clues left behind by the previous Dalai Lama. When the likely candidates, usually very young children, have been found, they are subjected to extensive tests, one of which requires them to identify possessions of the previous Dalai Lama from among an assortment of similar items.

the training of the dalai lamas

Historically, once the incarnation had been identified, the boy would be taken to Lhasa, the capital of Tibet, and installed as the Dalai Lama on his throne in the Potala Palace, often at a very early age. He would be raised and educated by highly qualified teachers from many of the great monasteries of Tibet, representing all the major traditions of Tibetan Buddhism. Many of these teachers might have been trained themselves by the previous Dalai Lama. This education program lasts more than twenty years and includes learning to read and write Tibetan and becoming adept in all the various traditions of Buddhist philosophy and ritual arts. During the Dalai Lama's minority, affairs of state would be handled by a regent appointed by the previous incarnation of the Dalai Lama or by the government.

In order to achieve his Master of Metaphysics degree, the young Dalai Lama would be expected to prove himself through extensive debate with Tibet's most respected scholars, before an assembly of thousands of highly educated monks from Sera, Drepung, and Ganden monastic universities.

the first dalai lamas

Gyalwa Sonam Gyatso was given the title Dalai Lama by the Mongolian king Altan Khan in 1578. Detail from an 18th-century Tibetan thangka.

The title Dalai Lama was first given by the Mongolian king Altan Khan to Gyalwa Sonam Gyatso during his visit to that country in 1578. Altan Khan granted this honor in recognition of Sonam Gyatso's great knowledge and compassion and out of gratitude for the positive influence he had had in turning the minds of the Mongolians toward Buddhism. *Dalai* is the Mongolian word for "ocean," while *lama* means "teacher of wisdom." Thus the title means "Teacher (like the) Ocean," or "Ocean of Wisdom." Interestingly, until only recently the Tibetans themselves never used this term but referred to him instead as Kundun ("in the Presence of"), Yishin Norbu ("Wish-fulfilling Gem"), or Gyalwa Rinpoche ("Precious Victorious One"). Today, due to the influence of Westerners, he is also referred to as His Holiness.

Even though Sonam Gyatso was the first person to receive the title, he was actually the Third Dalai Lama, since he was an identified reincarnation of the great Gyalwa Gendun Gyatso, who was himself a reincarnation of the renowned Gyalwa Gendun Drub. These two were posthumously named the First and Second Dalai Lamas.

The First Dalai Lama, Gyalwa Gendun Drub, was born in 1391 to nomadic peasants in central Tibet. After the death of his father when Gendun Drub was seven, his mother placed him in a monastery to be educated. He became a disciple of Tsong Khapa in 1415 and soon demonstrated his greatness as both a scholar and a realized master, as his fame spread throughout Tibet. In 1447, he established Tashi Lhunpo Monastery at Shigatse, which eventually became one of the most important monastic universities of southern Tibet. The First Dalai Lama died in 1474 at the age of eighty-three, while sitting in meditation.

The next year Gyalwa Gendun Gyatso was born, also in central Tibet, to a renowned yogic practitioner of the Nyingma tradition. He was recognized at the age of four as Gendun Drub's reincarnation, and, posthumously, was called the Second Dalai Lama. He studied at Tashi Lhunpo and Drepung Monasteries and became the abbot of Drepung. There he built a residence for himself called Ganden Phodrang (Joyous Palace).

Gyalwa Gendun Gyatso's principal focus was on practicing the tantric tradition, but he wrote extensively on practices from several distinct major lineages of Tibetan Buddhism. He discovered the power of Lhamo Latso (Lake of Visions), which is reputed to foretell events, and he established an important monastery on its shore.

It was at this time that what was to become Namgyal Monastery became associated with the Dalai Lamas. One account tells us that there was a monastery called Phende Gon, which was struck by an epidemic that left only eight monks alive. These monks then abandoned their home and set out on a pilgrimage to perform rites at various holy sites for their deceased companions. En route, they encountered Gyalwa Gendun Gyatso, who was also traveling for religious purposes. They found their meeting propitious and decided to stay together.

In 1542, at the age of sixty-seven, Gendun Gyatso passed away, like his predecessor, while sitting in meditation.

the establishment of namgyal monastery

In 1543, Gyalwa Sonam Gyatso, the Third Dalai Lama, was born near Lhasa and was soon recognized as the reincarnation of Gendun Gyatso. Educated at Drepung Monastery, he was renowned throughout Asia for his great wisdom as a teacher and scholar. The Namgyal monks, though they were not yet so named, received formal recognition as being associated with the Dalai Lama only when Sonam Gyatso established Phende Lekshe Ling in 1564-65. This monastery had its roots in Phende Gon and later became known as Namgyal Monastery. From that time on, the monks became responsible for performing prayers for the welfare of the land and people of Tibet and for assisting the Dalai Lama in performing religious rites.

The name Namgyal came into use in 1571 when the king Altan Khan of Mongolia became very ill and requested that his teacher, the Third Dalai Lama, perform long-life prayers for his recovery. The Dalai Lama instructed his monks to perform the sacred long-life prayer of the goddess Namgyalma, and from that moment on, Phende Lekshe Ling Monastery was also known as Namgyal Monastery.

Famous for combining the teachings of the Nyingma and Gelug lineages of Tibetan Buddhism, Sonam Gyatso established monasteries throughout Tibet, Mongolia, and western China, bringing their traditions to these lands as he traveled and taught. When he finally left Mongolia, he promised to return sometime in the future. He passed away in 1588 at the age of forty-five.

The next year, Gyalwa Yonten Gyatso was born in Mongolia to a direct descendant of Altan Khan. He was the only Dalai Lama to have been born outside of Tibet, demonstrating that the selection of the Dalai Lama goes beyond race, country, or class. It was not until he was twelve years old that he was brought to Tibet as the Fourth Dalai Lama. He spent his short life in study, practice, and teaching, declining, as did his predecessor, the many invitations sent by the emperor of China to visit the Manchu court. He passed away in 1617 at the age of twenty-eight.

the great fifth

The Fourth Dalai Lama's relatively modest contribution was amply made up for by the Fifth Dalai Lama, Gyalwa Ngawang Lobsang Gyatso, who is known as "The Great Fifth." Born in 1617, soon after the passing of the Fourth, this great leader reunited the three regions of Tibet in 1642, areas that had been functioning as separate kingdoms since the mid-9th century.

For the first time, a Dalai Lama became the spiritual and political leader of all of Tibet. In that same year, he declared Lhasa to be the capital of Tibet, and he named the government *Ganden Phodrang* in honor of the Second Dalai Lama, whose residence bore this name. This government, which divided authority equally between the

The goddess Namgyalma, protector deity of Namgyal Monastery. Cast bronze, 20th century, India.

clergy and the laity, continues today in exile under the leadership of the Fourteenth Dalai Lama. As the new head of Tibet, the Fifth Dalai Lama appointed governors for the various districts and ministers to form a new government. He also instituted a national system of medical care, as well as a program of national education. He visited Peking in 1652, at the request of the Ching emperor, in order to restructure the Buddhist monasteries there.

The Great Fifth Dalai Lama, Gyalwa Ngawang Lobsang Gyatso (1617-1682). 7^7/$_8$" high, gilt bronze, central Tibet, 17th century.

The Great Fifth was known for his spiritual power and personal dynamism. He produced voluminous scholarly writings, especially on history and classical Indian poetry, and he clarified and improved upon the rituals of Namgyal Monastery. He introduced to Namgyal many meditation practices influenced by the Nyingma order, added forms of sacred dance and chanting based on ancient Tibetan traditions, and established Namgyal as one of the few Tibetan monasteries to include the ritual practice and study of all four lineages of Tibetan Buddhism. The Great Fifth Dalai Lama traveled and taught widely, and he became famous for his statesmanship.

The Fifth Dalai Lama had a beloved teacher named Lobsang Chokyi Gyaltsen, who was a fourth-generation disciple of Tsong Khapa. When Lobsang Chokyi Gyaltsen died, the Dalai Lama recognized a boy as his incarnation and gave him the title of Panchen Lama (*panchen* means "great teacher"). The Panchen Lama became the abbot of Tashi Lunpo Monastery, founded by the First Dalai Lama, and all subsequent Panchen Lamas have held this position. The Panchen Lama is considered second in stature only to the Dalai Lama, and whichever one is the elder has traditionally served as teacher to the younger. The Panchen Lamas have figured strongly in the transmission of the Kalachakra Tantra, and the Third Panchen Lama is especially noted for having written one of the most important guidebooks to Shambala.

an astonishing palace is built

It was the Great Fifth Dalai Lama who began construction of a magnificent palace in Lhasa in 1645 upon the ruins of Tritse Marpo (Red Mountain), which had been the castle of King Songtsen Gampo, built in A.D. 636. It became known as the Potala, named for the pure land where the bodhisattva Avalokiteshvara resides.

Knowing that he would die soon, the Great Fifth Dalai Lama called Desi Sangye Gyatso, prime minister of the government, to his side to tell him to keep his death a secret and to give him instructions on how to govern the country once he had passed on. In 1682, at the age of sixty-eight, the Fifth Dalai Lama passed away, leaving the entire responsibility of temporal and spiritual administration in the hands of his prime minister.

An important part of the Dalai Lama's instructions dealt with the necessity of completing the Potala Palace. In order to accomplish this, Desi Sangye Gyatso had to keep the Dalai Lama's death secret lest the people stop working on the palace, as well as to avoid occupation of Tibet by the Mongolian and Manchu emperors.

The First Panchen Lama (1567-1662) was recognized by the Fifth Dalai Lama as the reincarnation of his teacher. Thangka painting, Tibet, 18th-19th century.

Overwhelmed by his new responsibilities, the young Desi despaired of fulfilling them without the Dalai Lama's direction, and he cried out in great grief at his ruler's death. Suddenly the Dalai Lama came back to life for a moment and said, "Don't worry. The

small things you can decide for yourself. Whenever there are important matters that you don't know how to handle, just stand before this image of (the protector deity) Penden Lhamo and ask her for direction."

Desi Sangye Gyatso told the people that the Great Fifth was in a prolonged meditation retreat. When high Mongolian officials, who

The Potala Palace in Lhasa, Tibet, photographed during the New Year's celebration in 1890. A great appliquéd banner is displayed down the front face of the palace. This first known photograph of Tibet was taken by a Buryat Mongolian with a camera brought from Russia.

The goddess Penden Lhamo, protector deity of the Dalai Lamas and the Tibetan government. 6", cast silver inlaid with semiprecious stones, 17th century, Tibet.

had traveled a great distance, demanded to see him, one of the monks of Namgyal Monastery, who looked somewhat like the Dalai Lama, was placed on the throne to impersonate him.

In this manner, the Desi kept the Great Fifth Dalai Lama's death a secret from the people of Tibet for thirteen years, until the completion of the Potala Palace in 1695. Today a prayer that the young prime minister secretly carved into a stone palace wall still proclaims his wish for the Dalai Lama to be reincarnated.

the poet dalai lama

The Sixth Dalai Lama, Gyalwa Tsangyang Gyatso, who was born in 1682 in southern Tibet, was unique in his own way. He was the only Dalai Lama who chose not to follow monastic discipline, preferring sports and social life instead. Enthroned in 1697 at the age of fifteen, he refused to become a monk and moved out of the Potala when he was twenty years old. He was much loved by the people of Tibet for his lightheartedness, romantic poetry, and disregard for authority. But the Mongolian ruler Lhasang Khan invaded Lhasa in 1705, seized the young Dalai Lama and, according to one version of the story, murdered him in 1706. Tsangyang wrote to one of his lady friends as he was being forcibly taken away:

> *White crane!*
> *Lend me your wings*
> *I will not fly far*
> *From Lithang, I shall return.*

Lithang proved to be where the next incarnation was found.

Another version of the story says that the Sixth Dalai Lama, after being deposed by Lhasang Khan, sought refuge among the people, fading into anonymity, choosing life as a beggar, and making many pilgrimages to the holy places of Tibet, India, and China.

Gyalwa Tsangyang's unorthodox behavior with women came to be thought of as a tantric teaching of the greatest wisdom. It is said that even his love life followed advanced yogic practices. He wrote:

Never have I slept without a sweetheart
Nor have I spent a single drop of sperm.

Lhasang Khan enthroned a puppet ruler in place of the Sixth Dalai Lama and kept Tibet under his rule by occupying it with his Quogshot Mongol troops. But in 1717 the Dzungar Mongols entered Lhasa and killed Lhasang Khan. The monks of Namgyal Monastery were either executed or sent away. Those who survived founded a new monastery.

the seventh dalai lama

Gyalwa Kalsang Gyatso, who was to become the Seventh Dalai Lama, was born in 1708 in Lithang, as the Sixth Dalai Lama predicted, and was identified soon thereafter. Troubles with Mongolia prevented his official recognition until 1720, when Lhasa became liberated from Mongolian rule by popular rebellions aided by the Manchurians, who hoped to extend their interests in central Asia.

Despite this background of political intrigue, the Seventh Dalai Lama lived the life of a pure and simple monk and was dearly loved by his people. He composed a new liturgy for the *tsok,* or feast offering, and is noted for introducing the Kalachakra Tantra to Namgyal Monastery. Realizing that the complete lineage of the Kalachakra Tantra propagated by Tsong Khapa was in danger of extinction, the Seventh Dalai Lama requested the aged and noted scholar Ngawang Chokden to collect and master it. Having done this through extensive retreat, Ngawang Chokden passed the endangered lineage on to the Seventh Dalai Lama, who in turn passed it on to thousands of monks.

When he was at last admitted back to the Potala in 1735, he reassembled the monks and reestablished Namgyal Monastery. Concerned with preventing any further degeneration of the tradition, the Seventh Dalai Lama appointed a group of monks to maintain the rituals of the Kalachakra Tantra—and they continue to be practiced to this day.

The Seventh Dalai Lama also instituted the practice among the Namgyal monks of performing a one-day Kalachakra prayer ritual

The Seventh Dalai Lama, who brought the Kalachakra Tantra into the lineage of the Dalai Lamas. This image, measuring 2³/8" high, is made of dark, reddish-brown clay, Tibet, 19th century.

on the eighth day of every Tibetan month. In addition, in the third month of the Tibetan year the monks perform the entire Kalachakra ritual in commemoration of the Buddha giving the Kalachakra. This includes the construction of the sand mandala and performance of ritual dances, as well as other rituals, including a concluding fire offering purification ceremony. The Kalachakra Earth and Offering dances were also taught to Namgyal monks by monks from Shalu Monastery in south central Tibet at the request of the Seventh Dalai Lama.

In 1751, Kalsang Gyatso regained full spiritual and temporal authority over Tibet, but he died just six years later at the age of forty-nine. In spite of the political turbulence of his time, the pious Seventh Dalai Lama's religious and scholarly achievements were extraordinary.

a quiet period

No major changes were made in the routines or traditions of Namgyal Monastery during the lives of the Eighth through Twelfth Dalai Lamas, whom the Namgyal monks continued to serve.

The Eighth Dalai Lama, Gyalwa Jamphel Gyatso, was born in central Tibet in 1758 and was brought to Lhasa in 1762. He exhibited spiritual qualities, along with a strong distaste for the political maneuverings going on around him. It was during his reign that the British Empire was making itself known in Asia, and Tibet's isolationist policy developed as a defense. This policy continued until the 1950s. In 1783, he built the Norbulingka (Jewel Park), the magnificent summer palace of the Dalai Lamas. He died in 1804 at the age of forty-six.

The Ninth through Twelfth Dalai Lamas—Gyalwa Lungtok Gyatso, Gyalwa Tsultrim Gyatso, Gyalwa Khedrup Gyatso, and Gyalwa Thinley Gyatso—each had a very short life, ranging from ten to twenty-one years. Whether they died from disease due to increased exposure to foreign contacts, natural causes, or as a result of political intrigue, the lack of effective leadership made the country weak and unstable. Many Tibetans believe that the degeneration of virtuous activities may have been responsible for the short and ineffective lives of these four Dalai Lamas.

a modern dalai lama

Gyalwa Thubten Gyatso, born in 1876 and enthroned as the Thirteenth Dalai Lama in 1879, was to become the strong spiritual and political leader Tibet needed in the changing times ahead. The coming of the 20th century brought to Tibet political pressure from its three great neighbors: Russia, China, and British India.

Around the turn of the century, the Thirteenth Dalai Lama became acquainted with a Buryat Mongolian monk named Agwan Dorjiev, who was not only a renowned scholar but also strongly connected to Czar Nicholas II of Russia. The Russians, like the British and the Chinese, were interested in Tibet for its strategic

The beloved Thirteenth Dalai Lama, Gyalwa
Thubten Gyatso (1876-1933), who brought Tibet
into the modern world. This photograph
was taken in 1911 in Darjeeling, India.

location. Dorjiev tried to convince the Dalai Lama that the Romanov czar was the king of Shambala, and a book published in Russia in 1913 supported this theory. The Dalai Lama believed that Russia could be an important ally, and gave Dorjiev a large financial contribution with which he had the Kalachakra Temple built in St. Petersburg between 1909 and 1915, and he sent artistic treasures with which to decorate it as well. It functioned as a Tibetan Buddhist monastery until it was closed by Stalin's secret police in 1935. It was used as a radio-jamming station during World War II and as a zoological garden by the Communist Party until 1989, when it began to function as a monastery and Buddhist learning center once again. Today it is headed by a young Buryat monk named Samaydev, who journeyed to New York in 1991 to receive the Kalachakra Initiation from the Fourteenth Dalai Lama.

Concerned over Tibet's friendship with Russia, Great Britain sent an expeditionary force to Lhasa in 1904, which resulted in peaceful trade agreements. This prompted the Manchus ruling China to send an army in 1910, and the Dalai Lama fled to safety in India. The Manchus ruled Tibet for only about a year. China became engaged in a revolution, and by 1912 the Tibetans had managed to defeat and deport any remaining foreign soldiers. With the aid of the British, the Thirteenth Dalai Lama negotiated the Simla Agreement of 1914, which placed Tibet under the suzerainty of China, meaning that China would be responsible for its foreign affairs but would not have the right to colonize Tibet or maintain troops there. China never ratified the agreement.

The Thirteenth Dalai Lama was the first to have extensive contact with the West. He traveled for long periods of time and was deeply loved everywhere he went. He prophesied in 1932 that Tibet would soon be invaded from the East, and he urged his people to prepare themselves. He sought to modernize the country but met with considerable resistance from the established power structure.

The Kalachakra Temple in St. Petersburg, Russia, built in 1909 under the patronage of the Thirteenth Dalai Lama with the permission of Czar Nicholas II. Above the entrance are two deer facing a dharma wheel, signifying Deer Park, where the Buddha first taught.

the recognition of the
fourteenth dalai lama

Strange cloud formations were noticed in the sky northeast of Lhasa some time after the Thirteenth Dalai Lama died in 1933. According to custom, his body had been seated in state on the throne in his summer residence, the Norbulingka, facing south. After a few days, the face had turned eastward. In addition, a large star-shaped fungus suddenly appeared on a wooden pillar on the northeastern side of the

The Norbulingka (Jewel Park) was the summer palace of the Dalai Lamas in Lhasa. It was built by the Eighth Dalai Lama in 1783. This photograph was taken during the Cutting Expedition in 1937.

shrine. The regent consulted the magical lake of visions, Lhamo Lhatso, where, after several days of prayer and meditation, he saw an image of a monastery with roofs of green and gold and a house with turquoise tiles. The regent also saw the Tibetan syllables *AH KA MA,* which were interpreted as clues to go to the Amdo region of eastern Tibet.

Portrait of the Fourteenth Dalai Lama at his installation on the Lion Throne in 1940. Oil on canvas, 34³/4"x25", by Indian painter Kanwal Krishna.

Parties set out in various directions throughout Tibet to search for a very special child. The party that traveled to Takster in eastern Tibet arrived without fanfare at a farmhouse with turquoise tiles, and the two-year-old baby of the family went immediately to the high abbot, who was disguised as a servant, and sat on his lap.

The child pulled at the abbot's rosary, which had belonged to the Thirteenth Dalai Lama, and said he wanted it. The abbot said he'd give it to him if the child could tell him who he was. The boy called him Sera Aga, which means "a lama from Sera Monastery." He also correctly identified the two others in the party. When they left, he wanted to go with them, and afterward he would often tell his mother he was packing to go to Lhasa. When the delegation returned, they showed the child a series of articles, some of which belonged to the Thirteenth Dalai Lama, including two rosaries, a small hand drum, and a walking stick. Each time, the boy chose the article belonging to the Dalai Lama. He did hesitate over the wrong walking stick, but it turned out that this stick had indeed belonged briefly to the Dalai Lama as well. Further testing proved remarkably successful, and the little boy was officially recognized as the Fourteenth Dalai Lama.

The only obstacle that remained was the warlord who ruled western China at the time. When he found out the new Dalai Lama had been discovered in Takster, he demanded an enormous ransom to let the child be taken to Lhasa. After the ransom was paid, the warlord demanded even more money and valuable objects, and again the Tibetans were forced to comply.

The present Dalai Lama, who was born Lhamo Dhondup on July 6, 1935, with his eyes wide open, was finally brought to Lhasa to be enthroned in 1940. When he was given his novice vows at the Central Cathedral, he was renamed Tenzin Gyatso, which means "Ocean Which Protects the Dharma." He gave his first teaching in 1946 at the age of eleven.

china invades tibet

The signs were ominous: warnings from the State Oracle, a comet with a bright tail (signifying war), and a tremendous earthquake that rocked southeastern Tibet, changing the course of the Brahmaputra River, which swallowed up hundreds of villages in the province of Kham. The sky glowed an unholy red.

Then in 1950 the newly formed People's Republic of China announced its plans to "liberate" Tibet. The Tibetan government, which was led by a regent due to the Dalai Lama's youth, knew that

Gyalwa Tenzin Gyatso, the Fourteenth Dalai Lama, took over the Tibetan government in 1950 at the age of fifteen.

The Dalai Lama greeted by Mao Tse-tung during a visit to Beijing in 1954.

Ling Rinpoche, the senior tutor to the Fourteenth Dalai Lama, gave him the Kalachakra Initiation in 1955. Here he holds a vajra and bell at the Kalachakra Initiation in Bodhgaya, 1973.

its limited military resources would be no match for the Red Army. Delegations were sent to Britain, India, Nepal, and the United States to appeal for support, to no avail. Chinese troops moved into the eastern provinces of Amdo and Kham, overwhelming the Tibetan army in spite of the able assistance of the renowned Khampa warriors. The United Nations refused to take up the question of Tibetan independence. The long years of isolation were taking their toll.

The Tibetan government consulted the State Oracle, whose message was clear: the Dalai Lama must take charge. Although he was only fifteen years old, he was the only leader who could unite the country during this time of crisis. On November 17, 1950, Tenzin Gyatso was granted full authority in a traditional ceremony at the Potala.

The Dalai Lama sent a delegation of officials to Beijing, where they arrived early in 1951. Zhou Enlai, the foreign minister of China, forced them to sign the Seventeen-Point Agreement agreeing that Tibet was part of China, under threat of both personal violence and large-scale retaliation against Tibet.

Chinese troops marched into Lhasa, taking over houses, fields, and animals, and demanding large quantities of food, soon overtaxing the fragile economy. Rumors of violent oppression were pouring in from the eastern provinces.

The Dalai Lama felt that the only hope for his people against such a powerful enemy was to persuade the Chinese peaceably to fulfill the promises they had made in the Seventeen-Point Agreement, such as not to interfere with the Tibetan political system or religious practices and to aid in agricultural development. He committed himself to the Buddhist path of nonviolence, advocating cooperation when it was possible and passive resistance when it was not. And he accepted an invitation to visit Mao Tse-tung in China in 1954.

The Dalai Lama returned to Lhasa with Mao's plan for a committee to prepare for regional autonomy, but soon realized the committee would be a mere puppet of the Chinese. The situation in the eastern border provinces was becoming desperate, and by mid-1957 the Khampas were in full-scale revolt. Chinese Communist troops were obliterating entire villages, publicly executing hundreds of people by the most brutal means imaginable, and destroying monasteries and their inhabitants. Refugees poured into Lhasa.

In spite of the political turmoil, the young Dalai Lama was already dedicated to the Kalachakra teachings. He gave the Kalachakra Initiation in Lhasa for the first time in 1956, and again in 1957, to more than 10,000 people. As was traditional, forty-four Namgyal monks assisted him with the rituals of the empowerment. In 1959, the Dalai Lama took his examinations upon completion of the highest level of religious training, undergoing intense day-long philosophical debates before thousands of onlookers in order to receive his degree.

Associated Press report from 1959: "FEARFUL JOURNEY: Pursued by Red Chinese troops, struggling against the harsh elements of the Himalayas, the God-King of Tibet—the Dalai Lama—is shown here on the fourth day of his flight to freedom. The 23-year-old ruler, wearing spectacles, is aboard the white horse. At this point, the escape party is crossing the Zsagola Pass in Southern Tibet on March 21st—four days after the Dalai Lama fled Lhasa, the sacred city, dressed in the drab robes of an ordinary monk."

A Chinese general invited the Dalai Lama to attend a theatrical presentation on March 10, insisting that he come without any government officials or armed escort. The rumor spread throughout Lhasa that the Chinese were planning to kidnap the beloved Tibetan leader. By the morning of March 10, 30,000 Tibetans had gathered in front of the gates of the Norbulingka to keep him from going. The general exchanged several letters with the Dalai Lama, finally asking where in the palace he would be, so that he would not be harmed. This confirmed popular fears that the palace would be shelled, and on March 17 the first shots were fired.

The Dalai Lama decided he must leave Tibet. Dressed in unfamiliar soldier's clothes, and without the glasses by which he would be immediately recognized, he left the Norbulingka preceded by his family and followed by a small party of ministers and attendants. Thus began a long and dangerous journey across Tibet and the Himalayas to asylum in India.

The Chinese occupation of Tibet resulted in the deaths of a reported 1.2 million Tibetans from military activities, starvation, torture, and the hard labor inflicted during long-term prison sentences. Six thousand monasteries were systematically destroyed, with their sacred art sent to Beijing, destroyed, or desecrated. Some of the Chinese policies which continue to oppress Tibetans into the 1990s are the dumping of nuclear waste in the eastern provinces, significant deforestation, forced population control, and a massive transfer of the Chinese population into Tibet.

The Dalai Lama has remained in exile since 1959 in an attempt to keep the Tibetan civilization alive and to maintain a sense of Tibetan identity for those Tibetans born outside of their native land. He has said repeatedly, "It's best for me to stay outside Tibet where I can speak on behalf of the six million people inside Tibet." The government of an independent Tibet continues to operate from Dharamsala, India, supervising an expatriate population of more than 150,000 in India and Nepal, with other Tibetan settlements in Switzerland, Canada, and the United States. All of the principal cultural institutions have been rebuilt in India, including the medical college and numerous monasteries, where texts are being painstakingly reproduced and art forms relearned. A prime example has been in the work of Namgyal Monastery.

the reestablishment of namgyal monastery in exile

Fifty-two Namgyal monks managed to escape to India with nothing, not even their sacred texts or begging bowls. The Dalai Lama encouraged them to preserve the monastery's traditions, which they did by writing down texts from memory. They found themselves in a land where the climate was quite foreign, where they did not speak the language or know the customs, and where most of their time was taken up by menial work on road construction crews, which was the only livelihood available to them.

The Dalai Lama was eventually able to bring all the exiled Namgyal monks together again in 1961 at his newly established residence in Dharamsala, India. In Tibet, there were as many as sixty-five Namgyal monks trained in the rituals of Kalachakra, and the annual routine of the monks included rituals that were performed in conjunction with the lunar phases, the third month of the lunar year being devoted to Kalachakra. The traditional sacred practices were gradually reestablished, and by 1963 the Namgyal monks were once again able to perform the Kalachakra rituals.

Also in 1963, an abbot was appointed by the Dalai Lama to be in charge of Namgyal Monastery for the first time. His name was Samten Chophel. In 1969, the Tibetan government-in-exile began to build the Central Cathedral of Thekchen Choling in Dharamsala, and twenty-eight boys were admitted to Namgyal Monastery as student monks.

Innovations were made in the course of study as well. The Dalai Lama introduced the teaching of philosophy, which was added to the regular studies in mandala construction, sacred dance, and other rituals. The monks' attire was simplified to a standardized robe of burgundy and yellow cotton or wool, doing away with the silk brocades often worn in Tibet.

Thekchen Choling, the Central Cathedral in Dharamsala, India, decorated for the Dalai Lama's return from Oslo, Norway, where he received the Nobel Peace Prize in 1989.

kalachakra beyond tibet

In 1971, in addition to many other Buddhist teachings and ceremonies, the Dalai Lama conferred the Kalachakra Initiation—for the
first time in exile—on the Dharamsala community at the newly
completed Central Cathedral. Two thousand people attended.

The night the empowerment was completed, the Dalai Lama
dreamed he was in the center of the mandala, with the assisting
monks reciting certain verses from the principal Kalachakra text,
when the mandala dissolved into and remained in a clear-light state.
Speaking of the dream, he said, "When I woke up, I knew that in
the future I would perform this ritual many times. I think in my
previous lifetimes I had a connection with the Kalachakra teaching.
It's a karmic force."

In 1972, he gave the initiation in south India, at the Bylakuppe
Tibetan settlement. He performed it again at the end of 1973 in
Bodhgaya, India. This time, 50,000 people attended, of whom
1,000 were Westerners. The Kalachakra Initiation was again given
by the Dalai Lama in 1976 at Leh in Ladakh, India.

In 1980, when the Chinese opened up the borders of Tibet for
travel, a number of the former monks of Namgyal Monastery
who were still in Tibet were invited to visit Dharamsala at the
monastery's expense. They participated in special prayer ceremonies
and some remained.

In July 1981 the Dalai Lama traveled to America to confer the
first Kalachakra Initiation in the West, in a cornfield outside of
Madison, Wisconsin, on 1,200 people, including many Tibetans
now living in North America. Sixteen Namgyal monks also journeyed from Dharamsala to Madison to assist in the many different
aspects of performing the Kalachakra Initiation ritual. In the Dalai
Lama's effort to simplify the rituals since coming into exile, he has
reduced the standard number of ritual assistants for the Kalachakra
Initiation from forty-four to sixteen.

In 1983 the Dalai Lama gave the Kalachakra Initiation twice in
India. In 1985 he gave it in Switzerland, and then in Bodhgaya for

150,000 people in December. This included more than 100,000 Tibetans living in exile and 50,000 who had journeyed from Tibet. In July 1988 he gave the initiation in Zan-skar, which is in Ladakh, India. At the same time, four Namgyal monks constructed, for the first time in history, the Kalachakra Sand Mandala as a cultural offering at the American Museum of Natural History in New York City.

The Dalai Lama returned to the United States in July 1989, and gave the Kalachakra Initiation to 3,000 people at the Santa Monica Civic Auditorium overlooking the Pacific Ocean. At the same time, four more Namgyal monks created the Kalachakra Sand Mandala at the Natural History Museum of Los Angeles County, again as a cultural offering.

Since 1978, the Kalachakra Initiation has been given throughout the world by a number of eminent lamas in exile who represent the various traditions of Tibetan Buddhism. Among them are Sakya Trizin Rinpoche, the present head of the Sakya lineage, the beloved Kalu Rinpoche, Chutgye Trichen Rinpoche, and Jamgon Kongtrul Rinpoche.

They and many other great Tibetan lamas of modern times, including the Dalai Lama himself, encourage the nonsectarian dissemination of the teachings of the Buddha. The Kalachakra Initiation, because it is often given to large groups, serves as an excellent vehicle for sharing the path of compassion with people of all backgrounds.

the international year of tibet

In 1991, as part of the International Year of Tibet, the Dalai Lama, assisted by the monks of Namgyal Monastery, conferred the Kalachakra Initiation on 4,000 students in the newly renovated Paramount Theater at Madison Square Garden in New York City, while another group of Namgyal monks demonstrated the Kalachakra Sand Mandala as part of the *Wisdom and Compassion* exhibition at the IBM Gallery.

The Kalachakra Sand Mandala was also demonstrated in conjunction with the *Wisdom and Compassion* show at the Museum of Asian

Kalu Rinpoche (1905-1989), renowned meditation master of the Shangba Kagyu lineage, conferred the Kalachakra Initiation to many thousands of students in North America, Europe, and India. His profound expression of the teachings of the Buddha and his ever-present compassion attracted students from all four schools of Tibetan Buddhism. He established numerous meditation and retreat centers throughout the world and taught at Namgyal Monastery at the request of the Dalai Lama.

Art in San Francisco and other cultural institutions across America, including the Mingei International Museum of World Folk Art at La Jolla, California; the Field Museum of Natural History in Chicago, Illinois; the Buffalo Museum of Science in New York State; and the Royal Academy in London, England. The Namgyal monks demonstrated other mandalas at the Newark Museum in New Jersey; Windstar Foundation in Aspen, Colorado; the Herbert F. Johnson Museum in Ithaca, New York; the St. Louis Art Museum in Missouri; and the Virginia Museum of Fine Art in Richmond, Virginia. They have also constructed mandalas in art galleries at Kutztown University and Dickenson College, and at Samaya Foundation and the Open Center in New York City.

Many people believe that the destruction of Tibet and the spread of Buddhism to the West were prophesied by the great Padma Sambhava in the 8th century, who said, "When the iron bird flies and horses run on wheels, the dharma will be carried to the land of the Red Man." And, in fact, there is an ever-growing interest in Buddhism in the West, evidenced by the growing number of Tibetan studies programs in major universities and the many Tibetan Buddhist meditation centers and monasteries that have emerged in recent years, as well as impressive museum collections of Tibetan art.

In 1992, Namgyal Monastery established a branch in Ithaca, New York, where the monastery's religious practices and sacred arts will be continued in conjunction with a new Institute of Tibetan Buddhist Studies. The institute, open to men and women from around the world, will provide an opportunity for the systematic education in English of Tibetan Buddhist studies in a traditional monastic setting.

religious activities of namgyal monastery

The Namgyal monks' main responsibility is to assist the Dalai Lama in his spiritual activities and to perform ritual prayers for the Tibetan government. Daily, the monks perform prayers of Penden Lhamo, the main protector deity of the government as well as of the

John Bigelow Taylor

His Holiness the Dalai Lama at the sunrise meditation celebrated in Central Park, New York City, October 1991.

left: Appliqued scroll painting of the diety Kalachakra with his consort Vishvamata. above: Ritual dance protecting and consecrating the site, performed during the Kalachakra Initiation outside Madison, Wisconson, 1981.

above: Western Tibetan Buddhist monks lead a Long Life prayer for the Dalai Lama following the Kalachakra Initiation at Bodh Gaya, India, 1973. right: Kalachakra Initiation at Bodhgaya, India, 1973.

©Marsha Keegan

above: 1,200 North Americans gather in a corn field outside Madison, Wisconsin to receive the Kalachakra Initiation in 1981.
right: Mountain people of Zanskar in northern India await the arrival of the Dalai Lama for the Kalachakra Initiation in 1989.

Vajra Vega, the wrathful emanation of Kalachakra.

monastery. In addition, they perform elaborate ritual ceremonies for one to two weeks out of every month for different deities and protectors, to request prosperity for the Tibetan government and nation.

A high point of the year at Namgyal is the New Year, which usually occurs during the Western month of February or March. After two weeks of preparatory ritual offerings, the Tibetan New Year celebration begins at 3:00 A.M. with special prayers and meditations in a private ceremony on the roof of the Central Cathedral in Dharamsala, with the Dalai Lama presiding. Later that morning, the Namgyal monks offer long-life prayers to the Dalai Lama, and approximately 500 government staffers join the ceremony to receive blessings from him. On the second day of the ceremony, as many as 10,000 people come to receive individual blessings from the Dalai Lama.

The Dalai Lama blessing children during the Tibetan New Year celebration near his residence in Dharamsala, India, 1985.

the course of study at namgyal monastery

Boys are admitted for entry into the monastery between the ages of ten and seventeen. The youngest and least educated among them are first schooled in reading and writing. To be admitted as trainees, they must be well behaved and able to learn to recite ten pages of religious text from memory in one month. The main study program includes memorization of ritual texts and philosophical dialectics, in addition to Tibetan and English grammar.

The memorization takes three to seven years, depending on individual ability. The students are tested upon completion of each of the ritual texts. Debating philosophical dialectics is learned in an ongoing process, with an exam at the end of each year. Once they have completed the memorization program, the young students begin to practice the ritual arts, becoming members of the monastery and advancing to the level of junior monk.

The junior monks are entitled to join in the daily prayers of the monastery as part of their training. At the completion of the thirteenth level, their formal philosophical studies end. This normally takes approximately five years.

the dalai lama in today's world

Inspired by the leadership of the Fourteenth Dalai Lama, Tibetans in exile have worked tirelessly with the growing support of the international community to stop the devastation of Tibet and to free their homeland. The Dalai Lama made his first visit to the West in 1973, with an eight-country tour of western Europe, including a special

Philosophical debate at Namgyal Monastery is an important part of the curriculum and often has moments of great humor.

stop in Switzerland where he officiated at several Buddhist ceremonies for the 2,000 Tibetans living in Rikon, outside Zurich.

In 1979, the Dalai Lama visited the United States and the American Buddhist community for the first time. Subsequently, he has traveled widely throughout the world, to Russia, Mongolia, Japan, Central and South America, Mexico, Canada, and throughout Europe and the United States several times. He presented his Five-Point Peace Plan in 1987 before the Human Rights Caucus of the United States House of Representatives and elaborated on that plan before the European Parliament in Strasbourg shortly thereafter.

In the face of China's continuing campaign to discredit his efforts, he has received countless awards—including the Albert Schweitzer Award, the World Management Council Award, the Raoul Wallenberg Award, and the 1989 Nobel Peace Prize—in recognition of his unremittingly nonviolent struggle for Tibetan independence, as well as his humanitarian effort on behalf of both inner peace and global survival. In spite of his protest that he is "only a simple Buddhist monk," Gyalwa Tenzin Gyatso has come to be recognized as that rare kind of leader who can inspire and change the world.

Tenzin Gyatso, the Fourteenth Dalai Lama,
receives the 1989 Nobel Peace Prize
in Oslo, Norway.

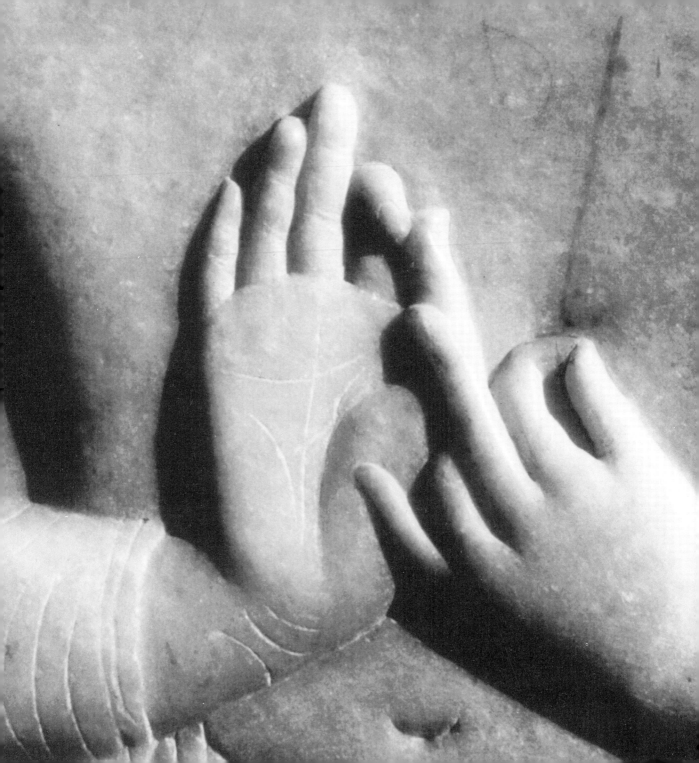

Tibetan

I vow to work for the benefit of all sentient

Buddhist

beings until the last one is enlightened.

Philosophy

The Bodhisattva Vow

the seed of compassion

IT IS SAID at the beginning of every Tibetan Buddhist text, at the start of every Vajrayana Buddhist initiation, by teachers both ancient and contemporary, that in order to practice and make progress on the path, the most important thing is to develop *bodhicitta,* the mind of compassion. This is the state of mind that wishes to attain enlightenment for the purpose of liberating all sentient beings from the cycle of suffering—birth, old age, sickness, death, and rebirth.

The hands of the Buddha teaching the dharma. Detail of life-sized statue of polished stone at Bodhgaya, India.

The word *bodhi* means "awake" and the word *citta* means "mind." Thus the word *bodhicitta* has been translated as "enlightened attitude," "awakened mind," "awakened heart," and, most commonly, "mind of compassion." It is interesting to note that the English word *compassion* means "feeling with." This sense of complete one-

Bodhisattva Avalokiteshvara. The eleven-headed, one thousand-armed form of the Bodhisattva of Compassion. 29¹/2"x20", silk and silver metal cord appliqué on silk, China, circa 1780.

ness with others is precisely what is at the core of the mind that is awake.

Another word that is relevant here is *bodhisattva,* or "awakened knowledge." A bodhisattva is a being who has attained enlightenment and has taken a vow to work for the benefit of all sentient beings. Moses, Jesus, and Mohammed are acknowledged by some Buddhists to be bodhisattvas—beings who have achieved liberation from the Wheel of Life but have chosen to be reborn in order to help others. Mahatma Gandhi, Martin Luther King, and Mother Teresa are recent examples. In addition, sincere Buddhist practitioners are considered to be aspiring bodhisattvas, on the path to realizing the state of perfection, or selflessness. The vow of the bodhisattva is renewed again and again.

To prepare students for the Kalachakra Initiation, the ritual master begins by giving teachings on developing compassion. This is regarded not only as a necessary foundation for receiving the empowerment, but also the essential requirement for attaining the enlightened state of mind. The Dalai Lama offers these preparatory teachings over a period of four days, before the students enter the initiation site.

The spirit of compassion is symbolized by Avalokiteshvara (known as Chenrezig in Tibet, Kuan Yin in China, and Kwannon in Japan), who is one of the best known and most beloved bodhisattvas of the Buddhist pantheon. Like all bodhisattvas, he can be visualized in colorful detail but is at the same time understood to be a symbol for an essential quality of Buddha mind.

According to legend, Avalokiteshvara vowed to free all beings from the cycle of suffering before his own liberation. The enormity of this task caused him to emanate in a form with one thousand arms reaching out in limitless compassion.

a question of motivation

Tibetan Buddhists examine and purify their intentions before every practice so that they may be fit vessels to receive the empowerment or instruction. On a daily basis, practitioners attune their motivation to the Buddha ideal of conducting all activities in a spirit of altruism.

The purpose of Tibetan Buddhist practice is not only to gain enlightenment in order to rise above earthly struggles. Practitioners must also have the sincere desire to alleviate the suffering of all sentient beings, placing others' well-being above their own just as a mother would that of her child.

Westerners, raised from birth on principles of individuality and independence, on values of personal achievement and material success, may find this very fundamental precept of compassionate motivation to be an alien concept. We may agree intellectually with the principle, which is in accord with the Judeo-Christian ethical tradition ("Love thy neighbor as thyself") and other spiritual practices. But the reality is that most of us, when we examine ourselves earnestly, find that we act primarily from self-interest.

How, then, can this most basic teaching of the Mahayana Buddhist path be considered to be even remotely attainable, as something relevant for each of us and not just for saints and spiritual devotees? The answer was given by the Buddha when he said that all beings possess the seed of enlightenment, and if that seed is properly cultivated it is only a matter of time before it will ripen. The path of the Buddha is intended to hasten that development.

The Buddha speaks of extremes as a cause of suffering, and therefore Buddhism is called the Middle Path, or Middle Way. Equanimity and moderation set the course by which to steer.

Ironically, some see the Buddhist ideal itself as an extreme. How can I work for the benefit of others, one might think, when it's all I can do to take care of myself? But working for the benefit of others is actually a path to personal satisfaction. If we have a genuine attitude of loving kindness and generosity toward others, people respond to us and we are rewarded in many ways. This is what the Dalai Lama calls being "wise selfish."

By taking the attention away from ourselves and thinking of others, we expand our vision of what the world holds for us, which benefits us and those around us.

Shakyamuni Buddha seated in his teaching posture. 24³/₄" high stone carving, Pala period, India, late 10th century.

the core of the teaching

The subject of altruistic motivation, or bodhicitta, brings us to the fundamental precepts of Mahayana Buddhism. The Buddha's first teachings after he achieved enlightenment were the Four Noble Truths, and the first of these is a recognition of the existence of suffering. This is often a stumbling block to people who are curious about Buddhism. They ask, quite understandably, "What relevance does this have to my life? If I'm happy, why do I need this? If I'm unhappy, how can this benefit me?"

However, the Buddha's observation cuts right to the root of the human condition: No matter what our station in life, no matter how favored we may be with material comfort or loving family and friends, no matter how powerful we are, we all grow sick, we all grow old, and every one of us will die. In addition, there are all the smaller, psychological sufferings of every moment—the frustration of not being able to do what we think we want, the anger of experiencing what we don't like, the envy of desiring what we don't have, the fear of losing what we do have.

The fact is, there isn't one of us who doesn't long for happiness, yet we are all constantly laying the foundations of unrest through the habitual conditioning of our own minds. When we realize that we are in a seemingly endless cycle of rising and falling emotions which offers no sense of fulfillment or lasting happiness, many of us look for a remedy.

Seeking another way to live, we listen to the words of the Buddha, and he begins with the subject of suffering. At first, this seems a rather bleak confirmation of our own painful experience. However, once we recognize that what we thought was a normal condition is in fact suffering, we begin to understand that there may be a remedy.

The Buddha explained the cause of suffering (the Second Noble Truth) to be attachment (desire) and aversion. Both causes of suffering are rooted in our belief in a self that exists apart from others, in the concepts of "me" and "mine." But underlying that is our fundamental ignorance of the nature of reality. Taking everything at face value and naively presuming that "I" am the most important object in "my" world, we blind ourselves to the truth that everything is interdependent. "My" very existence hangs upon a multitude of fortunate occurrences and could be extinguished at any time as easily as a candle flame in the wind.

Furthermore, what exactly is this "I" that is mistakenly conceived to be so permanent? Is the "I" that is reading this sentence, possibly relaxed and focused, the same "I" that is so upset when wrongly accused or threatened with physical danger? And does the enemy who wrongs me exist independently, or do I perceive him to be my enemy by virtue of some words or action which I interpreted as malicious? Were my enemy to speak kindly and offer assistance, would I not then call him my friend? This "I" that I am aware of "in here" is merely an illusion, an entity fabricated by the mind out of what is in fact a never-ending flow of consciousness. It is our self-centered attitude, at the root of which is our ignorance, that causes these reactions of liking/attachment versus not-liking/aversion.

understanding emptiness

When Buddhists speak about "emptiness," they do not mean the void. Emptiness is what is experienced in the absence of concepts, emotions, and other obstacles that prevent us from realizing the essential, pure nature of mind.

The Buddhist concept of emptiness is extremely difficult to translate into Western thought, because our philosophies have no comparable concept. Emptiness is not produced by the mind. One of the reasons we have so much trouble understanding it is its nondualistic nature; that is, it is beyond the references that we use to comprehend the world.

Buddhism encourages the cultivation of "mindful" activity, as a means to develop awareness of our actions. We are thus able to penetrate the ordinary mind, or what Buddhists call the coarse levels of consciousness, and begin to experience the subtle mind. Only the intuitive or subtle mind is capable of perceiving emptiness.

the elimination of suffering

This takes us right back to the Buddha's fundamental insight into the existence of suffering and its causes. Attachment and aversion, which are manifestations of the ordinary or coarse mind, stem from a distortion of our basic need for survival and result in our possessive drive to satisfy our desires. In daily life, we are continually grasping and clinging as a result of this conditioned reflex to possess. As this grows unchecked, what results is a cumulative effect in which we experience desire as a fixed, concrete condition of life. This perpetuates the basic delusion that getting what we want will make us happy; in reality, it only results in our wanting something else. While we are in a state of desire, reaching for something outside ourselves, we cannot find happiness. As long as we grasp at life to make it conform to our ideas of what it should be, and as long as we reject whatever we deem at the moment to be painful or unpleasant, we will always be in a state of suffering. We create our own suffering by the way we choose, consciously or unconsciously, to perceive the moment.

Our responses of attachment and aversion are deeply conditioned within us and, according to the Buddhist view, even continue through many lifetimes. So unless and until we "wake up" from our delusion, we are compelled to repeat our suffering throughout an endless cycle of rebirths.

All Buddhist disciplines are aimed at eliminating suffering. Often, we do not see how our emotions contribute to our suffering. Emotions are a construct of our own minds, which we alone are responsible for creating and for changing. The primary afflictive emotions, known to Buddhists as "the Three Poisons," are ignorance, greed, and hatred. They superimpose judgments of good and bad—judgments that exist entirely in our minds—and prevent us from experiencing the true nature of reality.

What we perceive as a problem often contains hidden opportunities. The Vajrayana path actually teaches us to use our disturbing emotions as a catalyst for transformation. As we actively replace our unwholesome mental activity with consciously chosen enlightened

responses, our old habits are naturally and spontaneously transformed. This is a way out, using suffering as a path to freedom.

the importance of practice

To understand the importance of setting out upon the path of liberation, practitioners reflect deeply upon the four fundamental meditations that turn the mind toward the dharma, or the teachings of the Buddha. These are (1) the preciousness of a human birth and the difficulty of attaining it; (2) the impermanence of all things; (3) the inexorability of karma; and (4) the pervasiveness of suffering in cyclic existence (life, death, and rebirth), or *samsara.*

Imagine the world as one large ocean with a single, doughnut-shaped, wooden yoke floating on its surface, blown about by the winds. Now suppose that a blind sea turtle were to poke its head out of the water once every hundred years in an attempt to find the center of that ring. While that may seem impossible, it is suggested that to obtain a human birth in the vast sea of beings is even more difficult.

According to Buddhist thought, there are six realms of existence. For instance, there is the hell realm, where conditions are so miserable that all one can think about is one's pain; there is the realm of hungry ghosts, in which beings hunger and thirst incessantly; and there is the animal realm, where stupidity and ignorance reign. Only human beings are in a position to realize the truth of the dharma and to choose to act on it.

Therefore a human lifetime is regarded as being precious indeed. Death may occur at any time; stability and certainty are mere illusions, so there is not a moment to waste. We must practice now.

The second meditation that turns one's thoughts toward the dharma is the reality of impermanence. This is the fact that nothing is static: everything is constantly in flux, being born and dying, even this very moment. Everything that seems so solid—monuments, empires, the earth itself—is in a continuous process of growth, decay, and dissolution. One season changes into the next; the body that once seemed so strong and healthy becomes weakened and eventually dies.

Opposite: *The Wheel of Transmigration.*
The center circle illustrates "the three poisons,"
represented by a cock (ignorance), a pig
(greed), and a snake (hatred). They are
surrounded by the six realms of existence,
which are in turn surrounded by
the perpetual cycle of life, or *samsara.*
43" thangka, Tibet,
19th century.

The third thought to contemplate is inexorable karma—the accumulation of our actions as governed by the law of cause and effect—which determines our destiny. Our actions, both positive and negative, accumulate in our karmic "account" throughout every second of our lives. No matter how insignificant they may appear, these actions affect not only the present but the future. We are, in fact, the summation of our collective karmic experience, all of which comes to bear on each moment. If we pay attention to our daily actions of body, speech, and mind, we can improve our karma in our present life and for our future lives.

The final subject for meditation that leads us to see the wisdom of practicing the Buddhist path is that the suffering of samsaric, or cyclic, existence is everywhere and it is unending. Whatever is left undone at the time of our death, whatever cravings or resistances were not recognized as illusion, whatever debts were owed in the course of harming others—all these things will coalesce once more into yet another lifetime of ignorance, greed, hatred, and continued suffering.

training the mind

The Buddha was recognized as the "Great Physician" not only because he was explicit in his diagnosis of the disease of suffering, but also because of his presentation of the Third and Fourth Noble Truths. The good news is that there is a cessation to the endless round, and the antidote, like the disease itself, resides in the mind.

Just as samsara arises from ignorance, so enlightenment is born of awareness. And this awareness is developed through hearing the teachings, contemplating them, and putting them into practice. Thus we can purify our minds of the "defilements" that keep us from perceiving the true nature of all beings and things. This purification allows the "pristine consciousness" of the enlightened state to enter into our lives, like sunlight shining through a newly washed window.

In the Kalachakra Tantra it says that "sentient beings are Buddhas, defiled by adventitious stains. When those are removed, all beings are Buddhas." Elsewhere in Buddhism, it is taught that the true nature of the mind is as clear as the sky. The stains or defile-

ments are not intrinsic to our nature but are collected through many lifetimes of ignorance and unwholesome actions. They are like clouds which, when removed, leave only the clear sky of our essential Buddha nature.

Monks seated beneath the bodhi tree during the 1973 Kalachakra Initiation at Bodhgaya, India. They are listening to a teaching by Ling Rinpoche, the senior tutor to the Dalai Lama.

To remind us that it is really quite possible (though not easy) to accomplish this, the Dalai Lama has said, "We human beings have a developed brain and limitless potential. Since even wild animals can gradually be trained with patience, the human mind also can gradually be trained, step by step. If you test these practices with patience, you can come to know this through your own experience. If someone who easily gets angry tries to control his or her anger, in time it can be brought under control. The same is true for a very selfish person: first that person must realize the faults of a selfish motivation and the benefit in being less selfish. Having realized this, one trains in it, trying to control the bad side and develop the good. As time goes by, such practice can be very effective. This is the only alternative."

one human family

We must recognize the necessity for a compassionate attitude. The Dalai Lama explains that each of us is essentially the same human being, made up of the same basic flesh, blood, and bone. Our differences of language, culture, social status, and gender are merely superficial and secondary. The most important thing we have in common is our desire for happiness, and we each have an equal right to its pursuit.

We are joined together in the same family, on the same planet, so it is necessary that each of us be a good and loving member of that family. Everyone, even the most cruel, appreciates being shown kindness and consideration. This is intrinsic to human nature, just as infants need to be held and touched with love in order to grow strong and survive. Thus we can all understand the basic human need for compassion.

Furthermore, we can recognize that we always feel friendlier toward someone who shows good will toward us, and we naturally feel uneasy when shown hostility, anger, or jealousy. Since we are in essence so much like one another, our own experience can tell us what everyone else must feel. The simple fact is that without a

The Dalai Lama teaches on compassion to prepare the students to receive the Kalachakra Initiation in Rikon, Switzerland, 1985.

newly affirmed sense of responsibility and cooperation toward one another, our very survival as a species is threatened.

realizing inner peace

The conclusion is unavoidable: The most important thing in life, the most primary and basic, is the practice of kindness and honesty. If we have the right attitude, we can face even tragedy with the inner peace that comes from love and trust in others, whereas a negative attitude will bring us only unhappiness.

What the Dalai Lama calls "universal responsibility" comes from the courage and self-confidence that replace fear and insecurity. Forgiveness, tolerance, and patience are evidence of true inner strength, and we can practice these states of mind consciously. Selfishness, on the other hand, is the result of ignorance and can only lead to suffering. The Dalai Lama teaches us that the cultivation of our positive human qualities takes constant effort, time, and mental determination. The need is urgent—more urgent than ever. And we must never give up hope.

The Tibetan Buddhist path is in no way passive. It is very much an active process of continually purifying the activities of one's body, speech, and mind, by reciting prayers and performing various ritual practices and meditations daily.

The accumulated thoughts, habits, and behavior patterns of this and former lifetimes are transformed by the continuous application of mental discipline. The effect of practicing altruism is a calming of the mind, which allows one to experience its finer, subtle levels. Eventually, this altruistic intention becomes a way of life from which love, compassion, and wisdom arise spontaneously. Through such continued and prolonged practice, the atomic structure of one's very being is altered.

The practice of Buddhism leads us beyond suffering by turning our attention away from our self-absorption and toward the ultimate truth.

The Kalachakra Initiation

THIS CHAPTER is a general introduction to the Kalachakra Initiation based primarily on *The Mandala Rite of Glorious Kalachakra,* written by Khe-Drub in the 16th century. For the practitioner, it will be useful in understanding the proceedings. For the reader who is unfamiliar with tantric Buddhism, it is intended to introduce a magnificent ritual that has remained a secret for centuries, until now. An attempt has been made to simplify and clarify this extremely complex, esoteric initiation, which has resulted in the omission of many details. Also, certain descriptions have been abbreviated. The reader wishing a complete

Monks perform a celebratory dance upon the completion of the Kalachakra Sand Mandala on the eighth day of the Kalachakra Initiation at Madison Square Garden, New York City, 1991.

description of the Kalachakra Initiation is referred to the Dalai Lama's book, *The Kalachakra Tantra,* translated by Jeffrey Hopkins, Ph.D. (London: Wisdom Publications, 1985).

Every step of the initiation process and every gesture of the ritual master is intended to help develop an attitude of compassion and generate the wisdom mind of pristine awareness. Even the simple act of reading about the initiation may provide a useful glimpse into the compassionate teachings of the Buddha.

tantric initiation

The Tibetan word for initiation is *wong-khor,* which literally means "giving permission," or granting the authority to practice the tantra. The person conferring the initiation is known as the ritual master or *vajra* master, because the vajra is the ritual implement that cuts through illusion and represents the indestructible mind. Since the tantra itself lives through direct transmission by the vajra master, the initiation fulfills the vajra master's pledge to pass on the tantra without diminishing it in any way, always for the benefit of all sentient beings.

During the initiation, the student makes a similar pledge to respect and uphold the teachings. In this way the student enters into the lineage.

Students may choose to take on different levels of commitment. One who maintains the commitment to a conscientious daily practice will achieve greater results, and the lineage will be strengthened. Or, the initiation may be received simply as a blessing.

introduction to the kalachakra initiation

The Kalachakra Initiation allows the student to hear the tantra, practice its path, and teach its wisdom. The goal is to attain the mental and physical "accomplishments" of the deity, the ultimate goal being bliss consciousness. The initiate who incorporates the tantra into his or her daily practice will achieve new levels of such

The second day of preparation for the initiation begins with the performance of a ritual dance "protecting and consecrating the site," in which interfering forces are summoned to protect and bless the mandala site. Madison, Wisconsin, 1981.

mental accomplishments as generosity, patience, and concentration. The physical accomplishments, which are achieved by opening the subtle energy channels of the body, include relaxation, strength, and healing.

The student, by generating himself (or herself) as the deity, is introduced to new mental patterns which help him to abandon old, destructive conditioning, thus bringing him closer to the experience of bliss consciousness of Kalachakra.

The entire Kalachakra Initiation comprises fifteen separate initiations. The first seven, referred to as the Seven Childhood Initiations, are described in this chapter. The Four High Initiations and the Four Higher Initiations are considered to be more secret in nature and are given to advanced practitioners.

The Kalachakra Initiation is generally given over twelve days. There are ten days of preparation rituals, of which the first eight are conducted by the vajra master, assisted by monks, without the students present. The students participate in the ninth day's activities, known as "The Preparation of the Disciple." The actual initiation ritual takes two days. There is one final day of ceremonies, which includes the dismantling of the sand mandala.

Throughout the initiation, the students repeat many basic steps, including the purification of body, speech, and mind; the verbal expression of one's intent to become enlightened for the benefit of others; and the rejection of one's misdeeds. This repetition plants the teachings clearly and firmly in the minds of the students.

the assumption rite

The assumption rite is the student's request for empowerment on the first day. The vajra master performs the rites to protect the initiate from external and internal obstacles until the time that the actual initiation begins. The assumption rites can be received by one or more representatives for the students.

The vajra master, who has generated himself as the embodiment of Kalachakra, makes torma (barley flour and butter) offerings to

Five *torma* offerings made of *tsampa* (toasted barley flour) and butter represent deities. In the foreground are offering bowls containing rice and incense.

Above: The tooth stick divination.
Right: On the first day, Richard Gere, as the representative of the students, makes the traditional supplication of the vajra master to bestow the Kalachakra Initiation. New York City, 1991.

spirits of the local area. He explains to the students the importance of their developing the three principles of the path: renunciation, bodhicitta, and the perfect view of emptiness.

The vajra master is visualized not as an ordinary person but as the deity Kalachakra. The empowerment site is seen not as an ordinary place but as the mandala itself, which is the mani-festation of Kalachakra's nondualistic mind. The students prostrate them-selves and recite verses to the vajra master, requesting the assump-tion rite.

The students or their representatives repeat the following vow after the vajra master:

To remove the nonvirtuous deeds which I have accumulated in many lives, I will maintain all individual vows. Do allow me to become Kalachakra.

Next, it is determined which of the six afflictive emotions re-quires particular attention for keeping the vows. This identification is made by dropping the "tooth stick" (a smooth twig from the fig tree, used in India as a tooth brush) on a specially painted mandala board indicating the six families of Buddhas. Each family is repre-

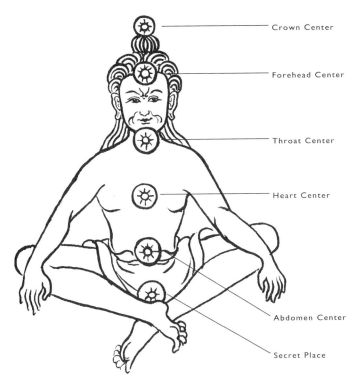

Crown Center

Forehead Center

Throat Center

Heart Center

Abdomen Center

Secret Place

Left: The six *chakras*, or energy centers.

Below: Purbas, or ritual daggers, protecting the mandala site.

sented by a different color which stands for an aspect of the wisdom of the Buddha.

The students request that the vajra master bestow the initiation upon them. In response, the vajra master spiritually anoints the students' six energy centers, or *chakras* (the crown of the head, the forehead, the throat, the heart, the abdomen, and the "secret place" or reproductive organs), with the Sanskrit "seed" syllables of the Buddhas, each syllable representing the essence of one of the six Buddha families. A seed syllable is the essence of a deity, the syllable from which the deity arises.

rituals of the site

Once the vajra master has agreed to confer the Kalachakra Initiation, the mandala site is prepared through a series of special rituals known as the Rituals of the Site:

On the second day, the vajra master prepares the "five substances" for the initiation. Here the Dalai Lama consecrates the ten vases filled with saffron water. New York City, 1991.

The chalk strings used to draw the mandala lines are blessed. The sand for the mandala is also consecrated at this time.

The vajras and bells used in the initiation are consecrated.

- "Testing the site" gains assurance through divination that the site is worthy of being home to the mandala.
- "Requesting the site" involves special prayers, which ask permission of divine beings and earthly authorities for use of the site.
- "Purifying the site" clears the area of extraneous objects and purifies it ritually. This includes invoking a circle of protective, ritual daggers known as *purbas,* which have been generated into protective deities, around the mandala site. The vajra master then meditates on emptiness. (This concludes the activities of the first day.)
- "Taking possession of the site" elicits permission from various divine beings to draw the mandala.
- "Protecting and consecrecating the site" summons and then disperses interfering forces through an elaborate ritual dance by the monks.

rituals of preparation

"Preparation of the earth goddess" consists of offering flowers and perfume to Tenma, the earth goddess, at the center of the mandala site.

"Preparation of the five substances" consecrates substances which will be used throughout the initiation. These are:

1. vases filled with purified water in which the deities will be generated
2. strings dipped in liquid chalk, to be used for drawing the mandala
3. the sand with which the mandala will be constructed
4. the vajra, a ritual implement symbolizing the indestructible mind
5. the bell, symbolizing the realization of emptiness.

The vajra master and his assistants visualize the Kalachakra Mandala, and then visualize lifting this meditated mandala into the space above the mandala base for its protection.

Above: Snapping the wisdom string. The vajra master and his assistants begin the construction of the sand mandala by defining the major axes and four base lines with the blessed chalk strings. New York City, 1991.

Left: At the completion of the second day's rituals, the four gatekeepers draw the sand mandala. Los Angeles, 1989.

During the "preparation of the chalk strings," the vajra master and his assistants draw the major axes and four base lines of the mandala, and then place grains of sand at each point where a deity will be represented.

In the "preparation of the deities," the vajra master summons the 722 deities from their abodes through prayer, asking them to take up residence in the mandala.

"Marking the mandala" calls for the preparation of a special thread made of five strands. The vajra master and his attendants visualize the five Dhyani Buddhas (the principal Buddhas of the five Buddha families) dissolving into the five strands and empowering them. The thread is then placed along the main outlines of the mandala, marking both the square mandalas and the outer, concentric circles into which the entire mandala is divided.

This completes the second day.

The four gatekeepers spend the next day drawing the mandala, including details such as the animals and the cushions for the deities, according to the Kalachakra text. The vajra master begins the third day by generating himself as Vajra Vega, the wrathful emanation of Kalachakra. He visualizes the syllable *HI* in each of his

Top: Vajra Vega, fierce emanation of Kalachakra. Detail from a contemporary Tibetan thangka.

Right: At the beginning of the third day, the vajra master generates himself as Vajra Vega and performs a dance opening the gates of the mandala. Here, a similar protective dance at the western gate is shown.

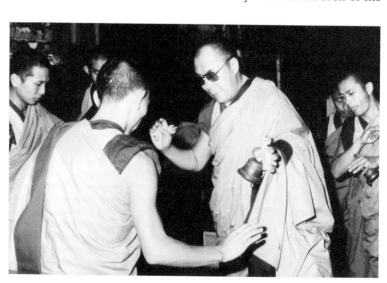

eyes. The syllable on his right eye becomes the sun and the one on his left eye the moon. He stands with his hands at his waist, reciting *HI HI* while smiling fiercely and turning his head from right to left. While doing this, the vajra master opens the three eastern gates by rubbing out the excess lines with saffron water. He repeats this process in the south, north, and west.

Now that the blessed string has fulfilled its function, the vajra master recites prayers to request that the five Dhyani Buddhas that had been invoked into the wisdom string now return to their sacred homes.

The next important step is known as the "preparation of the deities." The vajra master, reciting the mantra of all the deities, marks the seats of the 722 deities with scented water. First, the seat of Kalachakra in the center of the mandala is marked with a square, and the same is done for the four "ones gone thus" deities of the four directions, who sit at the cardinal points of the Mandala of Enlightened Wisdom. The seats of the other deities are symbolically marked with a circular motion. Then a grain of wheat is placed at each point to represent the flower that acts as a cushion for each deity.

The vajra master, facing the eastern gate, generates the entire mandala and all of the deities. He invokes the meditated mandala that was lifted into space on the second day and dissolves it into the generated mandala. Rituals are performed and blessings and offerings given.

The vajra master blesses his own tongue and generates it into the form of a one-pointed vajra, purifying his mouth and speech, and kneels on his right knee to supplicate Kalachakra as follows:

Grains of wheat indicate the placement of the 722 deities of the Kalachakra Sand Mandala.

> *Oh, victorious Kalachakra, lord of knowledge, I prostrate myself to the protector and possessor of compassion. I am making a mandala here out of love and compassion for my disciples and as an offering of respect to you. Oh Kalachakra, please be kind and remain close to me. I, the vajra master, am creating this mandala to purify the obstructions of all beings. Therefore, always be considerate of my disciples and me, and please reside in the mandala.*

Top: The vajra master holds the five colored strings representing the five Dhyani consorts.

Above: He and five assistants invoke the exalted wisdom of the consorts to enter the principal lines of the sand mandala.

Sitting on the eastern quadrant of the mandala, the Dalai Lama applies the first sand.
New York City, 1991.

The vajra master repeats this supplication three times and visualizes that Kalachakra grants him his authority by replying:

I grant your wish to you, holder of awareness.

The vajra master then visualizes lifting the deities and the mandala of preparation into the space above the mandala base. Thus the Rituals of Preparation are completed.

main ritual

The main ritual consists of "snapping the wisdom string," applying sand, placing vases around the mandala, decorating the thekpu, generating the entire mandala, making offerings, and, finally, conferring the initiation.

The ritual assistants begin by collecting the grains of wheat from the mandala. They clean the mandala and anoint it with sacred water. The vajra master, as Kalachakra, stands in the west, facing east, while five assistants stand opposite him, generated as Vajra Vega. They make offerings to the lifted mandala, which they visualize suspended in front of them.

The wisdom string is made of five strings of different colors representing the five Dhyani consorts. The vajra master wraps the strings around the forefinger of his left hand, starting with green at the bottom, followed by black, red, white, and yellow. Holding the string above his navel and reciting a mantra, he passes the other end of each of the colored strings to the assistants.

Reciting prayers, the vajra master and his assistants dissolve the common wisdom string into emptiness, from which they generate the five strings into the five consorts. The vajra master visualizes that each of the Dhyani consorts of the lifted mandala has at her heart center a Sanskrit syllable. These syllables are transformed into the five wisdom strings in the form of five colored rays. The vajra master generates rays from his heart center into the hearts of the consorts, activating the syllables in the form of wisdom string rays. These rays dissolve into the five colored strings held by the vajra master and his assistants.

The vajra master and his assistants twist the strands of the strings together, and then make offerings to the consecrated colored strings. The vajra master and an assistant, standing at the west and the east, hold the colored string above the mandala and recite a special mantra for snapping the string. They visualize the sound of the snap alerting the deities, who then descend from the lifted mandala and dissolve into the colored string in the hand of the vajra master. The vajra master and his assistant now hold the string directly over the east/west axis, and snap it while reciting the same mantra. At the sound of the snap, they visualize the nature of exalted wisdom in the form of the five colored strings descending and dissolving into the east/west axis line and blessing it. This procedure is repeated over the north/south axis, and then over the two diagonal lines, the four root lines, and all

The Dalai Lama holds a five-strand, multicolored string and a vajra at his heart as he leads the monks in prayer during the construction of the sand mandala. The other end of this string is tied around the top of each of the ten vases on the altar.

Above: Sand is applied to the mandala from the third through the seventh days of preparation for the Kalachakra Initiation. The monks begin by sitting on the mandala base and working from the center outward.

Right: Toward the end of the sand painting process, the monks stand on the floor, leaning forward to work near the perimeter of the mandala. Other monks join in to ensure that the mandala is completed by the end of the eighth day.

the other lines of the mandala until they have all been blessed. The vajra master then makes offerings to the colored wisdom string and requests that all the wisdom deities of the string return to their sacred home.

Now the applying of the sand begins. The vajra master sits on the east side of the mandala facing the center, reciting prayers. He applies white, red, and black sand to the foundation wall of the Mandala of Enlightened Mind. He paints a small portion of this wall to signify beginning the construction of the mandala with its foundation. The four gatekeepers and their assistants continue the process of sand painting in their respective directions.

By the conclusion of the third day, the assistants have completed applying the sand to at least the Mandala of Enlightened Great Bliss and the Mandala of Enlightened Wisdom.

The fourth through eighth days consist of ritual prayers and the construction of the sand mandala. Each day, before working on the mandala, the artisan monks generate themselves as the deities of the mandala, led by the vajra master.

After the mandala has been completed on the eighth day, it is blessed by the vajra master. Purbas symbolizing the ten directions are set around the completed mandala to protect against any obstacles which might disturb the initiation. Also set around the mandala are ten ritual vases, each representing a female deity (called a *shakti*) who personifies the wisdom of enlightenment. The shaktis will help in the empowerment of the student. A curtain is lowered on all four sides of the mandala house (*thekpu*) to shield it from the uninitiated, and a celebratory dance of the offering goddesses is performed by the monks. The students are invited to see the dance.

Two of the ten decorated vases, connected by the wisdom string, which are placed around the completed sand mandala. The vases represent female deities called *shaktis*, who will aid in conferring the initiation.

preparing the students

Before the students are initiated, they undergo a process of preparation which involves approximately forty steps. This process is generally referred to as "enhancement," or sometimes "enhancement of the students."

Throughout the enhancement and initiation processes, the student uses visualization to become acquainted with the mandala, and

to experience the qualities of the deities. "Becoming" the deities in this way helps students to transform their ordinary consciousness to that of Buddha mind. This practice is known as "deity yoga."

On the afternoon of the ninth day of the ceremony, the students officially enter the mandala site for the first time. In preparation, they have cleansed their bodies, dressed in clean clothes, and readied themselves for spiritual rebirth. Before entering the site, they rinse their mouths as a gesture of purification and respect, and they make prostrations to the vajra master, whom they visualize as the deity Kalachakra. The site itself is likewise visualized as a manifestation of the nondualistic mind of Kalachakra. The students recite a verse while making a *mudra,* or hand gesture, requesting that the vajra master give them the preparation for the initiation. This is called a "mandala offering."

The vajra master acts as a guide for the students. He introduces them to the deities of the mandala, the commitments, and the procedures for realizing the purpose of the initiation—achieving the enlightened mind of Kalachakra.

The vajra master explains the history, lineage, and essence of the Kalachakra Tantra, and he instructs the students on how to correct their motivation. He explains that for the initiation to be effective, vows of bodhicitta—the motivation to achieve enlightenment for the benefit of all sentient beings—must be taken.

internal initiation

The students now ask for spiritual rebirth as a child of the vajra master. They envision the vajra master as Kalachakra in union with his consort Vishvamata. Light rays radiating from the vajra master's heart draw the students into his body. They imagine themselves entering the vajra master's mouth, dissolving into light at his heart, moving downward through his body and into Vishvamata's womb, where they are dissolved into emptiness and, finally, reborn as Kalachakra with one face and two arms. Having emerged from the womb of the consort, the students visualize returning to their seats.

Above: This *mudra,* or hand gesture, is an offering mandala representing the universe. The students make this gesture as a supplication many times during the Kalachakra Initiation.

Opposite: The Dalai Lama as vajra master at the Kalachakra Initiation in Bodhgaya, India, in 1973. He sits on a throne facing the students in front of a thangka painting of Kalachakra. On the ninth day of the ritual, the students enter the mandala site for the first time. They will visualize the vajra master as the deity Kalachakra.

The students then supplicate the vajra master to bestow the pledges and the mind of enlightenment. The vajra master encourages them to keep a firm faith in the tantric teachings by implementing them in their daily practice.

the vows and blessings

Led by the vajra master, the students take two levels of vows: the common, or bodhisattva vow, and the uncommon, or mantra vow. Through meditation, the students generate the state of mind to practice the altruistic path of the bodhisattvas, and they repeat the verses of the bodhisattva vow three times:

> *I go for refuge to the Three Jewels,*
> *individually repent all misdeeds,*
> *rejoice in the virtue of others,*
> *will hold the mind of enlightenment.*

The uncommon mantra vow is taken by repeating additional verses three times.

The students are then symbolically blessed. First, they generate themselves as Kalachakra, and then they visualize six Sanskrit syllables, which represent the six Dhyani consorts (of the five Buddha families, plus the consort of Vajrasattva, Vajradhatvishvari) appearing on their six chakras. The six syllables, or goddesses, are imagined to dissolve into the chakras to purify them. The vajra master recites the syllables *HUNG AH OM* many times, and then touches the student with scented water, visualizing these syllables at the student's heart, throat, and forehead. This will bestow the seeds of Kalachakra and bless the three places, which represent mind, speech, and body. The vajra master then makes offerings to the students with flowers, incense, butter lamps, and food.

dropping the tooth stick

The student prays that his or her body, speech, and mind be cleansed in preparation for divination. The tooth stick ritual is repeated, with the same or different results, to determine the student's spiritual tasks to be accomplished.

the scented water and the kusha grass

A small amount of scented water is placed in the hands of the students. Three sips are taken to remove subtle defilements. They each then receive two reeds of kusha grass, because the Buddha was sitting on kusha grass when he became enlightened. The longer of the

two reeds is to be placed under each student's mattress to clear the mind of obscuring thoughts, while the shorter reed, to be placed under the pillow, aids in the generation of clear dreams.

As one of the forty steps in the "enhancement of the students," each student receives two reeds of kusha grass, used to clear the mind of obscuring thoughts and aid in the generation of clear dreams.

the protection cord

Students receive a red thread with three knots, which is tied around the upper arm. The Dalai Lama has explained its meaning: "As love increases in your mind, harmful forces do not affect you. Thus, the most effective method for protecting against harm is the cultivation of love. The best protection from one who is trying to harm you is to think, 'This being wants happiness just as I do. May this being attain happiness.' The thread is a reminder of this."

instructions for sleeping

The vajra master teaches about the cycle of suffering, which includes birth, death, and rebirth. He explains that it is a rare opportunity to be born in human form, even rarer to hear the teachings of the Buddha, and rarer yet to have access to the practice of the Kalachakra Tantra. Even if the student can't practice the secret mantra teachings, to see the sand mandala and circumambulate it will be of great benefit and is cause for rejoicing.

He then gives the students special instructions for the night. He suggests that they recite the Kalachakra mantra as many times as possible before going to sleep. They are to sleep on their right sides with their heads toward the mandala, or, if that is not possible, to imagine that the mandala is in the direction of their heads. This will keep them mindful of Kalachakra, of bodhicitta, and of the inherent emptiness of all things. It is explained that students are most likely to be in contact with the mysteries of subtle consciousness at dawn, and they are reminded to place the kusha grass under both mattress and pillow.

dream analysis

The next day, which is the tenth day of the ritual, the vajra master offers guidelines for analyzing the dreams of the previous night. He describes positive and negative symbols, and offers a means of overcoming troublesome dreams through meditation on emptiness, and by the generation of compassion and love toward the threatening forces in the dream. The vajra master then scatters water while recit-

On the tenth day, the vajra master gives representatives of the students the costume of the deity to instill in them a sense of the dignity of Kalachakra.

ing a special mantra associated with the "wisdom which understands emptiness," to disperse any negative effects.

The actual initiation begins here.

The vajra master gives general teachings on Kalachakra. The students, visualizing themselves as Kalachakra with one face and two arms seated at the eastern gate of the mandala, supplicate the vajra master to bestow all the vows, which are repeated.

To instill a sense of the dignity of the deity, the vajra master, reciting a mantra, gives several representatives of the students the costume of the deity: brocades, multicolored garments, and a three-tiered, red-haired knot crown.

Since they are not spiritually ready to see the mandala before receiving the initiation, the vajra master gives the students a red blindfold. The blindfold is placed symbolically over the forehead.

The vajra master recites a mantra and gives students a garland of flowers to offer to the deity upon entering the mandala.

The vajra master again gives the students three sips of scented water, as on the preparation day, to cleanse the three gates of body, speech, and mind.

Sprinkling scented water, the vajra master recites a mantra to remove obstacles and dissolve the students into emptiness. Within that emptiness, he generates them as Kalachakra with two hands embracing blue Vishvamata. The students focus on the emptiness of all phenomena. Then, imagining that all the Buddhas and bodhisattvas are present as witnesses, the students take the bodhisattva vow.

Students are then given further teachings on the five Buddha families and the Kalachakra Initiation itself. They take special tantric vows to train in the path of highest yoga tantra, in order to bring help and happiness to all sentient beings.

Students wear red blindfolds given to them by the vajra master to protect them from seeing the mandala before being initiated.

the twenty-five modes of conduct

The vajra master introduces the twenty-five modes of conduct, which include refraining from harming others, lying, killing, stealing, gambling, engaging in sexual misconduct, and becoming attached to sensory pleasures. A four-line verse expresses the students' motivation to maintain the rules of conduct forever.

The vajra master leads the students through an essential visualization process called the "generation of the all-encompassing

Flowers (here seeds from the bodhi tree) are given to the students by the vajra master to offer to Kalachakra upon entering the mandala. After the flower divination is performed, the flowers are placed on their foreheads to generate the wisdom of bliss and emptiness.

yogic mind." This mind of bodhicitta and emptiness generates the powerful seed which is the basis of the tantric path to achieve enlightenment. Students make pledges of secrecy—not to speak of the initiation to the uninitiated—as well as other pledges of correct behavior.

entering the mandala

While the vajra master recites mantras, the students (or their representatives) enter within the curtained mandala area. With blindfolds still on, they circumambulate the mandala while visualizing themselves as the Buddhas of the four entrance gates to the mandala. They repeat the secrecy oath. A complex visualization is led by the vajra master, in which deities are dissolved into blessings within the students, to the accompaniment of cymbals, bells, drums, and incense.

the flower garland initiation

Each student holds a single flower between his hands in prayer and visualizes offering a garland of flowers to Kalachakra. A representative drops a flower onto a painted mandala board that represents the sand mandala, which is too fragile to use for this purpose. As in the tooth stick divination, where the flower lands determines what the students' Buddha lineage is and what feats they will accomplish. The flower is also an offering to the deities of the mandala, who purify and transform the offering, "blessing it into magnificence." The flower, placed on the student's head afterward, help to generate the wisdom of bliss and emptiness. This initiation creates an auspicious bond between the deity and the students.

The vajra master exhorts Kalachakra to open the students' eyes. They remove their blindfolds, which symbolizes that the darkness of ignorance has been removed. They can now see the entire mandala.

The vajra master guides the students through a visualization of the three-dimensional mandala, introducing them to the deities.

explanation of the mandala

The outermost circle of the mandala is seen as brightly colored lights, representing a mountain of fire that completely surrounds and protects the mandala. This is the element of bliss consciousness, or pristine awareness. The green circle inside it represents space, with a chain of vajras seen as the indestructible mind protecting the mandala. Next comes the gray wind element, then the pink-red fire element, then the white water element, and finally the yellow earth element with its pattern of green swastikas, a benevolent symbol derived from ancient Indian culture representing stability and well-being.

These six concentric circles represent the six elements. Within the concentric circles is a square which represents the five-story palace of Kalachakra. Surrounding the palace are four crescent-shaped gardens, which contain various offerings to the deities.

The colors of the four quadrants of the square palace correspond to the four faces of Kalachakra. When the black quadrant is at the bottom, the viewer is facing the black face of Kalachakra, who resides at the center facing east.

The outermost square is the Mandala of Enlightened Body. Inside that are the Mandala of Enlightened Speech, the Mandala of Enlightened Mind, the Mandala of Enlightened Wisdom, and the innermost square, the Mandala of Enlightened Great Bliss.

description of the principal deity kalachakra

At the center of the mandala, on a green, eight-petaled lotus, is the principal deity—glorious Kalachakra with his consort Vishvamata. Kalachakra has a dark blue black body with three necks, the middle one black, the right red, and the left white. He has four faces, of which the main one is blue black and wrathful, with a fang. His right face is red, with an expression of desire; his left face is white, and very peaceful; and his rear face, depicted at the extreme left, is yellow, with a look of meditative concentration. Each face has three eyes. His hair is in the form of a topknot. The three-tiered crown is topped with the seal of the bodhisattva Vajrasattva and other ornaments, including a crescent moon and a double vajra. His body ornaments include vajra, jewels, vajra earrings, vajra necklace, vajra bracelet, vajra belt, vajra ankle bracelets, flowing vajra scarves, vajra garlands, and a skirt of tiger skin.

Kalachakra has six shoulders, three on each side, which are black, red, and white. Connected to each shoulder are two upper arms, and connected to each upper arm are two lower arms, each with one

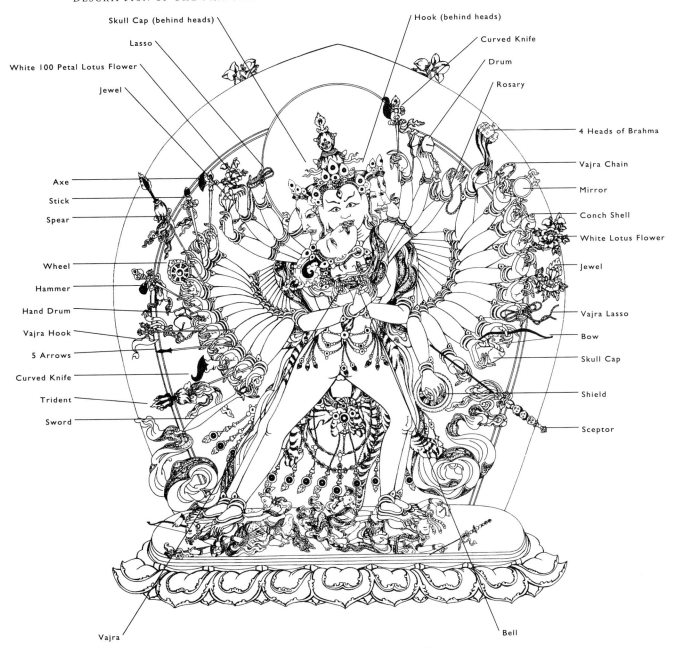

Skull Cap (behind heads)

Hook (behind heads)

Lasso

Curved Knife

White 100 Petal Lotus Flower

Drum

Jewel

Rosary

4 Heads of Brahma

Vajra Chain

Axe

Mirror

Stick

Conch Shell

Spear

White Lotus Flower

Wheel

Jewel

Hammer

Hand Drum

Vajra Lasso

Vajra Hook

Bow

5 Arrows

Skull Cap

Curved Knife

Shield

Trident

Sword

Sceptor

Vajra

Bell

The implements of the deity Kalachakra and his consort Vishvamata.

hand, for a total of twenty-four hands, twelve on each side. The different-colored arms, symbolizing the purified and enlightened body, speech, and mind of Kalachakra, are used to remove the obstructions of body, speech, mind, or wisdom. The lower eight arms are black, the middle eight are red, and the upper eight arms are white. The back side of all the thumbs are yellow, the first fingers white, the second red, the third black, and the fourth green.

The inside of the hand and the lower joints of all his thumbs and fingers are black; the middle joints are red, and the upper joints white. Each finger is adorned with a shining, radiant ring.

the implements of kalachakra

Kalachakra holds twenty-four implements. In his four right black hands are a vajra, a sword, a trident, and a curved knife. His four right red hands hold five arrows, a vajra hook, a hand drum, and a hammer. His four right white hands hold a wheel, a spear, a wooden stick, and an axe. The implements of his four left black hands are a vajra bell, a shield, a scepter, and a skull cup filled with blood. His four left red hands hold a bow, a vajra lasso, a jewel, and a white lotus flower. The implements of the four left white hands are a conch shell, a mirror, a vajra chain, and a four-faced head of Brahma. Kalachakra stands on the cushion of a lotus and moon, sun, Rahu, and Kalagni disc, with his outstretched red leg pressing on the heart of the demonic god of the desire realm and his left white leg pressing on an afflicted deity. The consorts of the demonic god of the desire realm and the afflicted deity prostrate themselves at the feet of Kalachakra.

kalachakra's consort vishvamata

Vishvamata has a yellow body with four faces. Her main face is yellow, and the other three faces are white, blue, and red. Each face has three eyes. She has eight yellow arms. The implements of her four right hands are a curved knife, a hook, a small drum, and a rosary. The implements of her four left hands are a skull cup, a lasso, a white, eight-petaled lotus flower, and a jewel. Her head is crowned by Vajrasattva, indicating her lineage. Her body is adorned with the five seal ornaments of the Buddha families. With her left leg out-stretched, Vishvamata is in embrace with Kalachakra.

Kalachakra, represented by a vajra, and Vishvamata, represented by a dot of colored sand, reside at the center of the lotus of the sand mandala. Inseparable from them are green Akshobhya with his consort Prajnaparamita, and blue Vajrasattva with his consort Vajradhatvishvari, who are present on layers of sand below Kalachakra and Vishvamata. Thus, there are a total of six deities residing at the center of the lotus flower. On the eight petals of the lotus flower surrounding Kalachakra and Vishvamata reside eight shaktis. These eight, plus Prajnaparamita and Vajradhatvishvari, who are both in the center, make ten shaktis. The ten shaktis represent the ten perfections: generosity, morality, patience, effort, concentration, wisdom, method, spiritual aspiration, spiritual power, and transcendent wisdom.

The place where Kalachakra, Vishvamata, and the eight shaktis reside is the Mandala of Enlightened Great Bliss, which is at the center of the Mandala of Enlightened Mind.

The students visualize having seen and met the 70 deities of the Mandala of Enlightened Mind, the 116 deities of the Mandala of Enlightened Speech, and the 536 deities of the Mandala of Enlightened Body.

The vajra master states that all of the 722 deities have the nature of light rays and the great bliss of the enlightened state of mind. The 722 deities of the Kalachakra Mandala also correspond to specific parts of the human anatomy and their functions. Kalachakra himself corresponds to the heart, which is the seat of the subtle mind.

Having entered the mandala and having been introduced to the deities, the students sing a song of joy. This concludes the ceremony of the tenth day.

the seven childhood initiations

The students prepare for the Seven Childhood Initiations with offerings and supplications. The vajra master dispels all inauspiciousness.

Each of the seven initiations empowers the student to attain a particular spiritual goal, and each is analogous to an event in the development of a child.

The first two initiations, known as the Water and Crown Initiations, are associated with purification of defilements of the body. They take place at the northern gate of the Mandala of Enlightened Body.

The Silk Ribbon and Vajra-and-Bell Initiations are associated with purification of defilements of speech. They take place at the southern gate to the Mandala of Enlightened Speech.

The Conduct and Name Initiations are associated with the purification of defilements of mind. They take place at the eastern gate of the Mandala of Enlightened Mind.

The last initiation, that of Permission, is associated with the attainment of bliss, and takes place at the western side of the innermost Mandala of Enlightened Great Bliss. Thus, the Seven Childhood Initiations introduce the students to the deities of each mandala, allowing them to penetrate to the heart of Kalachakra.

There are twelve stages of realization to the practice of the Kalachakra Tantra. These are known as "bodhisattva levels," with the twelfth level corresponding to full enlightenment. The Seven Childhood Initiations authorize the students to achieve the first seven levels.

1. *Water Initiation.* Corresponds to a child's first bath.

The vajra master confers this initiation (and the others) as the embodiment of Kalachakra. He leads the students to the northern entrance of the Mandala of Enlightened Body, facing the white face of Kalachakra's "vajra body."

The purpose of the Water Initiation is to purify the student's five elements: wind, fire, earth, water, and space. The students make a mandala offering to the vajra master and then supplicate him to bestow the Water Initiation upon them. Using a conch shell, he sprinkles them with water taken from the ten purified vases. This water is the substance through which the initiation will be conducted. The Water Initiation begins with what is known as the Internal Initiation. The student visualizes being drawn by a ray of light from

The initiation substance "water," represented by a conch shell, used in the first of the Seven Childhood Initiations.

Kalachakra's (the vajra master's) heart center into his mouth, and through the vajra path into Vishvamata's womb. Then, after being transformed into emptiness, the student is generated as Kalachakra's "vajra body." A ray of light from Kalachakra's heart center then draws Kalachakra himself into the student, who becomes one with the deity. The heart rays then invite all the male and female Buddhas and bodhisattvas, known as the "conquerors." The vajra master makes offerings and supplications to them. The male and female conquerors melt in the heat of great desire into a substance called the "mind of enlightenment," which enters into Kalachakra's body through his crown and penetrates the womb of the consort. There the conquerors initiate the student. The student then emerges from the womb of the consort to take his or her initiation seat. This Internal Initiation is repeated at the gate of each mandala entered during the Childhood Initiations.

Next follows a complex visualization wherein the five elements of the students and the water from the vases are generated into deities. The elements and the water, as deities, are then initiated by the five Dhyani consorts of the mandala. The vajra master makes a gesture of touching the conch shell filled with water to the "five places" of the students: head, shoulders, arms, thighs, and hips. This symbolizes the purification of their five elements. He places water in the students' hands to drink. Drinking this water, the students experience a union of bliss consciousness and the realization of emptiness.

There is a concluding water ritual during this and several of the following Childhood Initiations wherein the student is anointed with sacred water in order to experience bliss consciousness.

The Water Initiation instills in the students the power to achieve the first bodhisattva level, known as "The Very Joyous Level," as its fruit.

2. *Crown Initiation*. Corresponds to a child's first haircut.

The students first make a mandala offering and a supplication to receive the Crown Initiation in order to purify each of their five "aggregates"—form, feeling, discrimination (perception), compositional factor (unconscious tendencies), and consciousness. The vajra master describes the auspicious nature of the event and the students envision a rain of flowers falling upon them.

Next follows a complex visualization in which the five Dhyani Buddhas who reside in the mandala confer the initiation while holding the initiation substance, which is the crown.

The vajra master touches the crown to the students' five places. At that moment, the students experience the nonconceptual mind of great bliss. At the conclusion of the Crown Initiation is a water ritual.

The Crown Initiation instills the power to achieve the second bodhisattva level, known as "The Uncontaminated Level," as its fruit.

The Water and Crown Initiations purify the body elements and aggregates of the students. Just as these are initially formed in the womb, these two initiations, which take place at the northern gate to the Mandala of Enlightened Body, establish the seeds in the students for attaining the exalted "vajra body."

3. *Silk Ribbon Initiation.* Corresponds to a child having its ears pierced.

The vajra master, as the embodiment of Kalachakra, leads the students to the southern gate of the Mandala of Enlightened Speech, facing the red face of Kalachakra's "vajra speech."

The students make a mandala offering and then a supplication to receive the Silk Ribbon Initiation. This initiation purifies the ten winds circulating through the body, which are associated with speech. Again, the vajra master describes the auspicious nature of the event and the students envision a rain of flowers falling over them. An Internal Initiation follows, generating the students into the "vajra speech" of Kalachakra. Then, through a complex visualization, the ten shaktis of the mandala, holding the silk ribbons, initiate the students, purifying their ten winds.

The vajra master touches the silk ribbons to the students' five places and then ties the ribbons to their headdresses (crowns). This blesses their ten winds into magnificence and generates the exalted wisdom of great bliss. A concluding water ritual follows.

The initiation substance "crown."

The initiation substance "silk ribbon."

The Silk Ribbon Initiation instills the power to achieve the third bodhisattva level, known as "The Luminous Level," as its fruit.

4. *Vajra-and-Bell Initiation.* Corresponds to a child's talk and laughter.

The vajra represents compassion, or the male principle, while the bell represents wisdom (the realization of emptiness), or the female principle. Thus the vajra and bell together form an important symbol of the essence of Tibetan Buddhism, the union of wisdom and compassion (referred to in the Kalachakra Tantra as the union of "empty form and immutable bliss").

The students make a mandala offering to the vajra master, and supplicate to receive the Vajra-and-Bell Initiation in order to bind the two main (right and left) channels of energy into the central channel.

After the vajra master clears away all obstructions, he instructs the students to visualize their right and left channels. The right becomes Kalachakra and the vajra; the left becomes Vishvamata and the bell. Both channels are purified as the two deities confer the initiation. Since all words move through these channels in order to form speech, this is a step of preparation for the students' attainment of enlightened speech.

The initiation substance "vajra and bell."

The vajra master touches the vajra and bell to the students' five places, and the students experience the mind of great bliss that realizes emptiness. A concluding water ritual follows.

The Vajra-and-Bell Initiation purifies the students' internal sun and moon, and authorizes them to achieve the accomplishments of the two principal deities. The power is instilled in the students to achieve the fourth bodhisattva level, known as "The Radiant Level," as its fruit.

Just as the winds and channels are formed in the womb, the Silk Ribbon and Vajra-and-Bell Initiations, given at the southern gate facing Kalachakra's yellow face of exalted speech, purify the defilements of speech. They plant in the initiates the seed of "vajra speech."

5. *Conduct Initiation.* Corresponds to the child's first enjoyment of the five senses.

The vajra master leads the students to the eastern gate of the Mandala of Enlightened Mind, facing the black "vajra mind" face of Kalachakra.

The students begin with a mandala offering and supplicate to receive the Conduct Initiation in order to purify the sense powers and their objects.

The students visualize themselves becoming the deities of the Mandala of Enlightened Mind and are granted an Internal Initiation.

Then the senses and sense objects, along with the vajra thumb ring, which is the initiation substance, are generated into bodhisattvas and their consorts, who reside in the mandala. They grant the initiation, blessing the five internal senses into magnificence. The thumb ring acts as a symbolic restraint upon the finger, and thus the senses.

As the vajra master touches the five places of the students with the thumb ring, they experience the exalted wisdom of the union of emptiness and great bliss. A concluding water ritual is also performed.

The vajra master reminds the students not to allow their senses to obscure their knowledge of the essential emptiness of objects. This is described as being the essence of the Conduct Initiation, wherein the students may achieve the fifth bodhisattva level, known as "The Difficult to Overcome Level," as its fruit.

6. *Name Initiation.* Corresponds to the naming of a child.

The students make a mandala offering to the vajra master, and supplicate to receive the Name Initiation in order to purify their "action faculties" (mouth, arms, legs, and reproductive, urinary and defecatory organs). The wrathful deities in the mandala comply, holding the initiation substance "bracelet."

The students then visualize a rain of flowers falling upon them. The vajra master touches the five places of the students with the bracelet, and they experience nonconceptual wisdom. A concluding water ritual follows.

The Conduct Initiation substance
"thumb ring."

The students then receive names from the vajra master, who stands wearing a special robe. The names, which are derived from the Buddha families, are determined through flower divination. When the vajra master speaks the student's lineage name, the student visualizes becoming enlightened, generating great bliss and exalted wisdom.

It is prophesied that each student will become a Buddha with this particular name in the future.

This initiation enables the students to overcome the four demons through the four immeasurables, which are as follows:

1. Love—the mind that wishes all sentient beings happiness
2. Compassion—the mind that wishes all sentient beings liberated from suffering
3. Joy—the mind that wishes that all sentient beings achieve happiness and not be separated from it
4. Equanimity—the mind that wishes all sentient beings free of discrimination regarding friends, enemies, and others.

The Name Initiation instills the power to achieve the sixth bodhisattva level, known as "The Approaching Level," as its fruit.

Just as the sense organs and action faculties are formed in the womb, the Conduct and Name Initiations are in the area of the eastern gate of the Mandala of Enlightened Mind, facing Kalachakra's black face, planting in the students the seed to achieve the exalted "vajra mind."

7. *Permission Initiation* (and "Appendages"). Corresponds to a child's first reading lesson.

The vajra master leads the students to the western gate of the Mandala of Enlightened Great Bliss, where they face the yellow face of Kalachakra's "vajra pristine consciousness."

The students present an offering mandala to the vajra master and supplicate to receive the Permission Initiation. The purpose of this initiation is to purify the defilements of wisdom through the initiation substance called "the five hand symbols" (vajra, jewel, sword, lotus, and wheel).

The Name Initiation substance "bracelet."

The vajra master dispels obstructions and expresses the auspicious nature of the occasion. The students visualize a rain of flowers falling upon them.

The students are generated into "vajra pristine consciousness" deities in an Internal Initiation. They are then generated, along with the five hand symbols, into Vajrasattva and Prajnaparamita, who reside at the center of the mandala. These deities bestow the initiation, holding the hand symbols. This helps the initiates to teach the tantra according to the interest and disposition of their students.

The vajra master touches each of the five places of the students with the five hand symbols, generating the exalted wisdom of great bliss. A water ritual is performed. The vajra master then gives each initiate an individual authorization to teach, which is done by recitation:

> *Turn the vajra wheel (teach the dharma)*
> *in order to help all sentient beings*
> *in all worlds, in all ways*
> *Turn the vajra wheel*
> *in accordance with the needs of the people*
> *in order to help all sentient beings . . .*

The Permission Initiation substance "the five hand symbols"—vajra, jewel, sword, lotus, and wheel.

As the recitation continues, a conch shell is placed in the students' right hands, the sound of which is symbolic of spreading the sound of the Buddha dharma. Then a Kalachakra text is presented. Next, a bell is placed in their left hands, symbolic of wisdom and emptiness, with the instruction that the teacher of the doctrine should always keep the knowledge of emptiness in mind and view all things as illusion.

A wheel that symbolizes bringing about the welfare of others through the spread of the dharma is given to the students, and instruction is given as to the meaning of emptiness. The students then promise to work for the welfare of all sentient beings by always joining compassion with wisdom. There are several Permission appendages:

1. In the "mantra transmission," the students visualize that a rosary chain of mantras arises from the heart of the vajra master, who is the embodiment of Kalachakra. This chain of mantras comes out of his mouth to enter the mouths of the students and descend to their heart centers. The students repeat the mantra three times after the vajra master, visualizing the mantra circling a syllable at their hearts.

2. The students receive "eye medicine" from the golden spoon of the vajra master, so that they may visualize that the haze of ignorance has been removed and the wisdom eye opened.

3. The vajra master gives the students a mirror, which symbolizes the fact that all phenomena can be perceived as illusions. Like reflections in a mirror, they are empty of inherent existence.

4. A bow and arrow are given to the students. The arrow deeply implants the realization of emptiness into the students' minds, thus encouraging the swift attainment of enlightenment.

5. In the "initiation of the vajra master," the pledges of vajra, bell, and "seal" are given. First, the students and a vajra and bell are generated as deities. The vajra master recites verses and a mantra and places the vajra in the students' right hands. He says that the secret nature of the vajra is the exalted wisdom of great bliss. Holding the vajra will recall the true nature of the ultimate vajra, or what is called "method."

The vajra master places the bell in the students' left hands while reciting verses. The sound of the noninherent existence of all phenomena is proclaimed by the sound of the bell. Holding the physical bell will recall the true nature of the ultimate bell of exalted wisdom realizing the emptiness of all phenomena.

The students are presented with a wheel which authorizes them to spread the dharma for the benefit of all sentient beings. The wheel of the law shown here is a symbol of the office of the Panchen Lama. The sun, with its halo of flames, sets the law of Buddhism in motion. 20" high, silver repoussé, Tibet, 18th century.

Vajrasattva, the Buddha of Purification, is visualized by the students to purify defilements at the conclusion of the Seven Childhood Initiations. 9" high, cast brass, Kashmir, 10th–11th century.

Holding the vajra and bell, the students recite verses after the vajra master and ring the bell at the end of each verse. They make the gesture of embrace with the vajra and bell, contemplating the meaning of great bliss and the meaning of emptiness.

The students visualize themselves as the divine body of Vajrasattva, in whom this exalted wisdom arises.

The vajra master performs a water ritual, again to achieve purification, and offerings are made. He recites instructions on behavior to the students, who are now of the vajra lineage.

The Permission Initiation empowers the students to achieve the seventh bodhisattva level as its fruit. This is known as "The Gone Afar Level."

The Permission Initiation, which takes place at the western gate of the Mandala of Enlightened Great Bliss, facing Kalachakra's face of pristine consciousness, corresponds to the wind of pristine consciousness which circulates just after a child is conceived. It purifies any defilements and plants the seed of Vajrasattva purity, granting the students the capacity to achieve the seventh bodhisattva level.

The students have now completed the Seven Childhood Initiations, the purpose of which are to purify the defilements of nonvirtuous activity. This empowers the initiates to practice the tantra and attain the highest accomplishments. Having received this empowerment, and having become "aspirants of the seventh level," they are now authorized to practice what is known as deity generation meditation, and to actualize all aspects of the mandala. One who can do so in this lifetime is said to become the "lord of the seventh level." One who is not able to actualize the tantra in one lifetime but practices all the virtues will become "lord of the seventh level" in seven lifetimes. The initiates recite a mantra and, while exalting in the glory of being the deity, visualize that they have attained the seventh bodhisattva level.

conclusion of the initiation

The exact time, date, and place of the initiation are determined by the vajra master according to the Kalachakra astrological system.

The vajra master instructs the students to abandon the fourteen root infractions:

1. Disturbing the mind of the teacher
2. Deviating from the teacher's word
3. Harboring anger toward vajra brothers and sisters (those initiated by the same teacher)
4. Abandoning love (for a sentient being)
5. Allowing the mind of enlightenment to degenerate
6. Deriding the tenets of other paths
7. Exposing the secrets to unripened persons
8. Abusing one's mental and physical body
9. Losing faith in the purity of phenomena (emptiness)
10. Associating with deriders of the dharma
11. Not remembering the view of emptiness
12. Influencing against the dharma
13. Forsaking commitments or vows
14. Deriding any woman.

The students express their intention to follow this behavior, and recite the verses:

> *Today my birth is fruitful.*
> *My being alive is also fruitful.*
> *Today I have been born in the lineage of the Buddhas,*
> *Now I have become the son of the Buddhas.*
> *An offering mandala is made.*

The vajra master and all the initiates together recite prayers of wish fulfillment, dedication of merit, and benediction.

The dedication of merit, performed at the end of every Mahayana Buddhist practice, is a request that any merit acquired by the practitioner be given away to benefit all sentient beings.

The vajra master and his assistants remain to perform the conclusion rituals, comprised of making offerings, and praising the deities with additional prayers of wish fulfillment, dedication of merit, and benediction.

This concludes the eleventh day.

A rice offering mandala is made by the ritual assistant at the conclusion of the eleventh day, Kalachakra Initiation while the students make offering mandalas with a mudra. These are offered to Kalachakra, as embodied by the vajra master, in gratitude for the initiation.

the dismantling of the sand mandala

On the twelfth day, the vajra master and his assistants perform self-generation, as on the other days, and make extensive tsok (food) and torma offerings to the deities. All the initiates are welcomed to circumambulate and view the sand mandala.

People from the surrounding mountain areas form a line to receive a blessing from the Fourteenth Dalai Lama and to view the Kalachakra Sand Mandala at the completion of the Kalachakra Initiation in Leh, Ladakh, India in 1976.

After the viewing of the mandala has been completed, the vajra master and his assistants stand at the eastern entrance of the mandala, bless both the external and internal offerings, and offer them to the deities with prayers and verse. The vajra master circumambulates the sand mandala three times, holding the vajra and bell. Back at the eastern entrance, facing the mandala, he expresses regret to the deities for any mistakes which might have been made during the initiation and recites verses for forgiveness.

The vajra master visualizes and requests the transworldly deities to enter into his heart. Snapping a finger of his right hand, he requests the worldly deities to return to their respective abodes.

The vajra master then meditates on emptiness. Reciting a mantra, starting from the east and going clockwise, he picks up the colored dots and Sanskrit syllables of sand representing the 722 deities and places them on a plate.

Again starting at the east, he cuts the major lines of the mandala with the point of a vajra. All the sand is swept up and put in a vase, which is then covered with the deity's costume and crown. The vajra master places a small portion of the sand on the crown of his head as a blessing, and then offers small amounts of the consecrated sand to the students.

The vase containing the sand is carried with great respect, to the accompaniment of auspicious verses, mantras, musical instruments, banners, and much ceremony, in a procession to a local river, lake, or ocean.

A special altar is placed near the water's edge. The vajra master and his assistants place special torma offerings for the *nagas* (water spirits) on the altar in front of the vase of blessed sand. They recite prayers while an assistant draws a small sand mandala of an eight-petaled lotus flower on a round offering mandala base. The symbols of Kalachakra and Vishvamata are placed at the center and the ten naga kings in the eight petals.

The vajra master generates the dots of sand as Kalachakra and Vishvamata and the ten naga kings, and performs a complex visualization invoking wisdom deities.

The vajra master visualizes that Kalachakra and Vishvamata dissolve into him. He visualizes that all the nagas, with great respect, receive the blessed sand. The sand from the small mandala is then added to the sand from the Kalachakra Mandala, and the vase is carried to the water. The vajra master pours the sand into the body of water, imagining that the blessed sand is being accepted by the water spirits and aquatic life, filling them with joy. The vajra master then rinses the vase, fills it with water, and returns to the mandala site.

After the students have viewed the sand mandala, the vajra master requests that the 722 deities return to their respective abodes. He then meditates on emptiness before beginning the dismantling process. The Dalai Lama at Bodhgaya, India, 1973.

Right: The Dalai Lama picks up the colored dots and Sanskrit syllables representing the 722 dieties of the sand mandala, placing them on a plate. New York City, 1991.

Below: Starting at the center of the sand mandala, the Dalai Lama cuts the energy of the major axes and base lines (eight directions in all) with the point of a vajra.
Los Angeles, 1989.

Above and left: Monks sweep up the sand
of the mandala.

Opposite: The Dalai Lama performs a ritual at a special altar at the edge of the Hudson River before pouring the sand into the water. Near the World Trade Center in New York City, 1991.

Above: Rinsing the vase after offering consecrated sand to the local river. Rikon, Switzerland, 1985.

Left: Offering blessed sand to the marine life of Santa Monica Bay. Los Angeles, 1989.

The Dalai Lama pours water brought back from
the river on the mandala drawing.
New York City, 1991.

pacification of the mandala site

The vajra master sprinkles the water around the mandala site and, with his assistants, removes all the chalk lines of the mandala by scrubbing the mandala base with this water.

Then, holding the vajra and bell, the vajra master recites a mantra, removes the ten purbas from their holders, and cleans the point of each with milk, symbolically liberating the spirits subdued by the purbas.

dedication of merit

The vajra master, sitting at the center of the mandala base and facing east, recites concluding prayers of dedication and benediction.

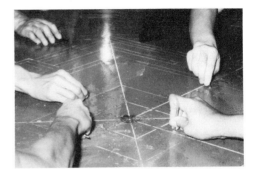

Above: The monks remove all the lines of the mandala drawing by scrubbing the base with river water.

Left: The Dalai Lama sits on the mandala base reciting concluding prayers. New York City, 1991.

175

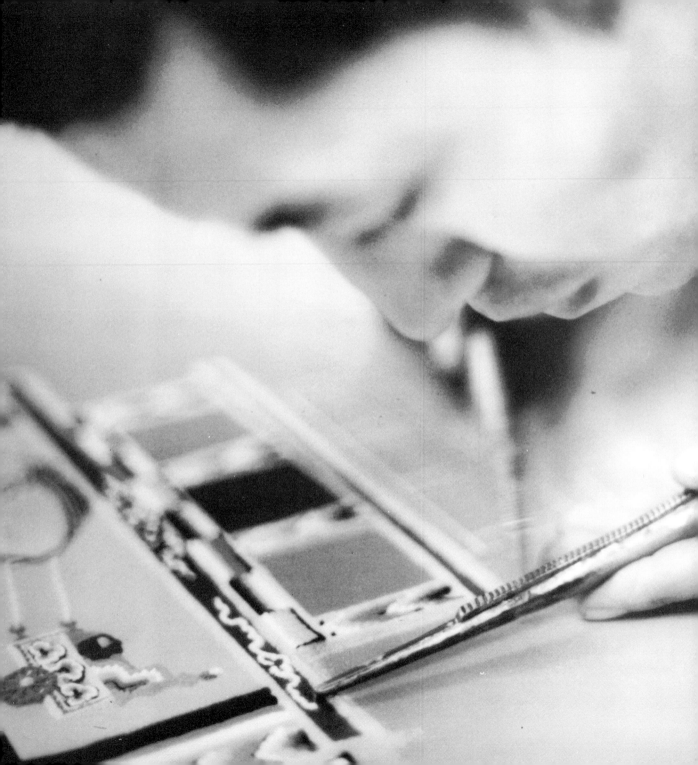

The Kalachakra Sand Mandala

THE KALACHAKRA SAND MANDALA is a two-dimensional representation of the five-story palace of the deity Kalachakra. It is one of the colored-particle mandalas, a generic term used to describe any mandala made of crushed materials such as jewels, flower petals, rice, or, most commonly, sandlike stone ranging in density from soapstone to marble.

In ancient times in Tibet, sand ground from brightly colored stone was often used. Today, white stones are ground

Namgyal monk Pema Lobsang Chogyen applies sand to the bottom beam of the western gate of the Mandala of Enlightened Body of the Kalachakra Sand Mandala. The American Museum of Natural History, New York City, 1988.

177

and dyed with opaque water colors to produce the bright tones found in the sand paintings. The basic colors are white, black, blue, red, yellow, and green. Each of the last four colors has three shades—dark, medium, and light—for a total of fourteen colors. The sand mandalas illustrated in this book are made from crushed white stones and marble dust dyed with opaque water colors.

Deities in the Kalachakra Sand Mandala are represented by Sanskrit syllables or dots. This detail of the southwest corner of the Mandala of Enlightened Body shows a peacock on which a lotus flower supports thirty deities, each represented by a dot.

Each of the 722 deities that resides in the Kalachakra Sand Mandala, as well as the mandala itself, is a manifestation of the principal deity Kalachakra. Each represents a different aspect of Kalachakra's enlightened qualities.

On seeing the Kalachakra Sand Mandala for the first time, people often ask, "Where are the deities?" and "Why are they represented by symbols?" It is important that full-body representations of deities be drawn exactly according to prescribed proportions or they cannot be blessed. Since spatial limitations prevent this, representative symbols are used in the mandala.

Here in the Kalachakra Sand Mandala, all deities are symbolized by either Sanskrit "seed" syllables or by dots. The exception is Kalachakra himself, who is symbolized by his own hand implement, the vajra, which is a diamond-hard or adamantine scepter, or "thunderbolt," as translated literally from the Tibetan word *dorje,* representing the indestructible mind.

Practitioners of the Kalachakra Tantra use the sand mandala as a diagram, or blueprint, to help them visualize Kalachakra's three-dimensional palace during the initiation ceremony and their daily meditation practices. It is said, and attested to by many, that by simply contemplating a mandala one can gain deep insight or inner peace, and that those who only see the mandala can establish a

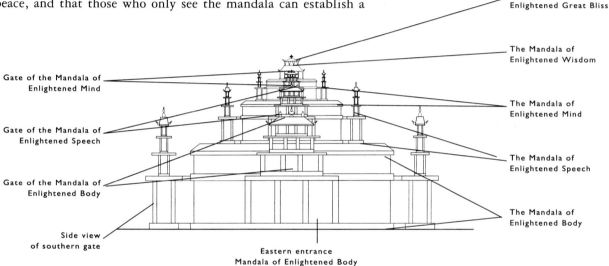

The Mandala of
Enlightened Great Bliss

The Mandala of
Enlightened Wisdom

The Mandala of
Enlightened Mind

The Mandala of
Enlightened Speech

The Mandala of
Enlightened Body

Gate of the Mandala of
Enlightened Mind

Gate of the Mandala of
Enlightened Speech

Gate of the Mandala of
Enlightened Body

Side view
of southern gate

Eastern entrance
Mandala of Enlightened Body

strong connection with the deity. This mandala also serves to purify the polluted environment and bring prosperity to the world.

The Kalachakra Sand Mandala consists of five square mandalas, one within the other, surrounded by six concentric circles. Each square mandala represents one of the five levels of Kalachakra's palace. The largest is known as the Mandala of Enlightened Body. Within it is the Mandala of Enlightened Speech. And within that is the Mandala of Enlightened Mind. These are characterized by elaborate gates at each of the cardinal directions.

Within the Mandala of Enlightened Mind, we find the Mandala of Enlightened Wisdom, and, at the very center, the Mandala of Enlightened Great Bliss. In the three-dimensional mandala, this is the

Elevation of the three-dimensional palace of Kalachakra. This drawing and those on pp. 183–92 were generated with an Auto-cad computer program by Daniel Maciejczyk under the supervision of Christian Lischewski.

The six concentric circles surrounding the square palace of Kalachakra represent the elements earth, water, fire, wind, space, and wisdom, or bliss consciousness.

uppermost or "penthouse" level of the palace. Here, the principal deity, Kalachakra, resides with his consort, Vishvamata, and eight female deities known as shaktis.

Each of the six concentric circles surrounding the palace represents one of the six elements. The innermost circle is the element of earth, upon which the base of the palace firmly rests. Going outward from the earth are the elements of water, fire, wind, and space. When the practitioner visualizes the mandala in its three-dimensional form, these elements are imagined directly below the palace, with that of space being all-pervasive. The sixth element, wisdom, or the light of blazing consciousness, is the outermost circle, described by the Dalai Lama as "pristine awareness."

orientation

The organization of the two-dimensional Kalachakra Mandala is based on the four cardinal directions, like a map. These directions are represented according to Buddhist orientation. We Westerners are accustomed to finding north at the top of every map, and east at the right. During the Kalachakra Initiation, the two-dimensional mandala lies flat, and students always circumambulate it beginning in the east, then continue walking around it in a clockwise direction. When a painted or photographic Kalachakra Mandala is hung on a wall, the black eastern quadrant is located at the bottom, so that the viewer is facing the central face of the deity.

The colors of the four quadrants of the Kalachakra Mandala correspond to the colors of the four faces of the deity Kalachakra. If the viewer is observing the mandala from the east, he is not only facing Kalachakra at the center, he is also facing the eastern quadrant, which corresponds to Kalachakra's central black face, associated with the element of wind. To the viewer's left, the red southern quadrant is associated with the element of fire, and corresponds to Kalachakra's red face. To the viewer's right, the white northern quadrant is associated with the element of water, and corresponds to

Kalachakra's white face. The yellow western quadrant is associated with the element of earth, and corresponds to Kalachakra's yellow face, which is actually his rear face.

preparation for ritual artists

In Tibetan Buddhism, altruistic motivation and the realization of emptiness are basic to one's practice. These are essential in performing ritual arts such as constructing the sand mandala, in both sacred and cultural contexts.

The creation of ritual art is both a meditative practice and a means of transmitting the message of the Buddha, which for Buddhists is the main source of happiness and prosperity for all sentient beings. With this in mind, the monks strive for perfection of their art as a means to perfect their minds and to maintain the authenticity of the teaching.

The monks begin their work each day by reciting special prayers of purification to cultivate a state of inner peace. The prayers reinforce the artists' motivation to work for the benefit of all beings. Through a visualization process, they generate themselves as the deity Kalachakra to remain mindful of their goal of perfection as they work.

As they paint they are conscious that the quality of their work reflects upon their spiritual lineage, as vital today as it has been since the time of the Buddha. Thus, their efforts toward perfection in constructing the sand mandala ensure that everyone, from the experienced Buddhist practitioner to the first-time viewer, will receive the blessings and teachings as the Buddha presented them more than 2,500 years ago.

While constructing the sand mandala, the monks work as a team, discussing the symbolic and philosophic meaning of the details they are painting, all the while offering one another advice and support. Each strives to do his best, enhancing his own spiritual practice through the development and perfection of mental and artistic activity.

drawing the mandala

In the Kalachakra Initiation, the mandala is drawn on the second day. As with other Tibetan mandalas, the drawing and design of the Kalachakra Mandala are taken from written instructions in ancient Buddhist texts and have remained unchanged since the Buddha taught them. The steps for drawing in this chapter use Western architectural language interpreted by Stan Bryant in conjunction with the system used at Namgyal Monastery, which is based on the Kalachakra text.

The drawing begins with the geometric outline of the mandala with chalk, charcoal, or pencil on a solid wooden platform, usually

Prajnaparamita, the holy teaching of transcendental wisdom. To the left and right of the text is painted the Kalachakra mantra known as the "Power of Ten." Gilt wood covers, 346 folios, colored ink and gold, 8.75"x 27" , 60 lbs., Tibet, 16th century.

painted red or blue. If the mandala base is square, the center of the base is the center of the mandala. The mandala can be made any size; its maximum diameter is determined by the shortest width of the mandala base. Some of the construction lines are drawn lightly, as they will be erased later.

STEP 1: Brahman Lines

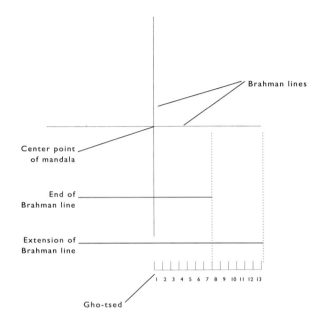

Brahman lines

Center point of mandala

End of Brahman line

Extension of Brahman line

Gho-tsed

1 2 3 4 5 6 7 8 9 10 11 12 13

STEP 2: Diagonal Lines

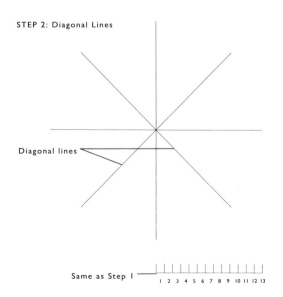

Diagonal lines

Same as Step 1

1 2 3 4 5 6 7 8 9 10 11 12 13

Step 1: Two lines are drawn perpendicular to each other with the center of the mandala as the point of intersection, and both are extended in each direction to the desired perimeter of the mandala. These two lines are the Brahman lines. The radius of the mandala is then divided along the Brahman lines into thirteen equal parts. The monks do not do this division mathematically but by trial-and-error, folding a strip of paper until it has thirteen equal parts totaling the length of the radius. The result is a scale with thirteen equal basic units for the Mandala of Enlightened Body, the largest of the five mandalas that compose the Kalachakra Mandala. The basic unit is called a *gho-tsed* in Tibetan. In each scale there are always thirteen gho-tseds, their length varying in proportion to the size of the mandala. The gho-tsed is also referred to as the entrance measurement because its measurement is the same as the width of the entrance to the mandala.

Step 2: Two diagonal lines are drawn through the center point of the mandala, defining eight equal pie-shaped spaces radiating from the center point.

Step 3: There are three gho-tsed measurement scales used in drawing the Kalachakra Mandala: that of the Mandala of Enlightened Body, the Mandala of Enlightened Speech, and the Mandala of Enlightened Mind. The scale of the Mandala of Enlightened Mind is one-half that of the Mandala of Enlightened Speech, and the scale of the Mandala of Enlightened Speech is one-half that of the Mandala of Enlightened Body. Within the Mandala of Enlightened Mind are the Mandala of Enlightened Wisdom and the Mandala of Enlightened Great Bliss, both of which use the scale of the Mandala of Enlightened Mind. Each gho-tsed is divided into six equal "small parts," or *chachung* in Tibetan.

Step 4: Starting at the center of the mandala, using the scale of the Mandala of Enlightened Body, a point measured one gho-tsed unit from the center determines the root line of the Mandala of Enlightened Mind. Two units out determines the root line of the Mandala of Enlightened Speech, and four and six units out determine the root line and parapet line respectively, of the Mandala of Enlightened Body. Eight units from the center locates the point at which the Brahman line will end, which is where the innermost of the six concentric circles will later be drawn. Thirteen gho-sted units out from the center of the mandala locates the perimeter of the entire mandala.

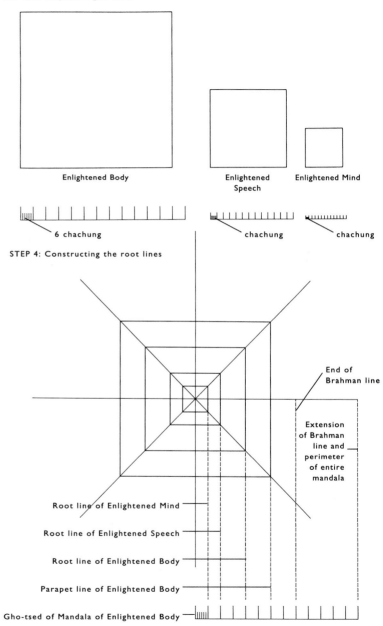

STEP 3: Proportional relationship of three mandalas and their respective gho-tseds

Enlightened Body

Enlightened Speech

Enlightened Mind

6 chachung

chachung

chachung

STEP 4: Constructing the root lines

End of Brahman line

Extension of Brahman line and perimeter of entire mandala

Root line of Enlightened Mind

Root line of Enlightened Speech

Root line of Enlightened Body

Parapet line of Enlightened Body

Gho-tsed of Mandala of Enlightened Body

STEP 5: The Mandala of Enlightened Mind

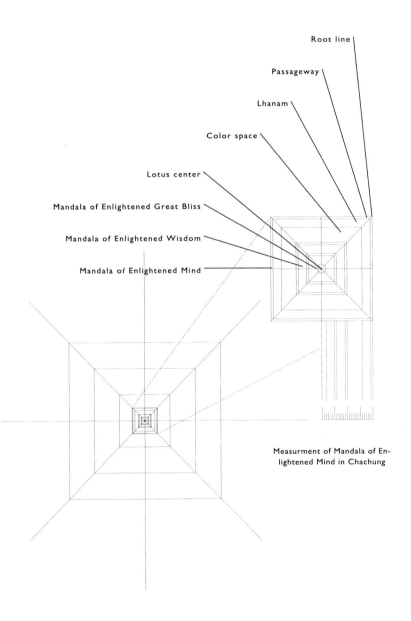

Root line

Passageway

Lhanam

Color space

Lotus center

Mandala of Enlightened Great Bliss

Mandala of Enlightened Wisdom

Mandala of Enlightened Mind

Measurment of Mandala of Enlightened Mind in Chachung

the mandala of enlightened mind

Step 5: Using the gho-tsed measure-ment scale of the Mandala of Enlightened Mind, a circle is drawn from the center point with a radius of 2 chachung, or "small parts"; this is the center of the lotus flower and the seat of Kalachakra and Vishvamata.

The following points are marked, mea-suring out in chachung from the center point along the Brahman line: 6, 7, 11, 12, 19, 23, and 24. From these points lines are drawn perpendicular to the Brah-man line and end at the diagonal con-struction line which represent:

• at 6 chachung, the inner square of the Mandala of Enlightened Great Bliss.

• at 7 chachung, the outer line of the inner square of the Mandala of Enlight-ened Great Bliss.

• at 11 chachung, the inner line of the square of the Mandala of Enlightened Wisdom.

• at 12 chachung, the outer line of the square of the Mandala of Enlightened Wisdom.

• at 19 chachung, the outer line of the area called the "color space" of the Man-dala of Enlightened Mind.

• at 23 chachung, the outer line of the area called the *lhanam* of the Mandala of Enlightened Mind.

• at 24 chachung from the center point, the root line, or outer line, of the passageway of the Mandala of Enlightened Mind.

Step 6: A circle is drawn with a radius of 6 chachung from the center point. This circle is divided into eight equal parts, rotated 22.5 degrees off the Brahman line, to define the eight petals of the lotus flower, which are the locations of the eight shaktis. To define the sixteen chambers that will house the eight pairs of deities and eight vases, the following points are marked along the Brahman line, in both directions out from the center: 2, 3, 6, and 7 chachung.

From these points lines are drawn perpendicular to the Brahman line 4 chachung long, located between the points 7 and 11 chachung out from the same Brahman line. Repeating this in all four directions creates the eight deity chambers, each 4 chachung wide, one in each of the four cardinal directions and one in each corner. It will also create the eight vase chambers, each 3 chachung wide and each separated from the adjacent deity chambers by pillars 1 chachung wide.

STEP 6: The Mandala of Enlightened Great Bliss and the Mandala of Enlightened Wisdom

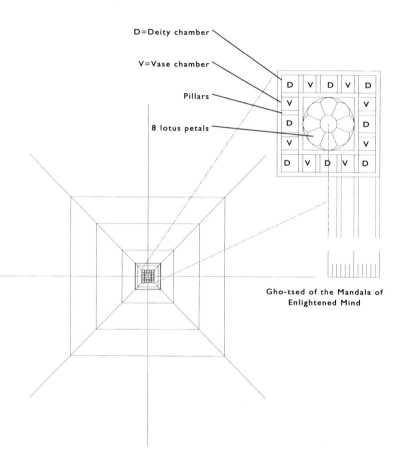

D=Deity chamber

V=Vase chamber

Pillars

8 lotus petals

Gho-tsed of the Mandala of Enlightened Mind

STEP 7: Entrance and parapet of the Mandala of Enlightened Mind

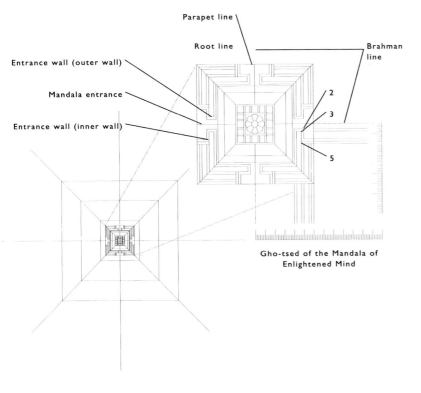

Parapet line

Root line

Brahman line

Entrance wall (outer wall)

Mandala entrance

Entrance wall (inner wall)

2

3

5

Gho-tsed of the Mandala of
Enlightened Mind

entrance and parapet of the mandala of enlightened mind

Step *7:* Note that the following descriptions and illustrations apply to all of the three mandalas of the Kalachakra Mandala; only the measuring scale is changed. All the measurements above are based on only one side of the entrance or Brahman line. The calculations are repeated on each side of the Brahman lines on all four sides of the mandala.

The following points are marked in chachung out from the center of the mandala along the Brahman line: $25^1/2$, $2^1/2$, 30, 33, $34^1/2$, and 36.

The width of the mandala entrance is 6 chachung wide, and is determined by measuring at the root line 3 chachung on either side of, and perpendicular to, the Brahman line.

At this location, the inner line of the entrance wall is begun. A line is drawn 6 chachung out from this point parallel to the Brahman line.

A line is drawn from this point 6 chachung away from the Brahman line, parallel to the root line.

A line is drawn parallel to the Brahman line 6 chachung out. The line ends at the parapet line.

At the point $4^1/2$ chachung from the Brahman line and $1^1/2$ chachung out from the root line, a line is drawn 3 chachung out, parallel to the Brahman line.

From this point, a line is drawn parallel to the root line and two points are located at a distance of $10^1/2$ and 12 chachung from the Brahman line. From these two points, lines are drawn parallel to the Brahman line $7^1/2$ chachung out, ending at the parapet line.

Again the point is located $4^1/2$ chachung from the Brahman line and $1^1/2$ chachung out from the root line. A line is drawn parallel to the root line ending 26 chachung from the Brahman line, where it meets the diagonal construction line.

The foundation wall and pillars adjacent to the wall have now been completed.

Now all construction lines within the entrance, walls, and pillars are erased. The entrance, wall, and pillar lines are then drawn heavily, as all other major mandala lines constructed up to this point.

gate of the mandala of enlightened mind

Step 8: To construct the gate, eleven construction lines are lightly drawn parallel to and measured out from the parapet line at these points (with corresponding letter identification): 1(A), 2(B), 6(C), $6^1/2$(D), $7^1/2$(E), $10^1/2$(F), 11(G), 12(H), 14(I), $14^1/2$(J), and 16(K) chachung. Each gate has three stories and a roof. Each story has a beam, a fence, and three chambers. The construction point measure-

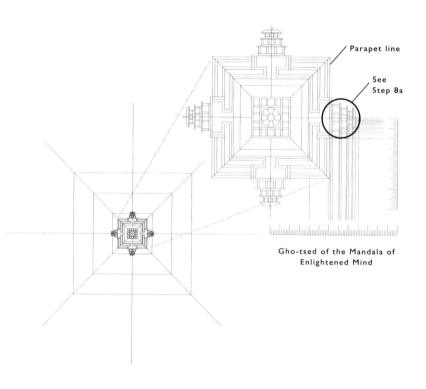

STEP 8: Gate of the Mandala of Enlightened Mind

Parapet line

See Step 8a

Gho-tsed of the Mandala of Enlightened Mind

STEP 8a: Gate of the Mandala of Enlightened Mind

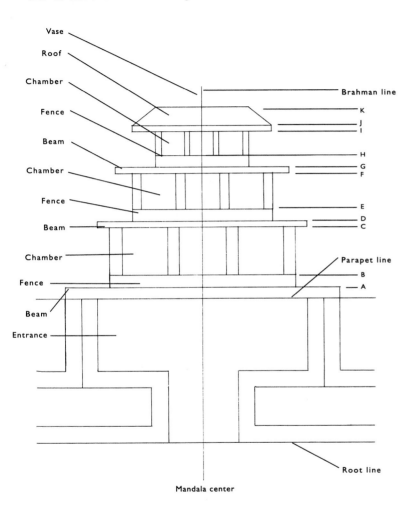

ments (dimensions between each successive point), line designations, and part names are given below.

Step 8a: The following lines are drawn parallel to and measured from the Brahman line. All of the measurements are based on only one side of the Brahman line. To complete the gate, the same measurements are duplicated on the other side of the Brahman line.

A line from the parapet line to A, 12 chachung from the Brahman line.

A line from A to C, 8 chachung from the Brahman line.

Three lines from B to C, 2, 3, and 7 chachung from the Brahman line.

A line from C to D, 9 chachung from the Brahman line.

A line from D to F, 6 chachung from the Brahman line.

Three lines from E to F, $1^1/_2$, $2^1/_4$, and $5^1/_4$ chachung from the Brahman line.

A line from F to G, $7^1/_2$ chachung from the Brahman line.

A line from G to I, 4 chachung from the extension of the Brahman line.

Three lines from H to I, 1, $1^1/_2$, and $3^1/_2$ chachung from the Brahman line. Note that the Brahman line ends at line H.

A line from I to J, 6 chachung from the extension of the Brahman line.

A point is located on line K, 4 chachung from the extension of the Brahman line. A line is drawn from this point to a point on line J, 6 chachung from the extension of the Brahman line.

At the intersection of the Brahman line extension and line K, a vase is drawn 2 chachung tall.

All the lines noted above are darkened. Between these darkened lines, all lines parallel to the root line are darkened. The gate to the Mandala of Enlightened Mind has now been completed.

STEP 9: Gate of the Mandala of Enlightened Speech

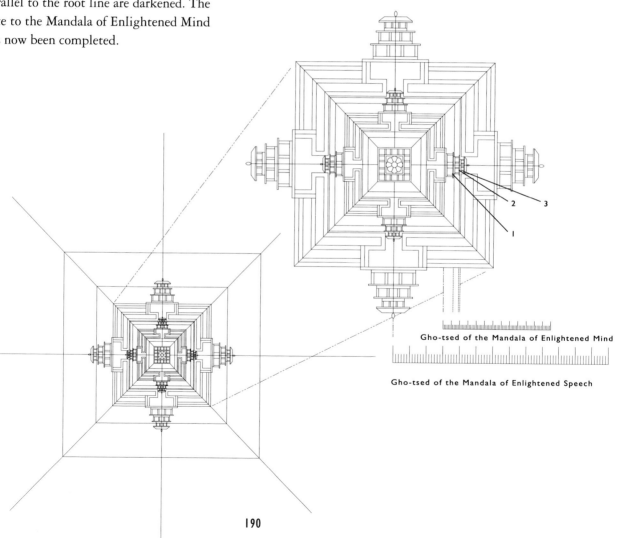

Gho-tsed of the Mandala of Enlightened Mind

Gho-tsed of the Mandala of Enlightened Speech

STEP 10: The Mandala of Enlightened Body

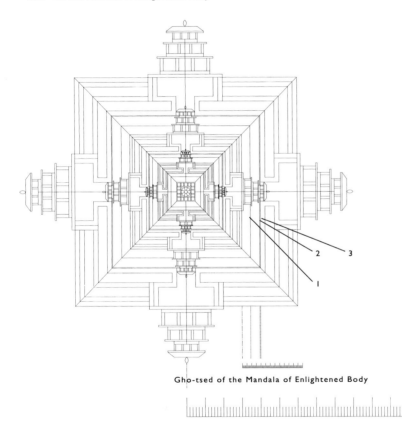

Gho-tsed of the Mandala of Enlightened Body

the mandala of enlightened speech

Step 9: Two measurement scales are used in drawing the Mandala of Enlightened Speech.

Using the gho-tsed measurement scale of the Mandala of Enlightened Mind, three construction lines are drawn parallel to and measured out from the parapet line of the Mandala of Enlightened Mind at these points: 7, 11, and 12 chachung, ending at the diagonal construction line.

Using the measuring scale of the Mandala of Enlightened Speech, the steps from the root line to the top of the mandala gate are repeated as shown in Steps 7 and 8, to complete the construction lines for the Mandala of Enlightened Speech.

the mandala of enlightened body

Step 10: As with the Mandala of Enlightened Speech, the Mandala of Enlightened Body uses two gho-tsed measurement scales.

Using the gho-tsed measurement scale of the Mandala of Enlightened Speech, three construction lines are drawn parallel to and measured from the parapet line of the Mandala of Enlightened Speech at these points: 11, 23, and 24 chachung, between the diagonal construction line and the mandala gate.

Using the measuring scale of the Mandala of Enlightened Body, the steps are repeated from the root line to the top of the mandala gate as shown in Steps 7 and 8 to complete the construction lines for the Mandala of Enlightened Body.

Step 11: Now that the drawing of the palace of Kalachakra has been completed, the six concentric circles are drawn. The innermost of these is located at the end of the Brahman line, 8 gho-tseds from the center using the scale of the Mandala of Enlightened Body. This is at the top of the fence of the highest gate of the Mandala of Enlightened Body.

The remaining circles are constructed at the following points out from the center: $8^1/_2$, $9^1/_2$, $10^1/_2$, $11^1/_2$, 12, and 13 gho-tseds.

Once the circles are drawn, all remaining construction lines are erased, including the diagonal lines, except for the segment within the color space. All the lines are enhanced with ink. This completes the drawing of the Kalachakra Mandala.

STEP 11: The Six Concentric Circles of the Kalachakra Mandala

End of Brahman line

End of Brahman line extension

Gho-tsed of the Mandala of Enlightened Body

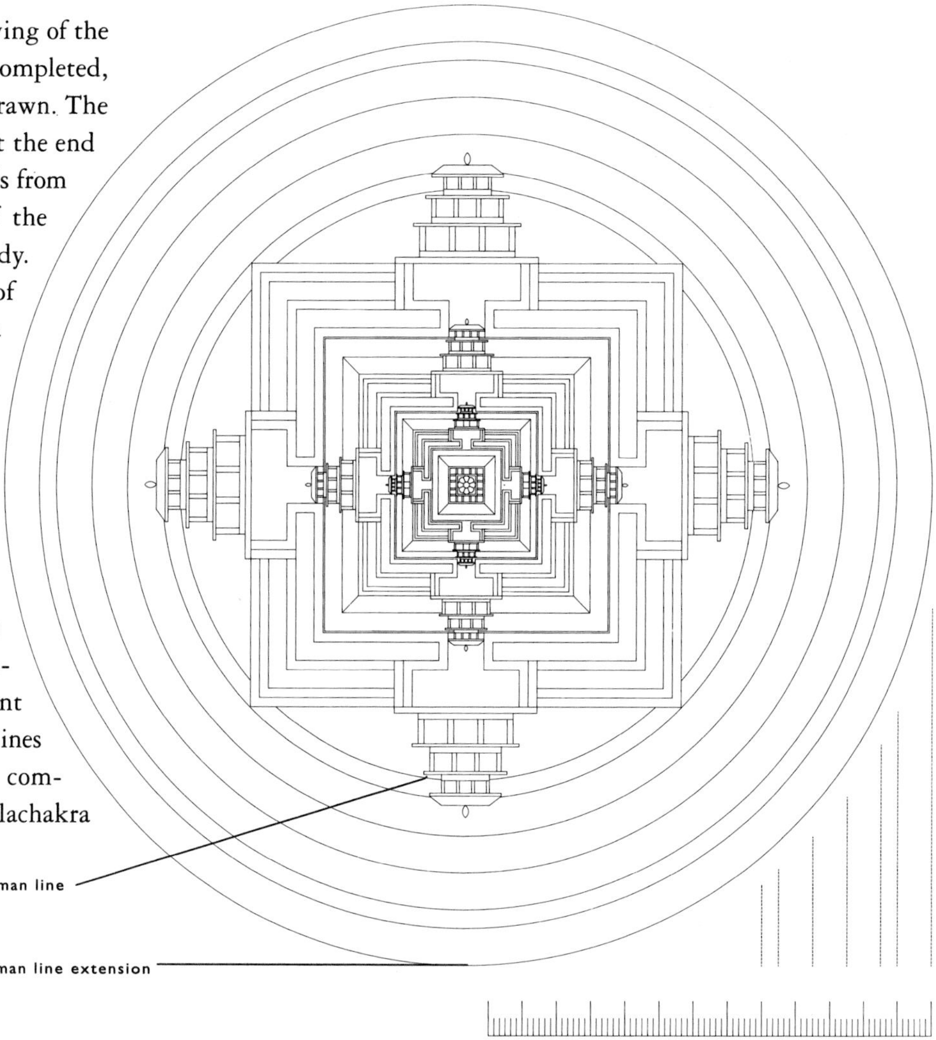

painting the mandala

During the initiation, four monks begin applying the sand to the Kalachakra Mandala. They are joined by four more monks as the mandala grows larger. The drawing of the mandala is completed on the second day and from the third to the eighth day the monks apply the sand for a total of seven days' work. When the mandala is presented as a cultural offering in a museum or gallery, the drawing

is completed before the exhibition is open to the public. The painting with sand by four monks takes from three to five weeks, depending on the schedules of both the facility and the monks.

The Kalachakra Sand Mandalas depicted in this book measure 6^{1}/$_{2}$ feet in diameter. No matter what the mandala size, the work of applying sand is always started at the very center and progresses out-

With fixed concentration, Namgyal monks seated on the mandala base apply sand to the eastern and western gates of the Mandala of Enlightened Mind.

ward. In the early stages of painting, while the sand mandala is smaller than three feet in diameter, the monks sit on the outer part of the unpainted mandala base, always facing the center.

In the tantric teachings, it is said that if one steps over or on or sits on a ritual instrument, image of the deity, scripture, or mandala, it is not only a sign of disrespect but is also equivalent to the breaking of one's vow. To avoid such an incident, the monks recite prayers each day, visualizing the lines of the drawing of the mandala as being lifted above the mandala base and remaining suspended above it until the workday is completed. When the mandala is about halfway completed, the monks then stand on the floor, bending forward over the base in order to apply sand.

Traditionally, one monk is assigned to each of the four quadrants. At the point where the monks stand to apply the sand, an assistant joins each of the four. Working cooperatively, the assistants help by filling in areas of color while the primary four monks outline the other details with sand.

The monks memorize each detail of the mandala as part of Namgyal Monastery's training program. It is important to note that the mandala is explicitly based on the scriptural text, and that there is no creative invention along the way. Any creative inspiration is manifested within the perfecting of skill.

At the end of each work session, the monks dedicate any artistic or spiritual merit accumulated from this activity to the benefit of others. This practice prevails in the execution of all ritual arts.

There is a good reason for the extreme degree of care and attention that the monks put into their work: they are actually imparting the Buddha's teachings. Since the mandala contains instructions by the Buddha for attaining enlightenment, the purity of their motivation and the perfection of their work allows viewers the maximum benefit.

Each detail in all four quadrants of the mandala faces the center, so that it is facing Kalachakra. Thus, from the perspective of both the monks and the viewers standing around the mandala, the details in the quadrant closest to the viewer appear upside down, while those in the most distant quadrant appear right-side up.

previous page: The Kalachakra Sand Mandala at the American Museum of Natural History, 1988.
left: Namgyal monk Lobsang Samten applies sand to the Kalachakra Mandala. above: Shinga, or wooden scraper, used to adjust sand.
overleaf, left: The four faces of Kalachakra, which correspond to the four quadrants of the Kalachakra Mandala:
black = wind / East, red = fire / South, yellow = earth / West, and white (rear face) = water / North.
In the foreground is the yellow face of Vishvamata.

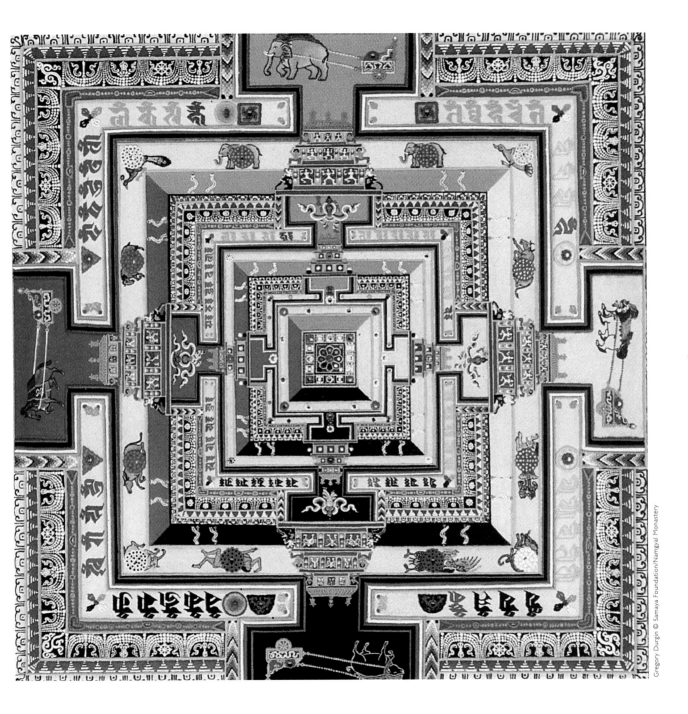

above: The western gate of the Mandala of Enlightened Body.

right; Detail of the western gate. Male and female "probable humans" seated in devotion beneath a sweet-smelling yellow tree.

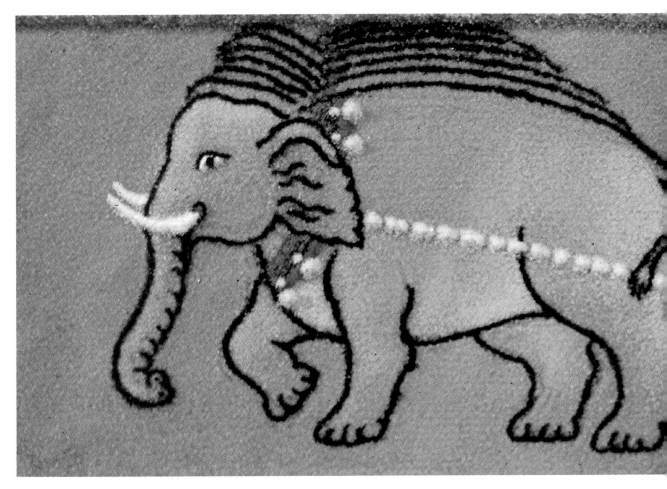

Seven animals at each entrance of the Mandala of Enlightened Body draw a chariot with a green lotus flower which serves as a cushion for male and female wrathful protective deities represented by a pair of colored dots.

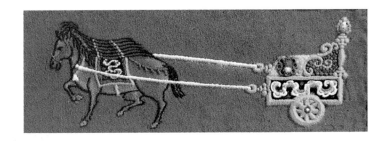

Gregory Durgin © Samaya Foundation/Namgyal Monastery

top: In the West, seven elephants against a yellow background. left: In the South, seven horses against a red background.
middle: In the East, seven boars against a black background. right: In the North, seven snow lions against a white background.

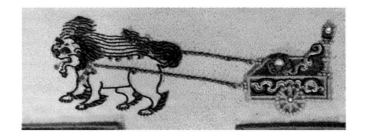

left: Bowl of fruit offering.

above: Offering garden surrounding the eastern gate of the Mandala of the Enlightened Body of the Kalachakra Mandala.

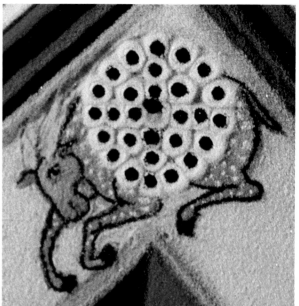
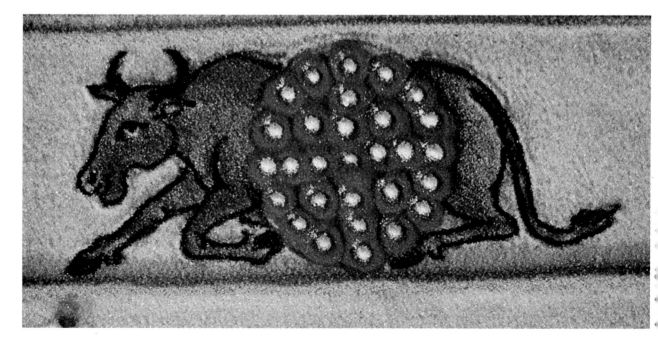

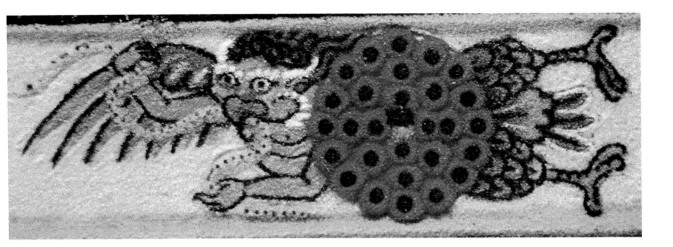

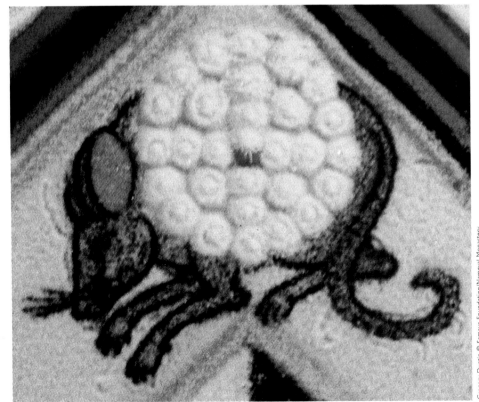

Twelve animals act as mounts
for 360 deities symbolized by
dots of colored sand,
representing the calendar
according to the Kalachakra
system. The five animals pictured
here are: the peacock, ram,
Garuda, bull, and mouse.

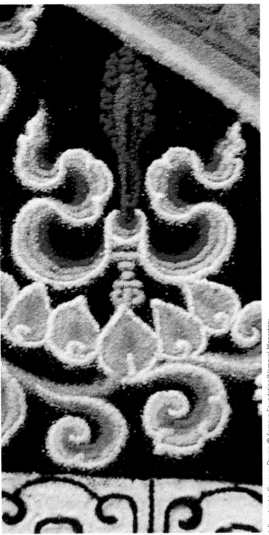

left and right: Gregory Durgin © Samaya Foundation/Namgyal Monastery

left: Detail of the eastern gate of the Mandala of
Enlightened Body and the adjacent offering garden.
above: Detail of offering garden of the
eastern gate; A blue sword with red flames,
used to cut through ignorance.

above: Offering goddess offers her dance at the northern gate of the Mandala of Enlightened Speech.

right: Wheel symbolizing cemetery grounds where the elements of fire and wind meet.

The wheel serves as a cushion for two protective deities represented by dots at the center.

left: The king of the bird kingdom, Khading Anila, in the East. above: The snow lion Senge Kangpa Gyepa in the West. These two mythical animals, depicted in the water element, are actually visualized above and below the mandala.

Dismantling the Kalachakra Sand Mandala. left: Here, the Dalai Lama cuts the energy of the mandala at the Kalachakra Initiation at Madison Square Garden, New York City, 1991. above: Namgyal monks, led by Tenzin Yignyen, sweep up sand at the Natural History Museum of Los Angeles County, 1989.

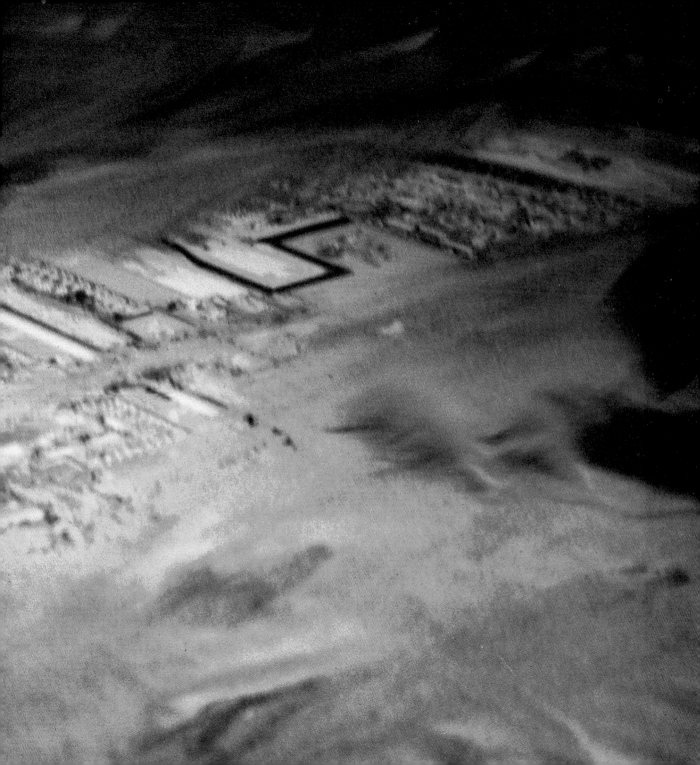

Generally, each monk keeps to his quadrant while painting the square palace. When they are painting the outer six concentric circles, they work in tandem, moving all around the mandala. They wait until an entire cyclic phase or layer is completed before moving outward together. For example, they complete the Mandala of Enlightened Mind before starting the Mandala of Enlightened Speech. This insures that balance is maintained, and that no quadrant of the mandala grows faster than another.

In the tradition of Namgyal Monastery, sand is applied through the end of a long, narrow metal funnel, or *chakpu* in Tibetan. Each chakpu is part of a pair; one is used to rasp a corrugated metal strip attached to the other, which is filled with sand. This rasping vibrates the chakpu, causing the sand to be released through the smaller opening.

There are different sizes of chakpus. Those with larger openings, through which sand flows liberally, are used for filling in background space and making thick walls and borders. Other chakpus with smaller openings for the elaboration of fine details, release sand grains in more delicate streams. The flow of sand is also controlled by the speed and pressure used in rasping. Slow, soft rasping causes the sand to trickle out, even just a few grains at a time, while harder, faster rasping causes it to pour out in a steady stream. Mastery of this technique takes great patience and diligent practice.

The chakpu is not grasped; rather, it lies flat in the open palm of the left hand (assuming one is right-handed), with the thumb placed on top to balance it. The rasping side is facing up. The hand itself is supported by the mandala base, which allows for ease of lateral movement from the wrist. The right hand holds the second chakpu, which does the actual rasping. The monks interpret the sound of the hollow metal chakpus being rubbed together as an expression of the Buddhist concept of emptiness, or the interdependence of phenomena.

The two chakpus symbolize wisdom and compassion; their action symbolizes the Buddhist practice. The result of their action, the completed mandala, symbolizes the enlightened state.

A monk uses an elongated metal funnel called a *chakpu*, which is filled with colored sand. It rests in the palm of his left hand, secured by his thumb and guided by the movement of his wrist. In his right hand, he holds a second chakpu, used to rasp the corrugated surface of the first. This causes a vibration that releases the fine grains of sand from the tip of the instrument.

Traditionally, in ancient times, the Indian Buddhist sand painters used their fingers to apply sand, as monks in some Tibetan monasteries do today. The chakpus used by the Namgyal monks were invented in the 18th century by the Tibetans.

Special wooden scrapers, known in Tibetan as *shinga,* usually measuring one to four inches wide, are used to adjust and straighten lines of sand into narrow, raised walls and other demarcations. The shinga are also used to remove excess sand.

Within Namgyal Monastery, before a monk is permitted to work on constructing a sand mandala he must undergo at least three years of technical artistic training and memorization, learning how to draw all the various symbols and studying related philosophical concepts.

Because of the monks' level of concentration and the high degree of cooperation among them as they work, mistakes or accidents are rare. But occasional errors made within the mandalas may be discov-

Above: The *shinga,* a wooden scraper, is used to straighten the edges of the sand and to remove stray grains from the work area.

Right: Young monks learn to draw the Kalachakra Sand Mandala in a class at Namgyal Monastery in Dharamsala, India.

ered too late for correction by the wooden scrapers. In such a case, a piece of cloth is placed over the large end of a chakpu, and a monk will gently suck up the sand of the mistake into the chakpu.

Viewers of the sand mandala often ask, "What keeps the sand in place?" The answer is that the layers of sand simply rest one upon the other. Gravity is the only adhesive used.

196

entering the mandala

During the Kalachakra Initiation, the ritual master introduces the students to the deities. His description of the mandala begins at the outermost concentric circle, moving inward toward the center of the innermost mandala, wherein he describes the principal deity Kalachakra and his consort Vishvamata.

We begin our description of the mandala in the center and move gradually outward, the way it is painted. Every motif depicted in the mandala has symbolic meaning and can be interpreted on various levels.

the mandala of enlightened great bliss

The Mandala of Enlightened Great Bliss represents the transcendent experience of enlightened awareness. To the practitioner, this is understood as the consummate union of Kalachakra and Vishvamata; that is, the union of wisdom and compassion.

1. The mandala represents the fifth and uppermost level of the five-story, three-dimensional palace of Kalachakra.

2. A solitary monk sitting in the eastern quadrant of the mandala begins by painting the outline of a small circle at the center, which is the center of the lotus flower. He paints the outline of the eight petals with light blue sand.

3. In the center of the lotus flower, five layers of colored sand are painted, one on top of the other. At the bottom is green, then white, red, blue, and finally yellow, which is the only one we can see. They symbolize, respectively, a lotus flower, the moon, the sun, Rahu, and Kalagni (lunar nodes in the Tibetan cosmology). These layers serve as cushions for the central deities, Kalachakra and Vishvamata, and together they represent the central themes of Buddhist practice: renunciation, bodhicitta, and the realization of emptiness.

4. The lotus flower represents renunciation, the letting go of all attachments. Just as the lotus grows in the muddy water but is not

The first step in painting the Kalachakra Sand Mandala: a monk seated in the eastern quadrant outlines the central lotus flower.

defiled by the muck, renunciation, which is born of the suffering of cyclic existence, bears none of the qualities of the suffering. The lotus flower also represents the pure nature of the mind.

5. The next layer is the moon, symbolizing the pure nature of bodhicitta which cools the disturbing emotions and their results.

6. Directly on top of the moon layer is that of the sun. The sun symbolizes the realization of emptiness, which eliminates one's delusion or ignorance, a primary cause of suffering. Thus, it represents the fire of enlightened awareness which consumes all confusion and distortion caused by human ignorance.

7. On top of the sun layer is a Rahu disc, which symbolizes the wisdom unique to the Kalachakra Tantra, that of immutable bliss.

8. The last and topmost layer, the Kalagni, totally covers the layers just painted. It symbolizes the special method of the Kalachakra Tantra, empty form.

9. Next, a blue vajra is painted on top of the raised mound of layered sand. It represents the mandala's principal deity, Kalachakra. The vajra itself is Kalachakra's main ritual implement, symbolizing the indestructible mind of the Buddha, which has the ability to cut through illusion. The blue color of the vajra, symbolizing Kalachakra's blue body, represents immutability; Kalachakra dwells in an unending state of being, far beyond any kind of degeneration, impairment, or exhaustion.

10. The monk, still sitting in the eastern quadrant, then paints a yellow orange dot to the right of the blue vajra. This dot represents Kalachakra's consort, Vishvamata. Yellow is associated with the earth element and with the fulfillment of one's potential through spiritual practice.

Although we see only the symbols of Kalachakra and Vishvamata, residing in that same space and inseparable from them are two male deities, Akshobhya and Vajrasattva, embraced by their consorts Prajnaparamita and Vajradhatvishvari, respectively. In all, six deities reside in the center of the lotus flower.

The green color to the left of the blue vajra represents Kalachakra's cloak.

11. Like all of the deities represented in pairs throughout the mandala, Kalachakra lives in perpetual embrace with his consort. Their position symbolizes the simultaneous union of compassion and wisdom, which in the Kalachakra Tantra refers to empty form and immutable bliss, the state of enlightenment.

12. The eight petals surrounding the center of the lotus flower are filled with green sand. The petals serve as seats for the eight shaktis. They (with Prajnaparamita and Vajradhatvishvari, who reside at the center with the four other deities) represent the spiritual powers which are the purification of ten winds and represent, in turn, the ten perfections. Each shakti is represented by a symbol—in this case, a dot of color for the seed of the deity's essence or vitality. The term for this in Tibetan is *tigley* and in Sanskrit *bindu,* which translates into English literally as "drop." The colors of the dots correspond to the quadrants of the mandala in which the shaktis reside.

13. The square that surrounds the eight-petaled lotus is now filled with blue sand. This color reflects that of the central vajra or Kalachakra.

14. In each corner of the central square, colored dots representing Kalachakra's

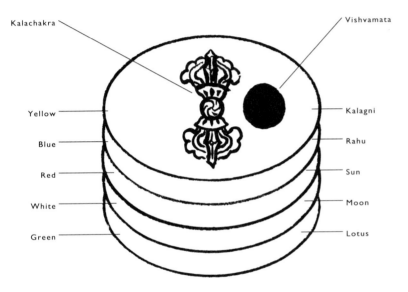

Cross section of the five layers of sand at the center of the lotus flower of the Mandala of Enlightened Great Bliss.

qualities of body, speech, mind, and wisdom consciousness are placed upon the blue background. The white dot (northeast corner), symbolizing a white conch shell, represents his body; the red dot (in the southwest corner), symbolizing a wooden ritual gong sounding the dharma, represents his speech; the black dot (in the southeast corner), symbolizing a precious black jewel, represents Kalachakra's mind; and the yellow dot (northwest corner), symbolizing a wish-fulfilling tree, represents his wisdom consciousness.

15. A sky-blue border of sand forms a square surrounding the eight-petaled lotus flower. A second sky-blue border surrounds the first. The space between these borders is filled with a chain or rosary of black vajras which represents beams supporting the ceiling of the Mandala of Enlightened Great Bliss. These decorated beams mark the outside boundary of this innermost mandala. It is inhabited by a total of fourteen deities, although only ten are visible here.

the mandala of enlightened wisdom

The Mandala of Enlightened Wisdom represents the subtle mind.

1. The mandala represents the fourth level (second to the top) of the five-story palace of Kalachakra.

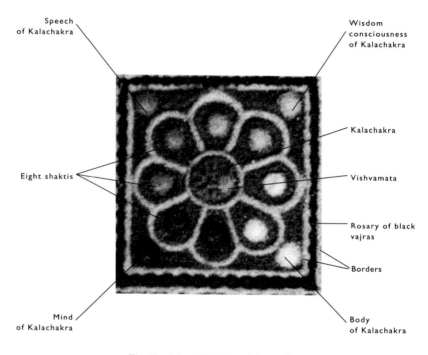

The Mandala of Enlightened Great Bliss.

200

2. It contains sixteen black pillars, four in each direction. These pillars, symbolic of the sixteen different kinds of emptiness, are decorated with dots of sand which represent black swords (east), red jewels (south), yellow dharma wheels (west), and white lotus flowers (north).

Surrounding these sixteen pillars are two light blue borders like those surrounding the previous mandala. Between these borders is a chain or rosary of green vajras symbolizing the indestructible nature of the enlightened mind. The spaces between these pillars form sixteen chambers.

3. Four of the sixteen chambers are located in the four cardinal directions and four in the four corners. Each houses an eight-petaled lotus flower, which acts as a cushion for a pair of male and female peaceful deities represented by dots of colored sand. The lotus flowers in the four cardinal direction chambers are white and those in the four corner chambers are red. The sixteen deities residing in this mandala are called the "Ones Gone Thus."

4. The remaining eight chambers located between the chambers of the eight pairs of deities house eight white vases, each between two white lotus flowers. The vases are filled with a nectar of purified substances of the human body, such as blood and bone marrow. Along with the

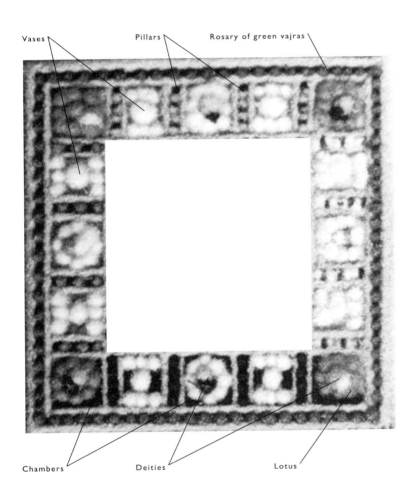

Vases Pillars Rosary of green vajras

Chambers Deities Lotus

The Mandala of Enlightened Wisdom.

two vases located at the eastern and western entrances to the Mandala of Enlightened Mind, they are the vases of the ten directions. They represent the power of spiritual transformation.

the mandala of enlightened mind

The Mandala of Enlightened Mind represents the coarse mind, which perceives relative truth and absolute truth as one. It houses 70 deities.

1. The Mandala of Enlightened Mind represents the third level of the five-story palace of Kalachakra.

2. The area surrounding the light blue border of the Mandala of Enlightened Wisdom, which appears as four trapezoids, is called the "color space," because the colors of this area correspond to the colors of their respective directions.

3. The white square surrounding the color space is called the *lhanam,* which, in Tibetan, means the actual place where the deity resides. This lhanam is home to twelve pairs of deities, represented by colored dots, residing on four red lotus cushions at each corner and eight white lotus cushions between the four corners. These twenty-four deities are bodhisattvas.

4. The area immediately beyond the border surrounding the white lhanam is a very narrow passageway in the colors of the four directions.

5. Surrounding the passageway are the foundation walls, composed of three parallel lines. From the inside out, white, red, and black give shape to the four entrances. These three foundation walls represent the three vehicles or paths: the Theravada, the Mahayana, and the Vajrayana.

6. At each of the four entrances, a pair of wrathful deities resides on a red or white lotus flower. At the eastern entrance, an additional pair of wrathful deities sits on a second lotus. These ten wrathful deities act as protectors of the entrances to the Mandala of Enlightened Mind.

Opposite: The Mandala of Enlightened Mind, inside of which are the Mandala of Enlightened Wisdom and the Mandala of Enlightened Great Bliss.

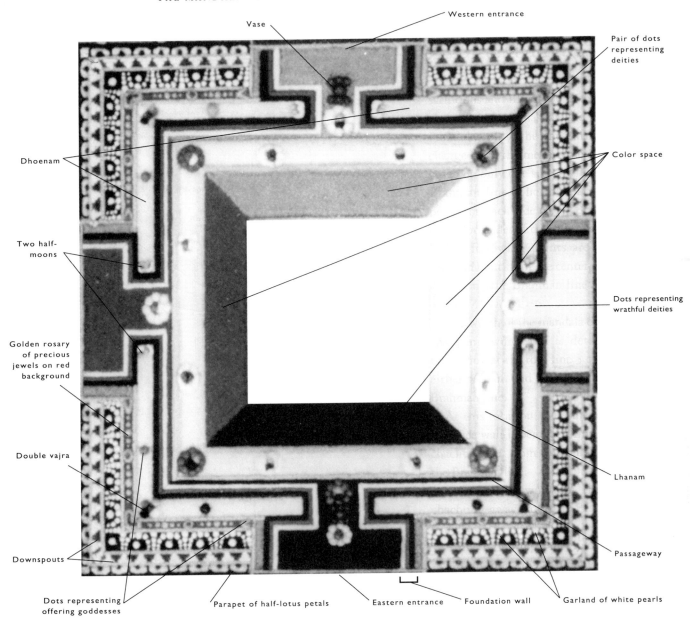

Vase

Western entrance

Pair of dots representing deities

Dhoenam

Color space

Two half-moons

Dots representing wrathful deities

Golden rosary of precious jewels on red background

Double vajra

Lhanam

Downspouts

Passageway

Dots representing offering goddesses

Parapet of half-lotus petals

Eastern entrance

Foundation wall

Garland of white pearls

203

Also at the eastern entrance, a green vase is found between two lotuses, and in the western entrance is a blue vase. As mentioned above, these two vases, plus the eight vases in the Mandala of Enlightened Wisdom, are the vases of the ten directions.

7. The white areas just beyond the foundation walls are known in Tibetan as the *dhoenam*. Two offering goddesses represented by dots reside on each of the four L-shaped white dhoenam, which are at the exterior of the foundation walls. These eight offering goddesses, plus four located in the entrance of the Mandala of Enlightened Speech, are part of a group of six pairs of offering goddesses.

8. At each of the four corners of the dhoenam there is a multicolored double vajra, which symbolizes the four means of a bodhisattva to gather students. They are:

- giving whatever is necessary
- speaking pleasantly
- speaking in accordance with the doctrine
- practicing the doctrine

The colors of the four points of the vajras and their centers represent the five Buddha families—Akshobhya (blue), Vairocana (white), Ratnasambhava (yellow), Amitabha (red), and Amoghasiddhi (green). The vajras also represent stability.

At either end of the dhoenam, situated next to the entrance, are two white half-moons connected to yellow half-vajras, adorned with a red jewel where they meet. These symbolize the Four Noble Truths.

9. The red area outside the dhoenam is decorated with a golden rosary of precious jewels. This area symbolizes wisdom, and the jewels represent method.

10. The next three areas beyond this red area contain architectural decorations and offerings. In the first, on a black background, hang garlands and half-garlands of white pearls. They symbolize the particular qualities of the Buddha which are not shared by others. These pearls spill out of the mouths of decorative sea monsters, which are represented by a dot of white sand in each corner.

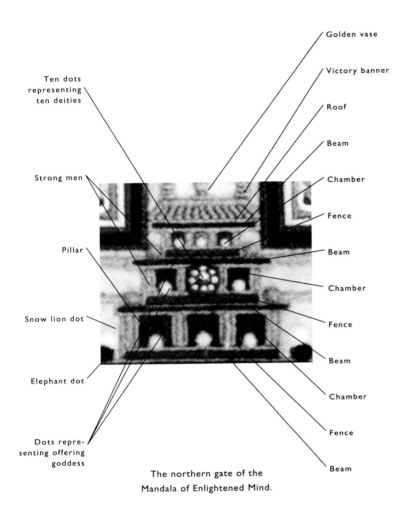

Ten dots representing ten deities

Strong men

Pillar

Snow lion dot

Elephant dot

Dots representing offering goddess

Golden vase

Victory banner

Roof

Beam

Chamber

Fence

Beam

Chamber

Fence

Beam

Chamber

Fence

Beam

The northern gate of the Mandala of Enlightened Mind.

At the ends of the garlands are offerings, represented by dots, symbolizing mirrors, bells, yak-tail fans, half-moons, flowers, etc. And inside the garlands are many more offerings represented by white dots. The mirrors represent the emptiness of all phenomena. The bells ring the sound of emptiness. The yak-tail fans remove the heat of suffering.

Moving outward, the blue area representing the sky contains white lines forming triangles, which represent downspouts that release rainwater from the palace roof.

The last and outermost detail of the Mandala of Enlightened Mind is a white parapet with the design of a half-lotus petal outlined in black. The parapet symbolizes protection from afflictive emotions and fortifies one against obstruction on the path. There are yellow pillars to the left and right of each entrance.

the gates of the mandala of enlightened mind

1. There are four gates in the Mandala of Enlightened Mind. Each is made up of eleven levels which appear as three stories. Each story has a beam, fence, and chambers, totaling nine levels, all crowned by a beam supporting the roof and the roof itself. These eleven levels represent the levels leading toward the realization of Buddhahood. Each story has three cham-

bers, for a total of nine chambers separated by yellow pillars. Each gate has a golden roof with a golden vase, flanked by golden victory banners.

2. In each of the nine chambers of each gate, a playful offering goddess makes offerings to Kalachakra. Here, they are represented by white dots.

3. The gray and white dots seen at either side of the lower level of each gate symbolize elephants and snow lions, which help to support the gate. The elephant represents empty form and the snow lion represents immutable bliss. On either side of the two upper levels, light flesh-colored dots represent strong men, who help to support the upper beams. The strong men at the lower of these two levels represent the union of empty form and immutable bliss which is dependent on ongoing learning; the strong men at the upper level represent the union of empty form and immutable bliss that requires no more learning; that is, the state of Buddhahood, or enlightenment.

4. On either side of the gate, near the corners of the parapet of the Mandala of Enlightened Mind, are two banners attached to golden poles set in golden vases, with a half-moon and a half-vajra at the top of each. These banners (here depicted as white) appear superimposed over the color space of the Mandala of Enlightened Speech. They wave from the roof of the palace and symbolize conquest over all afflictions that cause suffering.

the mandala of enlightened speech

The Mandala of Enlightened Speech represents the pure qualities of the Buddha's speech. This quality of enlightened speech enabled Shakyamuni Buddha to teach both sutras and tantras, so that disciples of all levels and dispositions could attain realization. The speech of the Buddha is considered most supreme, because it is through speech that he was able to teach and liberate sentient beings. This mandala houses 116 deities.

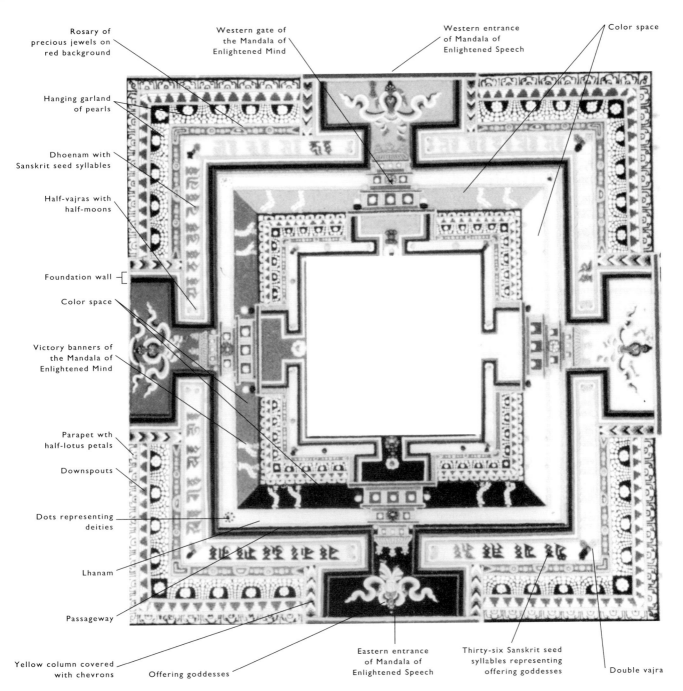

Rosary of precious jewels on red background

Western gate of the Mandala of Enlightened Mind

Western entrance of Mandala of Enlightened Speech

Color space

Hanging garland of pearls

Dhoenam with Sanskrit seed syllables

Half-vajras with half-moons

Foundation wall

Color space

Victory banners of the Mandala of Enlightened Mind

Parapet wth half-lotus petals

Downspouts

Dots representing deities

Lhanam

Passageway

Yellow column covered with chevrons

Offering goddesses

Eastern entrance of Mandala of Enlightened Speech

Thirty-six Sanskrit seed syllables representing offering goddesses

Double vajra

The Mandala of Enlightened Speech.

1. The Mandala of Enlightened Speech is the second level of the five-story palace of Kalachakra.

2. The color space, the white lhanam, and the narrow passageway of the Mandala of Enlightened Speech are the same as those of the Mandala of Enlightened Mind.

3. This lhanam contains 80 deities. It has eight lotus flowers, each with ten deities, represented by colored dots. A female deity resides on each of the eight petals, and at the center of each are a male and female deity in union. The lotuses at the four corners are white. At the cardinal directions, superimposed on the middle chamber of each of the four gates, is a red lotus. These 80 deities are called *yoginis* of the Mandala of Enlightened Speech.

4. Five parallel colored lines beyond the narrow passageway serve as foundation walls of this mandala, giving structure to the four entrances. These walls represent the five cognitive faculties: faith, effort, mindfulness, concentration, and wisdom. The colors of the walls (green, black, red, white, yellow) are symbolic of the five wisdoms of the Buddha, which correspond to the five Buddha families. They are as follows:

- Vairocana: Wisdom of Ultimate Reality = Purification of Ignorance
- Akshobhya: Mirror-like Wisdom = Purification of Anger/Hatred
- Ratnasambhava: Wisdom of Equanimity = Purification of Pride
- Amitabha: Wisdom of Discrimination = Purification of Attachment/Desire
- Amoghasiddhi: Wisdom of Accomplishment = Purification of Jealousy

5. In each of the four entrances of the Mandala of Enlightened Speech are colorful offering goddesses, appearing to be directly above the gates of the Mandala of Enlightened Mind. They aren't shown here, due to spatial limitations, although they are actually two of the six pairs of offering goddesses, the first four of which were

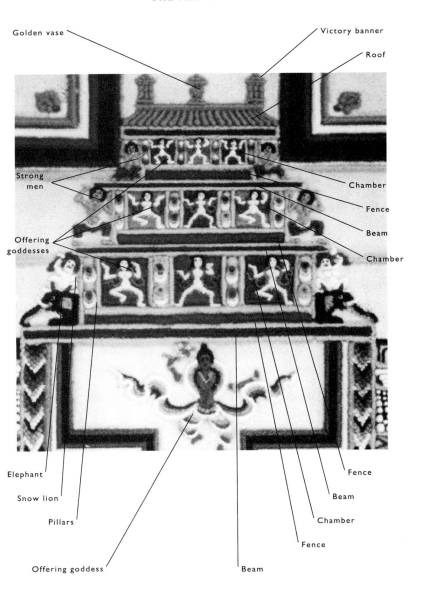

Golden vase

Victory banner

Roof

Strong men

Chamber

Fence

Beam

Offering goddesses

Chamber

Elephant

Snow lion

Pillars

Fence

Beam

Chamber

Offering goddess

Fence

Beam

The northern gate of the Mandala of Enlightened Speech. In the entrance, below the gate with the white background, is an offering goddess.

seen in the dhoenam of the Mandala of the Enlightened Mind (p. 204, Step 7).

6. The four white, L-shaped dhoenams (four Ls) found just beyond the five colored walls are home to 36 *dhoema,* or offering goddesses, represented here by Sanskrit seed syllables. The color of each syllable is the color associated with the goddess.

Just as in the Mandala of Enlightened Mind, double vajras appear in the corners of the dhoenam, and half-vajras with half-moons, each adorned with a red jewel, appear on either side of the entrance.

7. Beyond the dhoenam, the red area decorated with golden jewels, the black background areas containing garlands of white pearls, the blue area with white triangular-shaped downspouts, the parapets, and the victory banners are exactly the same as those of the Mandala of Enlightened Mind.

8. At either side of the entrance is a decoration of multicolored chevrons hung over the columns.

the gate of the mandala of enlightened speech

The four gates of the Mandala of Enlightened Speech are the same as the gates of the Mandala of Enlightened Mind, except the pillars are decorated with multicolored sand. The offering goddesses, elephants, snow lions, and strong men are represented in their natural forms rather than by dots.

Within the square chambers of the gates, offering goddesses make offerings, including the joy of their music and dance, to all deities of the mandala.

At the top of each gate is a golden roof with a golden vase flanked by golden victory banners.

the mandala of enlightened body

1. The outermost mandala, the Mandala of Enlightened Body, is the bottom level of the five-story palace of Kalachakra. Here are housed 536 deities, including the 108 deities depicted in the cemetery grounds.

The three areas surrounding the parapet of the Mandala of Enlightened Speech are, moving outward, color space, lhanam, and the narrow passageway of the Mandala of Enlightened Body.

2. 360 deities reside in this lhanam. Here we see 12 animals, each carrying one of the 12 months of the year.

Each animal bears a lotus with 28 petals. Each of the 28 petals supports a deity representing one day of the 28-day lunar cycle, and a pair of deities in union, symbolizing the full moon and the new moon, resides at the lotus center. Thus, every figure bears a lotus flower which serves as a cushion to 30 deities representing the 30 days of the lunar month, totaling the 360 days of the lunar year.

Note that the lotus flowers in the corners of the lhanam are white and that the more central lotuses are red. These colors are the opposite of, and thus complement and balance, those found in the lhanam in the Mandala of Enlightened Mind. In Tibetan astrology, red is symbolic of the energy of the sun and white is symbolic of the energy of the moon. Red is identified with the female essence and white with the male essence.

3. The five colored lines surrounding the narrow passageway of the Mandala of Enlightened Body are the same as those of the Mandala of Enlightened Speech, which represent the walls. Here the five

walls symbolize the five powers: faith, effort, memory, concentration, and wisdom.

4. The four white, L-shaped dhoenam found just beyond the five colored walls are home to 36 offering goddesses, represented by Sanskrit seed syllables. The colors of the syllables correspond to the colors of their respective directions, with the exception of one syllable in each direction. East and north each have a single blue syllable, and the south and west a single green syllable. All of these goddesses are known as *Chir-Doema* in Tibetan.

5. Just as in the Mandalas of Enlightened Mind and Enlightened Speech, in each corner of the dhoenam of the Mandala of Enlightened Body double vajras are painted in four colors which correspond to each of the four directions. Half-vajras with half-moons, each adorned with a red jewel, appear on either side of the entrances.

6. In the dhoenam and in the space between the Sanskrit seed syllables and the half-vajras are geometric shapes symbolizing the six constituencies, which are the five elements (water, earth, fire, air, and space) plus the wisdom element. On either side of the eastern entrance, two gray crescent shapes symbolize the element of wind, and to the left of the entrance a green circle symbolizes space. On either side of the southern entrance, two red triangles symbolize fire. On either side of the western entrance, two yellow squares decorated with the green swastika (a symbol of stability) symbolize earth, and on the right side of the entrance a blue circle symbolizes the wisdom element. Two white circles on either side of the northern entrance are symbolic of the element of water.

These four geometric shapes represent the types of tasks performed by the Buddha and the protective deities:

- pacifying (circle)
- increasing (square)
- empowering (bow)
- enforcing (triangle)

The geometric shapes in all four directions bear green lotus flowers at their centers. These each act as a cushion for a male *naga* deity

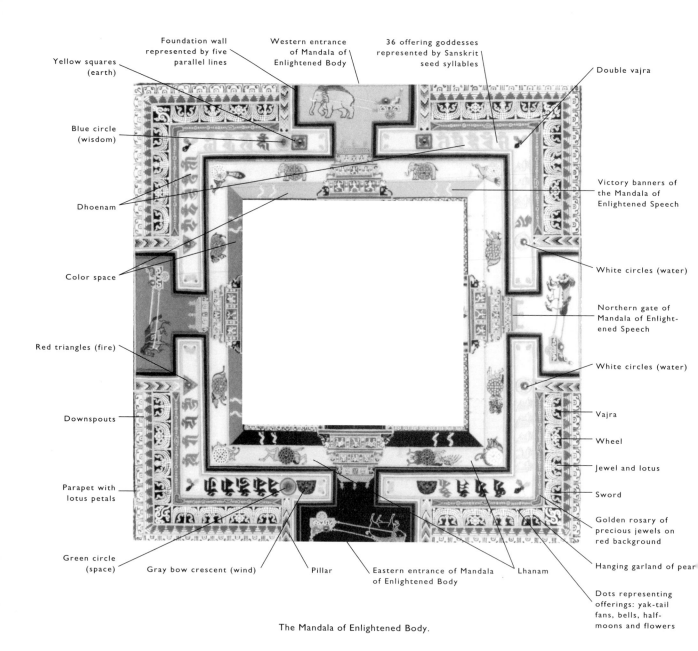

Yellow squares (earth)

Foundation wall represented by five parallel lines

Western entrance of Mandala of Enlightened Body

36 offering goddesses represented by Sanskrit seed syllables

Double vajra

Blue circle (wisdom)

Dhoenam

Color space

Red triangles (fire)

Downspouts

Parapet with lotus petals

Green circle (space)

Gray bow crescent (wind)

Pillar

Eastern entrance of Mandala of Enlightened Body

Lhanam

Victory banners of the Mandala of Enlightened Speech

White circles (water)

Northern gate of Mandala of Enlightened Speech

White circles (water)

Vajra

Wheel

Jewel and lotus

Sword

Golden rosary of precious jewels on red background

Hanging garland of pear

Dots representing offerings: yak-tail fans, bells, half-moons and flowers

The Mandala of Enlightened Body.

Opposite: Detail of the Mandala of Enlightened Body showing the twelve animals residing in the lhanam. They serve as mounts for the 360 deities that represent the calendar according to the Kalachakra system.

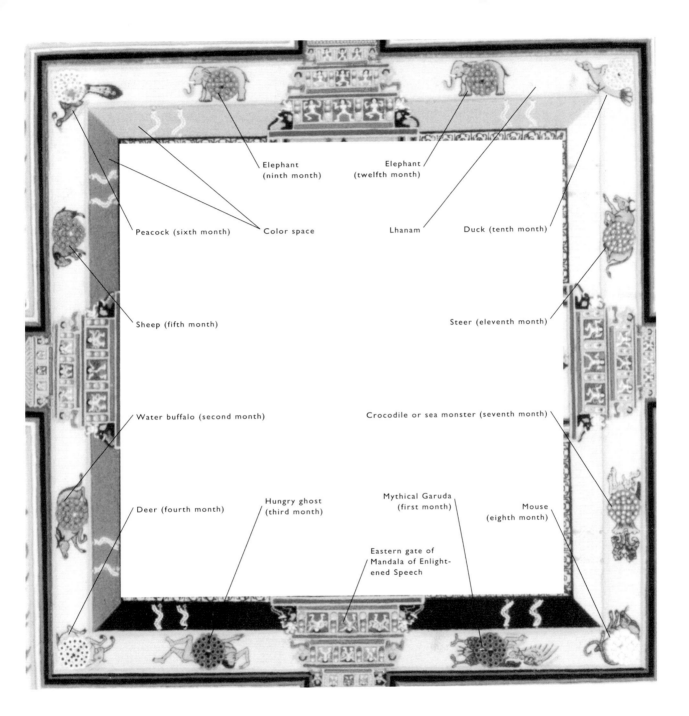

Elephant
(ninth month)

Elephant
(twelfth month)

Peacock (sixth month)

Color space

Lhanam

Duck (tenth month)

Sheep (fifth month)

Steer (eleventh month)

Water buffalo (second month)

Crocodile or sea monster (seventh month)

Deer (fourth month)

Hungry ghost
(third month)

Mythical Garuda
(first month)

Mouse
(eighth month)

Eastern gate of
Mandala of Enlight-
ened Speech

(associated with water and jewel treasures) in embrace with a very fierce female deity. The green circle in the east and the blue circle in the west have no lotus flowers, although the deities are the same as described above. There are 20 deities residing in these elements.

7. Just as in the Mandala of Enlightened Speech, the red area beyond the dhoenam is decorated with a golden rosary of precious jewels. The red area symbolizes wisdom, and the jewels represent method. The different shapes of the jewels represent the four tasks performed by the Buddha, described above.

8. The next three areas beyond this red area contain offerings to Kalachakra, which are the same as those of the Mandala of Enlightened Mind and the Mandala of Enlightened Speech, but with more space available, they are portrayed with different and even more elaborate designs. In the first, a black background is filled with hanging garlands and half-garlands of white pearls, symbolizing the qualities particular to the Buddha which are not shared by others. These pearls spill out of the mouths of decorative designs meant to evoke sea monsters. At the ends of the garlands are offerings symbolized by dots representing mirrors, yak-tail fans, bells, half-moons, and flowers. Inside the garland of white pearls are offerings symbolizing the implements of the five Buddha families, which are:

- a vajra (Akshobhya)
- a wheel (Vairocana)
- a jewel (Ratnasambhava)
- a lotus placed under the jewel (Amitabha)
- a sword (Amoghasiddhi)

These symbols are repeated two times in each direction.

The choice of what kind of offerings to depict here is left to the artists, as an expression of their devotion to Kalachakra. They can draw symbols representing the five sensual objects, eight auspicious signs, eight auspicious substances, seven precious royal emblems, or (as here) the five Buddha families.

If the mandala were viewed as a three-dimensional structure, we would see that the garlands described above adorn part of the upper wall of the palace. In the three-dimensional mandala, viewed from

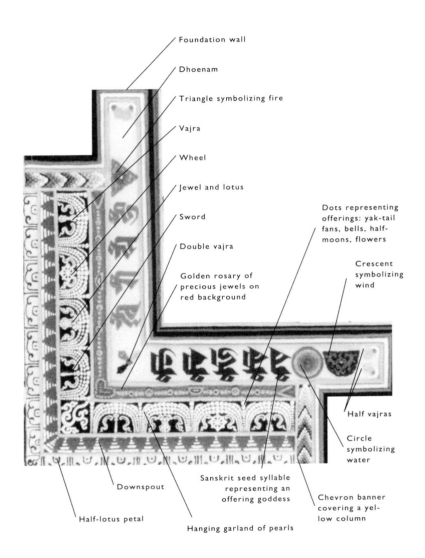

Foundation wall

Dhoenam

Triangle symbolizing fire

Vajra

Wheel

Jewel and lotus

Sword

Double vajra

Golden rosary of
precious jewels on
red background

Dots representing
offerings: yak-tail
fans, bells, half-
moons, flowers

Crescent
symbolizing
wind

Half vajras

Circle
symbolizing
water

Downspout

Half-lotus petal

Sanskrit seed syllable
representing an
offering goddess

Hanging garland of pearls

Chevron banner
covering a yel-
low column

Foundation and wall detail of the northeast corner
of the Mandala of Enlightened Body.

the exterior, most of the details are obscured; these garlands are among the few design details that are clearly visible in the photograph of the three-dimensional mandala shown on pages 58 and 218.

The next area, painted blue and representing the sky, contains triangular shapes representing downspouts, which release rainwater from the palace roof.

The last and outermost detail of the Mandala of Enlightened Body is a white parapet with a half-lotus petal design outlined in black. The parapet symbolizes protection from afflictive emotions as well as fortification against obstructions on the path.

On either side near the corners of the parapet are two victory banners, depicted here as white, although they are often golden. The banners are set in golden vases and supported by golden poles, with a half-moon and half-vajra on top of each.

entrances of the mandala of enlightened body

At the entrance of each of the four quadrants of the Mandala of Enlightened Body, seven animals pull wheeled chariots, each carrying a pair of wrathful protective deities on a green lotus flower cushion. These chariots are symbolic of attaining the realization of emptiness mind through the conceptual mind.

In the east, seven boars draw a chariot against a black background associated with the element of wind.

In the south, seven horses draw a chariot against a red background associated with the element of fire.

In the west, seven elephants draw a chariot against a yellow background associated with the element of earth.

In the north, seven snow lions draw a chariot against a white background associated with the element of water. In Tibetan astrology, the 28 animals that draw the chariots represent 28 constellations.

At either side of the entrance is a decoration of multicolored chevrons hung over the columns.

Due to spatial limitations, two additional pairs of deities included in this group are located in the second innermost concentric circle (the water element) surrounding the square palace, sitting on carts pulled by mythical animals (see pages 227 and 228).

Detail: Two victory banners of the Mandala of Enlightened Body in the garden of the western quadrant.

the gates of the mandala of enlightened body

1. Each gate has three stories separated by blue beams and red fences. Each story has three chambers, for a total of nine, separated by yellow pillars. Each gate has a golden roof with a golden vase flanked by golden victory banners. Starting at the bottom and working toward the top, each gate consists of eleven levels which include the beam, fence, and chamber (three times), the beam supporting the roof, and the roof itself.

2. The four gates here are essentially the same as those in the Mandala of Enlightened Mind and the Mandala of Enlightened Speech. Here the blue beams, red fences, and yellow pillars are decorated in beautiful multicolored designs.

3. On the lower level, on either side of the gates, elephants bear snow lions on their backs and together they support the beams. Additional support on the upper levels is provided by strong men. The nine chambers of each gate are the same as in the other two mandalas, with the exception of the middle chamber of the lower level.

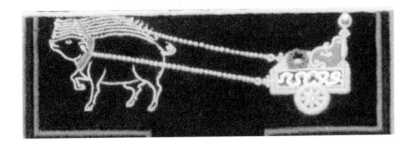

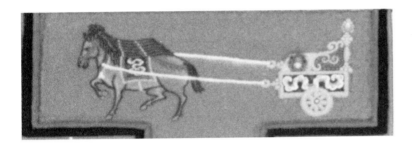

In each of the entrances of the Mandala of Enlightened Body are seven animals pulling a chariot that holds two protective deities.

Top to bottom: The seven boars in the eastern quadrant.

The seven horses in the southern quadrant.

The seven elephants in the western quadrant.

The seven snow lions in the northern quadrant.

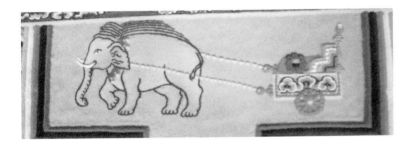

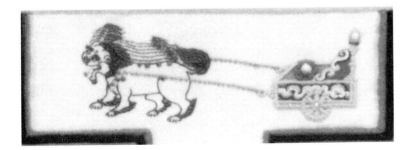

A gate of the Mandala of Enlightened Mind, a detail
from the three-dimensional Kalachakra Mandala in
the Potala Palace in Lhasa, Tibet.
12' in diameter, 18th century.

4. In the middle chamber of the lower level of the eastern gate,
two deer focus their attention on a dharma wheel. They symbolize
the instruction that the practitioner must completely concentrate on
the teachings without distraction. In this mandala, the black dharma
wheel symbolizes the Kalachakra teaching and the two deer symbolize the practitioner's generation and completion stages of the
Kalachakra Tantra.

In the middle chamber of the lower level of the southern gate, we
see a red offering vase, a conch shell, and a lotus flower. The vase
filled with nectar symbolizes the doctrine that, to practice the Buddha's teaching, one must first fill one's mind with the knowledge—
which is the nectar—of the Buddha dharma.

The standing conch-shell horn symbolizes the responsibility of the
practitioner not to possess the teachings but to pass them on to others. The lotus flower symbolizes spreading the teachings with the
motivation to benefit others.

In the middle chamber of the lower level of the western gate, a
yellow tree fulfills all aspirations. The tree is also a symbol of the
state of enlightenment. At the base of the tree, male and female
"probable humans" (a class of beings included within the realm of
the gods of desire) are kneeling, showing respect and devotion to
the tree. The male has the face of a horse, one of the traditional
ways of representing this type of spirit, which is attached to fra-
grance. Just as the sweet-smelling tree attracts the spirits, here it
symbolizes the qualities and knowledge of Kalachakra that attract
practitioners.

In the middle chamber of the lower level of the northern gate are a
hanging drum, a club, and a hammer. The sound of the drum symbolizes the awakening of sentient beings from the sleep of ignorance.
The club represents a support, symbolizing bodhicitta, necessary for
the attainment of enlightenment. The hammer symbolizes the realization of emptiness, which removes major obstacles on the path.

5. As in the other two mandalas, on top of the roof of each gate,
golden victory banners flank the central, golden offering vases.

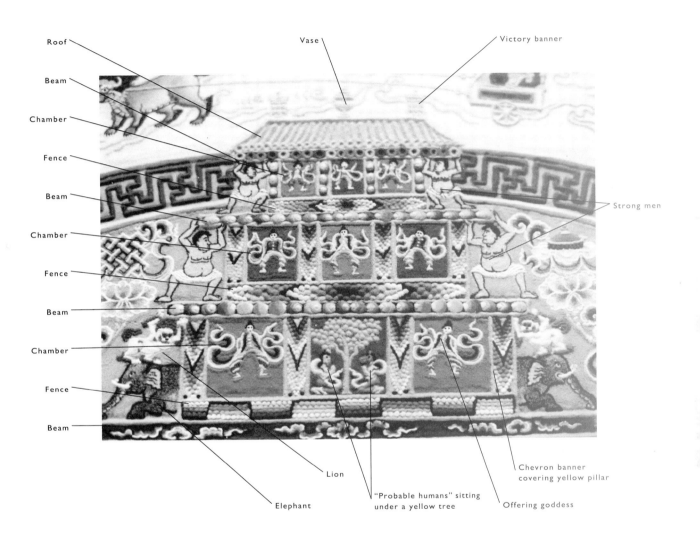

Roof

Beam

Chamber

Fence

Beam

Chamber

Fence

Beam

Chamber

Fence

Beam

Vase

Victory banner

Strong men

Lion

"Probable humans" sitting under a yellow tree

Elephant

Chevron banner covering yellow pillar

Offering goddess

The western gate of the Mandala of
Enlightened Body.

offering gardens

On each side of the square palace are four crescent-shaped gardens, formed by the innermost circle surrounding the palace. The background color of each garden—black, red, yellow, or white—corresponds to its respective direction. At the center of each garden is a gate as described above. Each crescent contains various offerings to the deities.

On both sides of the gates are golden vases from which grow vines with green leaves. Lotus flowers growing from these vines serve as supports for the offerings, and symbolize the act of making offerings with the selfless intention to benefit others. Each offering is wrapped in flowing cloths, similar to the way gifts are wrapped in decorative paper.

The purpose of these offerings is to generate great bliss in the deities, which results in the accumulation of merit for the practitioner and the increase of prosperity for all sentient beings.

Here the artists have the liberty to paint their own choice of offerings, usually representing the five senses, the five Buddha families, or teachings of the Buddha. Quadrant by quadrant, the Namgyal monks have painted the following offerings:

1. In the offering garden of the eastern quadrant, as viewed from the west, against a black background, are found from left to right, a red lotus flower representing a garland for the deity, an orange vajra representing indestructible mind, and a standing conch shell representing the melodious sound of the Buddha's speech. To the right of the gate are a white wheel representing the teachings of the Buddha; a multicolored jewel representing the wish-fulfilling gem; and a blue sword with red flames, used to cut through ignorance. The lotus, vajra, wheel, jewel, and sword represent the implements of the five Buddha families.

2. In the southern quadrant, as viewed from the north, against a red background, is seen from left to right, first a golden wheel representing the teachings of the Buddha. The next five offerings rep-

resent the objects of the five senses: a bowl of fruit for taste; a pair of cymbals for sound; to the right of the gate, a mirror for sight, which is form; and a conch shell on its side (filled with fragrant nectar) for smell. A cloth scarf representing touch is found surrounding all the various offerings. Continuing to the right, a standing (sounding) conch shell represents the melodious sound of the Buddha's teachings.

3. In the western quadrant, as viewed from the east, against a yellow background, moving from left to right, offerings include the eight auspicious signs: first, a yellow dharma wheel represents the teachings of the Buddha; second, a victory banner symbolizes the victory of body, speech, and mind over obstacles and negativities; third, an eternal knot symbolizes the interdependence of all phenomena, and the union of wisdom and compassion; fourth, a precious umbrella symbolizes protection from the heat of illness, obstacles, and harmful forces; fifth, two golden fish with colored fins

Opposite: The lower middle chambers of the four gates of the Mandala of Enlightened Body. From top are the eastern gate, southern gate, western gate, and northern gate.

Below: Two fish in the yellow offering garden of the western quadrant, together representing fearlessness, freedom, and spontaneity.

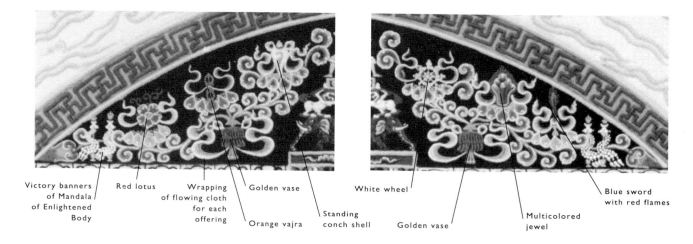

Victory banners
of Mandala
of Enlightened
Body

Red lotus

Wrapping
of flowing cloth
for each
offering

Golden vase

Orange vajra

Standing
conch shell

White wheel

Golden vase

Multicolored
jewel

Blue sword
with red flames

Black offering garden of the eastern quadrant.

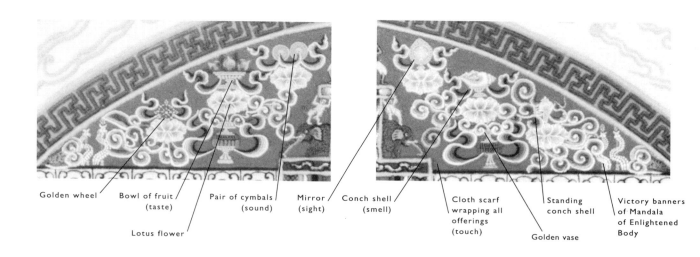

Golden wheel

Bowl of fruit
(taste)

Lotus flower

Pair of cymbals
(sound)

Mirror
(sight)

Conch shell
(smell)

Cloth scarf
wrapping all
offerings
(touch)

Golden vase

Standing
conch shell

Victory banners
of Mandala
of Enlightened
Body

Red offering garden of the southern quadrant.

222

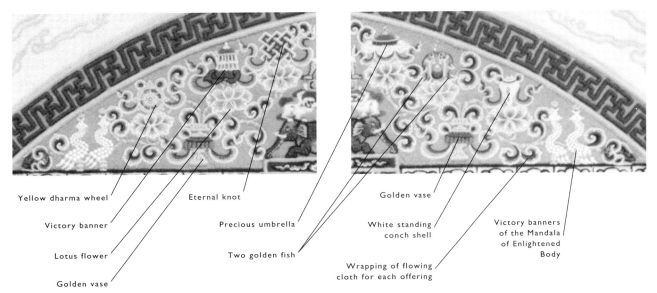

Yellow dharma wheel

Victory banner

Lotus flower

Golden vase

Eternal knot

Precious umbrella

Two golden fish

Golden vase

White standing
conch shell

Wrapping of flowing
cloth for each offering

Victory banners
of the Mandala
of Enlightened
Body

Yellow offering garden of the western quadrant.

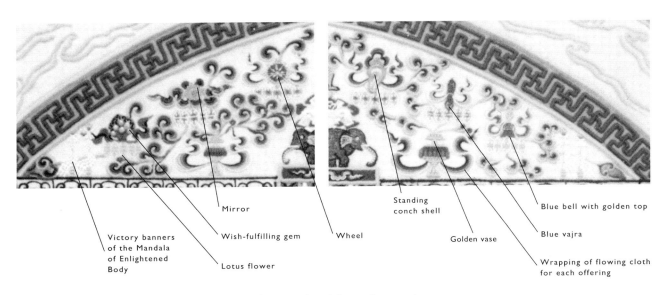

Victory banners
of the Mandala
of Enlightened
Body

Lotus flower

Mirror

Wish-fulfilling gem

Wheel

Standing
conch shell

Golden vase

Blue bell with golden top

Blue vajra

Wrapping of flowing cloth
for each offering

White offering garden of the northern quadrant.

together represent fearlessness, freedom, and spontaneity; sixth, a white standing conch shell sounds the call that urges practitioners to work for the welfare of others; seventh, lotus flowers that appear beneath all the offerings symbolize purification and the blossoming of wholesome deeds; and eighth, the golden treasure vases described in the eastern quadrant here also symbolize long life, wealth, prosperity, and all the benefits of liberation from suffering.

4. In the northern quadrant, as viewed from the south, against a white background, moving from left to right, are found a wish-fulfilling gem, a mirror, and a wheel. On the right side are a standing conch shell, a blue vajra (the description of these symbols is the same as in the other quadrants), and a blue bell with a golden top, which symbolizes wisdom and the sound of emptiness. Each of these offerings rests on a lotus flower.

the six outer circles

The six concentric circles that surround Kalachakra's square palace represent the six constituencies. From the innermost to the outermost circle are the elements of earth, water, fire, wind, space, and wisdom.

1. The first, innermost circle of earth is characterized by the earth color, yellow. An unbroken chain of green swastikas, or interlocking crosses, represents the earth's stability. In addition, the earth circle bears two symbols of the cosmos: a rising full moon in the northeast and a setting sun in the southwest.

2. The water circle is white, containing continuous, wavelike ripples and two mythical animals, each pulling a chariot. In the east we see Khading Anila, king of the bird kingdom; in the west is Senge Kangpa Gyepa, otherwise known as the "eight-legged lion." Each chariot bears a lotus flower upon which sits a pair of wrathful, protective deities in the form of dots. These deities are located above and below the square palace of Kalachakra in the three-dimensional mandala.

These two pairs of wrathful dieties are added to part of the four pairs that we have already seen (on page 218) in the four entrances of

Senge Kangpa
Gyepa (lion)

Cart with
pair of
deities

Wisdom

Sanskrit seed syllables
representing
protective deities

Wheel with pair of
protective deities

Space

Wind

Fire

Water

Earth

Setting sun

The six circles representing the elements at the
southwest corner of the Mandala of Enlightened
Body, including the setting sun on the innermost
circle (the earth element) and the mythical
animal Senge Kangpa Gyepa.

225

the Mandala of Enlightened Body, resting on chariots pulled by seven animals. Together, they make a total of six pairs of deities who protect the six directions (four, plus above and below) of Kalachakra's palace.

Above: Chain of swastikas representing stability in the circle of the earth element, which is surrounded by the water element.

Right: 88 Sanskrit seed syllables representing elemental spirits are found on the pink and gray circles (fire and wind) known as the cemetery grounds.

3 and 4. Beyond the water circle, the pink and gray circles represent the elements of fire and wind respectively. This whole area is known as the cemetery grounds. The ten wheels include one red wheel in each of the four cardinal directions, one white wheel at each corner, and an additional two red wheels, one each in the east and west. Seated on a lotus flower at the center of each wheel is a fierce female deity embraced by a male naga deity, each represented by a dot of sand. In each great cemetery are eleven Sanskrit seed syllables. These 88 seed syllables represent the main elemental spirits among millions.

5. Surrounding the dark gray wind circle is the green circle representing the element of space, which has an interlinking fence of golden vajras. The vajras depicted here have five points and are joined by a golden decorative design. This protective circle of vajras prevents evil spirits from harming the practitioner.

6. The outermost circle is also known as the "great protective circle," as well as the mountain of flames, circle of wisdom, or blazing light. Symbolic of the wisdom element, it has a design of 32 alternating sections of shaded colors. The red and yellow are drawn as

fire, whereas the blue and green are drawn as leaves. These four colors, plus white used in shading, represent the rays of the Buddha's five wisdoms in the form of a rainbow.

There is no border surrounding the great protective circle, illustrating that there are no limitations for the deeds of the Buddha and that his great compassion for all beings is extended with complete equanimity.

In the three-dimensional mandala, five of the six circles are actually layers upon which the mandala rests. The uppermost layer is earth, as the palace itself is constructed directly upon the earth. Below the earth is water, fire, wind, and finally space, which is all-pervasive. The sixth circle, the wisdom element, forms a protective sphere which totally surrounds the palace of Kalachakra.

This completes our description of the Kalachakra Sand Mandala.

Above left: The fifth and sixth circles, representing the space and wisdom elements. The space element displays a chain of vajras, while wisdom is represented by a symbolic "mountain of flames."

Above: Two red wheels, each serving as a cushion for two fierce deities, located in the southern quadrant, in the circles representing the fire and wind elements.

dismantling
ceremony

At the conclusion of the Kalachakra Initiation on the twelfth day, the sand mandala is dismantled. During its presentation as a cultural offering, the mandala is usually dismantled on the final day of the exhibition as follows:

1. Prayers request that the deities return to their sacred abodes. Once the monk presiding over the prayers is satisfied that the deities have left, the dismantling process is begun.

2. All 722 deities symbolized by the colored sands are skillfully picked up one by one by the head monk as he recites the Kalachakra mantra, and the sand is placed in an urn.

Deities that are singular or in a yab-yum grouping are picked up individually. For larger groupings of deities, the monk simply passes his fingers through them, picking up a portion of each. The disman-

tling is done in the reverse order of the making of the sand mandala. The head monk begins at the perimeter, picks up the protective deities in the cemetery grounds, and works clockwise toward the

Opposite and above: Namgyal monks dismantle the Kalachakra Sand Mandala. The American Museum of Natural History, August 1988.

center until he removes Kalachakra and Vishvamata.

3. Next, starting at the outer edge of the eastern quadrant, the head monk cuts through the mandala along the Brahman lines with a vajra, thus cutting the energy of the mandala. This is repeated, in turn, in the southern, western, and northern quadrants, and along the diagonal lines in the southeast, southwest, northwest, and northeast corners.

4. Standing in each of the four directions, the monks sweep the remaining sand into the center of the mandala. It is then placed in a specially prepared urn.

The monks carry the sand to the river or ocean, in a procession. At the water, the monks sit on a carpet with the vase containing the sand in front of them. In their prayers, they request that the protective spirits of the water accept the consecrated sand for the benefit of all beings. They visualize the aquatic life blessed by the essence of the sand. When the purified water rises from the ocean to the clouds and falls from the clouds as rain on the land, it purifies the environment and all its inhabitants. The monks then pour the sand into the water, saving some to give to those assembled in celebration of the event. Each person receives a small amount of blessed sand, which he is instructed to take home and place in a body of water or around the foundation of a house for protection.

Carrying the consecrated sand through the streets of New York City, 1988.

The dismantling of the sand mandala may be interpreted as a lesson in nonattachment, a letting go of the "self-mind." The ceremony reflects the Buddhists' recognition of the impermanence and transitory nature of all aspects of life. The monks believe that the dismantling of the mandala is the most effective means of preserving it.

Offering sand to the Hudson River through a tube that protects it from the wind.

World View According *to* Kalachakra

the universe of the mandala

THE COSMOLOGY REPRESENTED by the colored sand of the mandala is the complex view of the world according to Kalachakra. When the Dalai Lama states that Kalachakra is a vehicle for world peace, he is not speaking lightly. Behind his statement is not only a suggestion that world leaders come together with renewed motivation to work for the benefit of all beings and the survival of the planet, but also an implicit plea for a new understanding based on a larger, more comprehensive vision of the world. The depth of information contained in the Kalachakra Sand

Tibetan astrological calculations.

Mandala gives us an insight into the vast network of interrelationships comprising the physical, mental, and spiritual worlds in which we exist simultaneously.

There are three cycles of time outlined by the three main chapters in the basic Kalachakra text: outer, inner, and alternate. The outer concerns the astrological calculation of planetary movement and the geography of the universe.

The inner Kalachakra focuses on the functioning of the human body and mind. The body is dealt with at length, beginning with conception and embryonic growth, and proceeding through a physical analysis of the person in Buddhist terms. The mind is treated less extensively.

The third chapter, which is known by several names in English—other, secret, and alternate—has three subdivisions. The first is the Kalachakra Initiation itself. Second is the *sadhana,* or generation stage, which includes specific instruction on the meditation practice. And lastly there is the completion stage, or the way to attain realization.

All three cycles are interrelated, as the cosmos and the human physiology and mind are reflections of one another. At the Tibetan Medical and Astrological Institute in Dharamsala, India, it is considered essential for learning anatomy and the functions of the inner elements to know the outer Kalachakra, including the planetary movements and their effects. And advanced meditation practice is dependent upon the physical condition of the internal organs, as well as the influences exerted upon them by the heavenly bodies.

history of astrology in tibet

The first astrological theory and practice came to Tibet from China in the 7th century, when Princess Wencheng, the Chinese wife of Tibetan King Songtsen Gampo, brought with her various astrological and medical texts. A second wave of Chinese influence began in the 10th century. The Chinese system introduced what are known as "element" calculations, using a sixty-year, element-animal calendar cycle.

The Kalachakra system was brought to Tibet in the 11th century. It was blended with the Chinese influences by early masters of the Sakya and Kagyu traditions of Tibetan Buddhism. The first year of the Kalachakra sixty-year cycle is 1027, when the Kalachakra Tantra reappeared from Shambala.

One of the important Sakya scholars of astrological studies was Chogyel Pagpa Lama, who was the tutor of the Mongol ruler of China, Kublai Khan, in the 13th century. It was through his influence that the Kalachakra calendar became the official calendar of Tibet. Since the Chinese system was in use when the Kalachakra system appeared, the animals and elements associated with the Chinese years were adopted for naming the years in the Tibetan calendar although the two systems have different starting years.

Two different astrological systems based on the Kalachakra Tantra evolved in Tibet. The first is the Tsurpu lineage, developed by the Third Karmapa, also in the 13th century, which is followed by the Kagyu school to this day. The second, the Phugpa lineage, was developed in the 15th century and is followed by the Nyingma, Sakya, and Gelug schools. Both systems include broad Chinese-style calculations, known as the "yellow" system.

In the 17th century, during the reign of the Great Fifth Dalai Lama, Indian-style mathematics was developed and applied to Tibetan astrology. Another influence from India is derived from the Svarodaya (Arising from the Vowels) Tantra, in which a correlation is made between the vowels of the Sanskrit alphabet and the dates of the lunar month. By comparing the initial vowel of a person's name with that of a date, predictions can be made. This system is chiefly used for personal horoscopes.

The current astrological system, compiled in the 1980s at the Tibetan Medical and Astrological Institute, comes from these traditions, and continues to use the basic Kalachakra calendar.

It has been pointed out that the positions of the planets as calculated by the Kalachakra system do not always correspond to the calculations of Western science. However, the Tibetan system was never intended for use in navigation or for sending a rocket to the

A personal horoscope prepared for the author at the Tibetan Medical and Astrological Institute in Dharamsala, India.

moon. The practical application of the Kalachakra cosmology is to help clear away obstacles to health and happiness on our Karmic path to spiritual realization.

the tibetan horoscope

Astrological influences are seen to exist, not as independent heavenly bodies guiding us from afar, but in close relationship to the individual's consciousness, as a reflection of or in correspondence to one's behavior and inner life. Therefore, calculations can tell what conse-

Above and opposite: Tibetan calendar.
Two pages from the *Astrological Handbook*,
10"x3", Tibet, 17th century.

quences may occur if corrective actions are not taken. This is all part of the elaborate system of cause and effect (*karma*) that composes the universe.

Tibetan horoscopes are less concerned with planetary influences on character and personality than Western horoscopes. What is presented is a picture of how one's life may unfold. There are a number of ways of calculating the life span; the original Kalachakra text used the maximum of 108 years. The possible life spans calculated by various techniques indicate the variety of karmic seeds which could ripen if nourished in particular ways.

The life span in a Tibetan horoscope is divided into nine periods, each ruled by one of the heavenly bodies. Since the teachings of the Kalachakra Tantra emphasize the precious nature of a human birth, the horoscope may inspire a person to find appropriate ways of overcoming unfavorable conditions by developing the most beneficial karmic seeds. Whenever an unpleasant development is predicted, a remedy is offered. For instance, it may be suggested that one give alms to the poor, or save a life, or sanctify a portrait of one's spiritual teacher. This advice is intended to help put one back on the path of altruistic motivation.

Another benefit of seeing the ups and downs of a lifetime charted in a complete picture is that it offers insight into suffering. A person with an overview of his or her own suffering may better understand

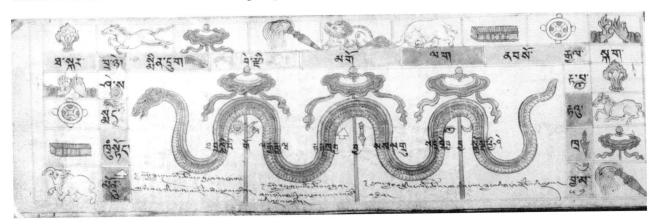

the suffering of others, and therefore develop the all-important karmic seed of compassion.

the tibetan calendar

Each year of the sixty-year cycle calendar system is ruled by one of twelve animals: the rat, steer, tiger, hare, dragon, snake, horse, sheep, monkey, bird, dog, and pig. These animal signs each correlate in turn to one of the five elements: wood, fire, earth, metal, and water. The element calculations are used for the purpose of making personal predictions, such as the prognosis and timing of illnesses, obstacles, marriage, births, and finally the timing of a person's death, including indications of which ceremonies to perform.

The Kalachakra Sand Mandala may be read as a calendar, with the twelve animals in the Mandala of Enlightened Body representing the succession of the twelve months. They each carry on their back a lotus flower hosting thirty deities, including the two in the center which represent the full moon and the new moon.

There are many complex aspects to the Kalachakra calendar, including solar days and lunar days. These refer to the precise amount of time it takes for either the sun or the moon to travel one specific unit of an entire cycle. The solar days last from dawn to dawn and are numbered by the dates of the month. Lunar days, named by the days of the week, are based on the phases of the moon and are of unequal lengths. Lunar and solar days do not correspond exactly to one

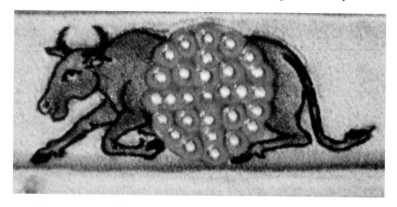

Right: The steer, one of the twelve animals in the Kalachakra Sand Mandala representing the succession of the months of the year, located in the northwest area of the Mandala of Enlightened Body.

Opposite: Model of the universe according to the Kalachakra teachings. At the center is Mt. Meru, surrounded by symbols of the four continents. The orbiting circles represent the movement of the planets and the months of the year. The twelve animals ruling the sixty-year calendar cycle surround twenty-seven constellations.

another. This makes for days with double dates, omitted dates, and an occasional additional month, which is something like our leap-year day.

A feature shared with the ancient Greek system is the naming of the days of the week after the planets—Sunday for the sun, Monday for the moon, and so on. In fact the Tibetan word for "weekday" (*gza*) is the same as that for "planet."

There are many days in the Tibetan calendar that are recognized, for various reasons, as being auspicious or inauspicious. Astrology is popularly used among Tibetans to determine dates for weddings, journeys, and business ventures. Physicians use astrology to determine the best date for administering medical treatments. And it is important for setting dates to make offerings and observe other religious rituals. For instance, it is considered auspicious to begin a

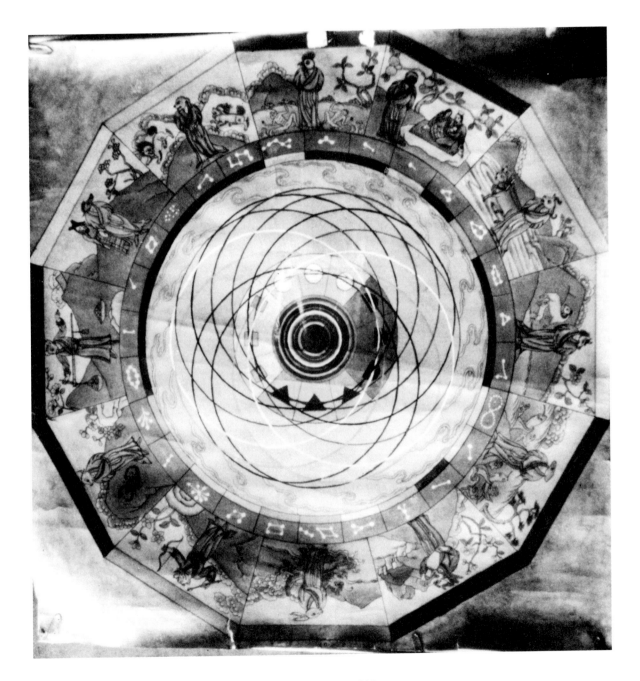

spiritual practice as the moon is waxing, so that the benefit of the practice will also expand. The Kalachakra Initiation is always given on the day of a full moon.

An astrological prediction is used much like a weather forecast. It determines the likelihood of things going well or badly according to the cosmological factors, which can always be influenced by one's behavior.

the external kalachakra

The Kalachakra system of astrology, sometimes known as the "stellar calculations" or "star studies," and the Greek (or Western) systems share a common pan-Indian source, so there are similarities. As in Western astrology, the Tibetan zodiac is divided into twelve signs and twelve related houses. The signs bear the same names as those in the modern West (Aries, Taurus, Gemini, and so on), but they are referred to as houses (*khyim*).

What we in the West would call the houses—those areas of the sky or horoscope that denote the various "departments" of a person's life (the physical body, personal finances, siblings and relatives, etc.)—are known as periods (*dus-sbyor*) and carry slightly different meanings.

As in the modern Western system, ten "planets" are used, but in this system only seven of these are heavenly bodies. (This was true as well in the older Western system, before the age of the telescope.) These are the seven visible bodies of the sun, the moon, Mercury, Venus, Mars, Jupiter, and Saturn. The remaining three in the Tibetan system are the comet, and Rahu and Kalagni (known as *Ketu* in the Hindu system), which are the north node and the south node of the moon. The comet is not used in horoscopes, but the lunar nodes are important for predicting solar and lunar eclipses.

the internal kalachakra

In the internal Kalachakra, emphasis is placed on the functioning of the human body and of the coarse and subtle minds. It is very im-

Sun

Moon

The sun and the moon depicted in the Kalachakra Sand Mandala.

Top: The sun sets in the earth element at the southwest corner of the Mandala of Enlightened Body.

Bottom: The full moon rises at the northeast corner.

portant for the Kalachakra student to know that the internal winds are in motion, just as the planets are. That is why meditators who study the Kalachakra Tantra first learn the external Kalachakra, which details the movements of the sun and the moon.

The importance of these two heavenly bodies in the tantra is underlined by their representation by the principal deities themselves, Kalachakra (the moon) and Vishvamata (the sun). The purpose of the practice of Kalachakra—to achieve the purified mind of the deity—requires harmonizing one's inner being with the structure of the cosmos.

In the internal Kalachakra, the sun and the moon correspond to, or "rule," the right and left channels of the body. It is necessary to know the solar and lunar days and how to calculate them to work effectively with the variable sun and moon energies, which affect the passage of the winds through the body.

In Kalachakra, as in other Buddhist tantras and in Tibetan medicine, the subtle energy of the body is pushed by the "winds" through the "channels" of the human anatomy. Although these concepts do not have direct correlations in Western medicine, Tibetan doctors tell us the channels are part of the nervous system.

The channels are divided into left (*kyangma*) and right (*roma*), which correspond to the polarities of male and female. The sun is female in the Tibetan astrological system and the moon is male. The pull between these polarities is the reason we experience various inclinations of energy, mood, and mind/body balance. The central channel (*ooma*) is the pathway of balance and stability.

The deity Kalachakra has three colored necks representing the three wind channels. The right (*roma*) is red and influenced by the sun, and is the channel through which the sun-wind passes. The white neck is the left channel (*kyangma*); it is influenced by the moon, being the channel through which the moon-wind passes. The blue neck (*ooma*) is the neutral and central channel.

The neutral wind corresponds to the lunar nodes, Rahu and Kalagni. This neutral wind (known as "Rahu's wind"), which is not always present, is important for the practitioner of the generation and completion stages of Kalachakra, and generally it is experienced only by accomplished meditators. The Kalachakra Initiation provides the empowerment for binding together the winds of the left and right channels into the central channel.

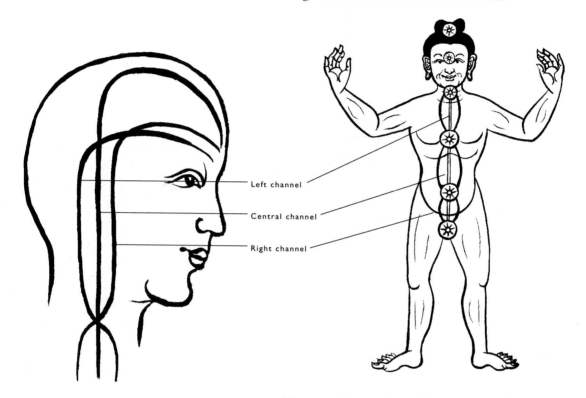

Left channel

Central channel

Right channel

The left, right, and central channels of the body. The goal of the Kalachakra practitioner is to bind together the winds of the left and right channels into the central channel, thereby stilling the ever-changing mind.

The practitioner who achieves control of the ever-moving winds inside the body, and especially the subtle winds, can still the ever-changing mind. But until that time, the winds act to agitate consciousness.

The axis and balance of the regenerative fluids are also influenced by the planetary movements. For instance, the red, female regenerative fluid, or blood, is influenced by the sun; the white, regenerative fluid of the male, or semen, is influenced by the moon.

the alternate kalachakra

When we speak of the alternate Kalachakra, we are referring to the stages of initiation, generation, and completion. The chapter in this book on the Kalachakra Initiation provides more detail about the first of these three stages.

The alternate Kalachakra is the path of transformation. The initiation forms the basis for developing the actual practice. During the generation stage, the practitioner develops a clear visualization of himself or herself as the deity Kalachakra, including his abode, the Kalachakra Mandala. This can only be done sketchily at first, but the meditator continues until he or she is able to maintain a precise visualization of the entire mandala with all its details in a space the size of a pea, for as long as desired.

The generation stage, in turn, provides the basis for the completion stage. Once the meditator can maintain the self-visualization as the deity in the mandala, he or she employs advanced techniques to actualize the visualization. This requires manipulation of the physiological processes, including control of the winds and the endocrine system. The realization of the state of mind produced by this practice is not yet the end of the path; it is but the first of twelve stages leading to the ultimate goal of enlightenment, or Buddhahood.

It is clear why the Kalachakra is among the highest levels of tantra, requiring dedicated practice based on firm motivation. This is why the Dalai Lama says that before we can bring about world peace, we must work to attain our own inner peace, always motivated by the desire to benefit all sentient beings. We must go beyond the illusion that we are each a single entity at the mercy of powerful physical forces. The Kalachakra Tantra makes it clear that attaining enlightenment affects not only our inner being but our bodies, the stars, and ultimately, our entire cosmos as well. We are all an integral part of the interrelated universe, the Mandala of Kalachakra. Our very survival depends on our awakening to this truth.

Transformation

of

Consciousness

"IN THE SEVENTEEN YEARS I've been here," said Dr. Malcolm Arth, director of the Department of Education of the American Museum of Natural History, of the Kalachakra Sand Mandala exhibition and demonstration, "I don't think I've ever experienced this combination of quiet and intensity among the public. The average museum visitor spends about ten seconds before a work of art, but for *this* exhibit, time is measured in minutes, sometimes *hours*. Even the youngsters, who come into the

Namgyal monk Lobsang Samten helps a child try her hand at sand painting at the American Museum of Natural History. New York City, 1988.

245

museum and run around as if it were a playground—these same youngsters walk into this space, and something happens to them. They're transformed."

Even the Dalai Lama has asked why people who are not Buddhist practitioners have such a strong response to the experience of seeing the Kalachakra Sand Mandala. After all, here is an aspect of one of the most advanced, most complex of all the Indo-Tibetan Buddhist tantras, a tradition that is bafflingly "foreign" to most Westerners and extremely difficult to understand even for longtime Buddhist students. Yet thousands of people every day would wander in from the hot summer sun and become transfixed, speaking only in whispers if at all, for long periods of time.

The reactions of the museum visitors demonstrated that something was being communicated. One man noticed, "You do feel calm—I mean *everybody*. Nobody's talking loud. There's no screaming and yelling. The kids are behaving themselves. It's amazing." Another said, "It has a very peaceful, very calming, and very centering impact on me, especially if I've come from the subway. To come here makes my day."

The real impact of the exhibition seemed to come from the first-hand experience of observing the extremely intense concentration of the monks at work. People were most impressed by the meditative focus they maintained as they applied the sand through the funnels. One man, who likened their work to pastry decoration, was, like many others, impressed at how they could work undisturbed with so many people moving around them and asking questions.

Perhaps some of the bystanders were able to sense the grace and ease in the monks' use of their bodies—the careful positioning of their elbows, the way in which their hands and wrists were held—that expresses the inner calm of their contemplative focus. But most of the onlookers were not consciously aware of the monks' arduous preparation through years of meditation and prayers for the purification of their motivation.

A Namgyal monk in deep concentration.

transformation of consciousness

What is it that makes the Kalachakra Sand Mandala, a highly refined and esoteric ritual art form, so powerful a vehicle for communicating with contemporary Westerners? The training the monks receive is not merely drawing lessons, nor is their meditation only the kind that clears and pacifies the mind. Their mental activity is focused on developing their altruistic intention to be of benefit to all sentient beings. They generate this in their prayers at the beginning of the day, and it continues like the steady hum of a generator.

This causes an almost electric kind of energy to pervade the room. What surprised the Dalai Lama, museum administrators, and the media was the discernible effect of this force on a random Western audience in a secular setting.

Through the careful, mindful way in which he uses his body; through the continuous monitoring of the content of his speech and mind; and through meticulous attention to every detail of the iconography, the ritual artist becomes a selfless conduit for that which is so much larger than himself. And when these artisan monks construct the canonically specific images of the sand mandala or other ritual art forms, they inevitably meditate on their symbolic meanings, which thus have the potential to become an integral part of their beings. This heightened attention to detail and awareness of implicit meaning is repeated over and over again wherever Buddhists practice ritual art, whether for a Tibetan religious ceremony or in an American museum.

Attention to detail is critical throughout the entire construction of the sand mandala. If the artists are off by even a fraction of an inch, the whole mandala will reflect this, so an attempt at perfection must be made from the very beginning of the laborious process. Inevitably the monks are at the same time contemplating, both individually and in their conversation as a group, the philosophical significance of every detail, color, and placement. There is a vast, complex logic inherent in the design of the Kalachakra Sand Mandala, and the monks

A monk practices the ritual art of making *torma* offerings.

247

develop an understanding of its meaning over many years, both conceptually and experientially, in the act of constructing it. Each time they participate in a sand mandala they are expanding their knowledge of the tantra as well as their peace of mind.

If we make a mistake while painting in oil or gouache, we can simply paint over it. Of course there are ways of correcting some of the mistakes possible in a sand painting, but the sand is as delicate and fragile a material as could be worked with, and even a slight deviation can cause damage difficult to correct. As in all things, the monks themselves differ in their ability to do sand painting. There are some who draw or apply sand with exceptional grace, which is not only a reflection of their training but also of their state of mind.

By learning to focus on that which is beneficial to others as an integral part of the ritual, the monks enter into a state of union with the deity. Western athletes, whose performance is dependent on deep concentration, refer to such a state as "entering the zone." This is also what is meant by "the dancer becomes the dance." The intense degree of training and physical preparedness required of their discipline brings them to a level of consciousness where they are no longer distracted by personal preoccupations but are instead completely prepared for spontaneous and appropriate action.

The difference, however, between the Western athlete or dancer and the Tibetan ritual artist is in the motivation. Instead of doing his best in order to gain praise or win a competition, the ritual artist is motivated to make a perfect sand mandala as a means of achieving liberation from suffering for all sentient beings.

the art of simply being present

The curious analogy that can be made between ritual artists and athletes is evident in that both are completely compelling to behold in action. What accounts for this magnetism is their total lack of self-consciousness, something we rarely see in our society. When we see someone who is fully engaged in what he or she is doing, without falseness, without scattered or needless activity, and without preoccupation with appearance, we respond to it.

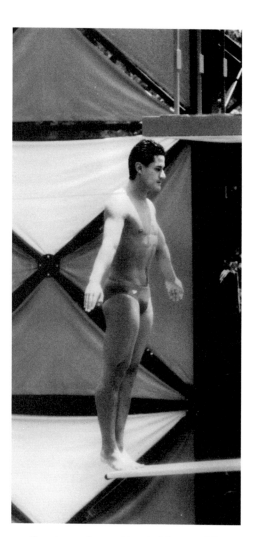

Greg Louganis: an athlete in "the zone." He visualizes the perfect dive before executing it.

In Zen terminology this is called "being present." It is the kind of attunement that always coexists with a heightened state of attention and that has been, for millennia, consciously developed in the ritual arts of cultures throughout the world.

"The dancer becomes the dance." Laura Dean Musicians and Dancers in performance.

Another way of speaking about it is as a state of surrender. One gives oneself over; one is totally there. This is an experience that can be found equally in the person who is creating the art or the performance and in the person who is viewing, hearing, or receiving it. Children as well as adults noticeably surrendered themselves to the experience of the sand mandala in the museum, foreign as it might have been to them.

Passersby watch the dismantling of the Kalachakra Sand Mandala at the IBM Gallery. New York City, 1991.

a lesson in impermanence

With all the hard work and intensity of focus devoted to the construction of the Kalachakra Sand Mandala during its presentation as a cultural offering at the various institutions, Western viewers expected to share in some expression of celebration as the work came to completion. Instead, there was none; the monks were visibly unmoved. This is because the completion of this spectacular mandala is not thought to be the end at all, but only one part of the larger ritual and only one step toward attaining the enlightened state of mind. It is important to note that the same degree of focus and mindfulness exhibited in the construction of the mandala is demonstrated in its dismantling process.

The tradition of the Kalachakra Sand Mandala continues as the sand is poured into the waters of Santa Monica Bay. Los Angeles, 1989.

Significantly, each time the mandala was swept up, regardless of how methodically or ritualistically this was done, Western onlookers reacted strongly, in many cases with great emotion. Many viewed the act not as a dismantling but rather as a destruction. What transpired was most unexpected, almost inconceivable, to the mind-set of our culture, which places such value on possession. The lesson we came away with—some of us less with the wisdom of understanding, perhaps, than with the shock of disbelief—was the Buddhist view of the impermanence of all phenomena. As the monks said,

"Just as foreign as it is to you to think of not preserving the sand mandala, so it is equally unthinkable to us to keep it. The best way of preserving this tradition is to dismantle it and come again to make another one."

The ritual art in its sacred context is unconcerned with "product," as it is always a part of the much larger ritual. In this case, the sand mandala is constructed primarily as the vehicle through which the ritual master confers the empowerment of the tantra to the student. Once this has been accomplished, it has fulfilled its function. Just as the deities were initially invoked into the sand mandala for the purpose of conferring the initiation, so at its conclusion the ritual master thanks them and requests that they return to their sacred home. Thus the deities are removed from the sand mandala, and the sand is swept up and poured into the local waters.

the heart of the matter

At the center of the process is the motivation of altruism. With this intention, the artist meditates on attachment to understand that the things we cling to are impermanent, and none is more insubstantial than the "I" which does the clinging. But the lesson conveyed is actually greater than that of impermanence. The idea of possessing any of the ritual arts, and holding on to either their form or the accomplishment derived from them, defeats the purpose. Rather, the emphasis is placed on perfecting the mind of the practitioner, who generates in himself or herself the body, speech, mind, and wisdom consciousness of the deity. With this as the objective, the idea of permanence in ritual art is as inconceivable as not wanting happiness.

It all depends on our point of view. If we see Buddhist ritual arts in the context of their sacred meaning, then we see them as an integral part of the ritual, which is itself part of the realization of the goal of the enlightened state of mind. But by trying to decipher their meaning through the context of those plastic arts whose intention is to express the artist's inspiration, and which have a beginning (creation) and an end (exhibition, presentation, demonstration, and even sale), we attach a very different meaning. If one is accustomed to preserving a work of art, or seeking material value for it, then of course the idea of creating art as part of a ritual for the sake of the benefit of others would seem foreign indeed. In that case, it would be logical to see the objective of the ritual arts as a lesson in impermanence, and a divergence from the context of possession, which implies attachment.

In fact, the monks object to the phrase "creating the sand mandala," because they claim that they are "constructing" it strictly according to the text. They cannot "create" that which already exists.

At the completion of the ritual, the artist goes a step further by offering any merit he or she has accumulated as a result of this activity to the benefit of others. This act of altruism serves to further the goal of nonattachment, since possessing the fruits of his or her action can also serve as an obstacle to attaining the goal of realizing Buddha mind. More than impermanence, it is a lesson in nonattachment. For the nonpractitioner, it is letting go of the beauty and material value of the object; for the practitioner, it is letting go of the accumulation of merit, joy, and bliss consciousness for the benefit of others.

product vs. process

There is a parallel here to what young children go through as they learn to hold a pencil and write their name or draw. At the end of the day, the child often comes home euphoric from this wonderful learning experience and shows his parents what he has done. Proud of the child, his parents put the work up on the kitchen wall as if to say to the neighbors and to the world, "My child has accomplished this." But this emphasis can easily be misunderstood by the child. What is fundamentally important to his development is not what he brings home, or even the approval of his parents, but what happened inside him during the learning process. The parents' kindhearted attempts to acknowledge the child appears to place value only on the tangible evidence of achievement.

In our product-oriented culture, part of us tends to get suppressed: that of the creative process itself. Children begin to feel they are loved for what they produce rather than for who they are, and who they are in reality is an ongoing process of learning and growing. They come to understand unconsciously that they have to create something that conforms to an external arbitrary standard, and

Young monks practicing a Kalachakra dance at Gomang Tashi Kyil Monastery in eastern Tibet, 1987.

within given time limits, rather than at their own natural pace. Intuitive knowledge gets repressed and often lost. They learn to compete with the other children in the class rather than to explore and appreciate their creative potential and to enjoy the excitement of the learning experience.

The children who come to the museum become transfixed watching the monks and the entire painstaking, unhurried process, and they leave with a sense of having experienced something beyond the day-to-day activity of their circumscribed worlds.

a transformation of values

The answer to the question of why people have been so drawn to the silent observation of a seemingly uneventful spectacle such as the construction of a sand mandala is perhaps that each one of us intuitively recognizes the importance of our own internal process. The sand mandala reminds us of something almost lost in our society: It is not only the intrinsic beauty of the piece that holds us, or the opportunity to assist in the preservation of an ancient living tradition, or even to marvel at the physical dexterity and perfection of mind required of the artist—though these are rare enough in today's mechanized world. What we are reminded of most forcefully, as we come into this space, is the depth and capability of the human mind.

The Dalai Lama agrees with the neuroscientists that we are probably using only one percent of our mental capacity. Tibetan Buddhism, through centuries of the most rigorous study, has learned to harness the power of concentration. Its exotic and mysterious rituals are all based on one all-encompassing "secret"—that the union of wisdom and compassion is the key to the attainment of great bliss. Now we have discovered that, if a handful of monks demonstrate a work of art based on the sincere motivation of compassion for others, even people stepping in from the teeming streets of New York or the freeways of Los Angeles will respond to that which resonates from deep inside us all.

Afterword

THE PRESENTATION of the material in this book is quite revolutionary. Secrets that are centuries old are not only revealed to a mass audience but also translated and interpreted so that their very esoteric concepts and terminology can be widely understood. Traditionally in Tibet, such material was read only by devoted scholars for the purpose of becoming enlightened. But today, the Earth is getting smaller and our cultural mixture is expanding. In this globalization of knowledge and wisdom, Kalachakra, like other Indo-Tibetan tantras, is finding its place. It is my hope that this book will add to its compassionate message, and to the Dalai Lama's statement that Kalachakra is a vehicle for world peace.

I asked the Dalai Lama if he could suggest a simple meditation for those readers who have never been exposed to Buddhist practice before. He said, "Just for a moment, concentrate on the infinite, deep blue sky. When we look at something like a table, our consciousness just stops on it. But when we look at deep space, there is nothing to stop our mind. Then, eventually, the mind automatically withdraws. The mind itself goes deep inside, stopping all thought and restlessness. Meditation is refreshment of the mind. Just breathe, and look at the sky."

I request the forgiveness of Kalachakra, the masters of the lineage, and the reader for any mistakes in this book. May any merit gained from this work be offered for the benefit of all beings.

Opposite: The stupa adjacent to the bodhi tree at the site of the Buddha's enlightenment at Bodhgaya, India. The Dalai Lama says that just as people are blessed by visiting such a place, so too is the power of the place increased by their presence. But he also reminds us that "the actual stupa exists in the heart center in each of us."

Picture Credits

THE FOLLOWING BLACK AND WHITE images have been reprinted with permission.

Front Matter

Pages ii–iii, *King Songsten Gampo and two wives.* Photo/copyright: Samaya Foundation. Courtesy Mokotoff Asian Arts Gallery, New York; vi–vii *Dalai Lama applies first sand.* Photo/copyright: John Bigelow Taylor/ Tibet Center.

Introduction

Pages xvi, *Monks at prayer, Bodhgaya.* Photo/copyright: John C. Smart; 3, *Lay people at Bodhgaya.* Photo/copyright: Moke Mokotoff. Courtesy Mokotoff Asian Arts Gallery, New York; 4, *Monk prostrating.* Photo/copyright: Moke Mokotoff. Courtesy Mokotoff Asian Arts Gallery, New York.; 5, *Monk with chakpu, Kalachakra Mandala (detail).* Photo/copyright: Ernst Haas. Courtesy Ernst Haas Studio, New York.; 7, *Bodhgaya crowds.* Photo/copyright: John C. Smart.

The Path of Kalachakra

Pages 8–9, *Kalachakra Mandala, Peking, 1932.* Photo: Basil Crump. Courtesy/copyright: Jacques Marchais Center of Tibetan Art, Staten Island, New York; 12, (left) *Avalokiteshvara.* Photo: Armen. Courtesy/copyright: Newark Museum, anonymous gift, 1981; 12, (right) *Vajrapani.* Photo: Armen. Courtesy/copyright: Newark Museum, gift Doris Weiner, 1969; 10, (both) *Manjusri.* Photo: Stephen Germany. Courtesy/copyright: Newark Museum bequest Estate of Eleanor Olsen, 1982; 15, *Kalachakra.* Photo: Jim Coxe, neg. no. 336754. Courtesy/copyright: Department of Library Services, American Museum of Natural History, New York; 16, (left) *Power of Ten.* Copyright: Kalachakra Program, Deer Park, 1981, David Patt, editor. Courtesy Deer Park, Oregon, Wisconsin; 16, (right) *Mani stone.* Courtesy/copyright: Newark Museum, Carter D. Holton Collection, 1936; 17,

Kalachakra mantra. Copyright: Kalachakra Program, Deer Park, 1981, David Patt, editor. Courtesy Deer Park, Oregon, Wisconsin; 19, *Shakyamuni Buddha, Tibet.* Photo/copyright: John Ford. Courtesy Berthe and John Ford Collection; 22, *Raktayamari Mandala.* Photo/copyright: John Bigelow Taylor. Courtesy Zimmerman Family Collection; 23, *Sand mandala, Tibet, 1937.* Photo: Cutting. Courtesy/copyright: Newark Museum, C. Suydam Cutting Collection.

The Sand Mandala as a Cultural Offering

Pages 26–27, *People viewing mandala at American Museum.* Photo: Gregory Durgin. Copyright: Samaya Foundation/Namgyal Monastery; 29, *Lobsang Samten/Guhyasamaja Mandala.* Photo: Barry Bryant. Copyright: Samaya Foundation/Namgyal Monastery; 30, (left) *Thekpu sketch.* Drawing: Gregory Durgin. Copyright: Samaya Foundation; 30, (center) *Thekpu structural schema.* Drawing: Stanley C. Bryant. Copyright: Samaya Foundation; 30, (right) *Detail of thekpu/brocades.* Photo: Barry Bryant. Copyright: Samaya Foundation/Namgyal Monastery; 31, (left) *Phuntsok Dorje painting thekpu.* Photo: Gregory Durgin. Copyright: Samaya Foundation; 31, (right) *Thekpu.* Photo: Barry Bryant. Copyright: Samaya Foundation; 32, *Monks praying, American Museum.* Photo: Barry Bryant. Copyright: Samaya Foundation/Namgyal Monastery; 33, (left) *People viewing completed mandala.* Photo: Gregory Durgin. Copyright: Samaya Foundation/Namgyal Monastery; 33, (right) *Viewing mandala on monitor.* Photo: Barry Bryant. Copyright: Samaya Foundation/Namgyal Monastery; 34, *Procession to river.* Photo: Warner Bryant Scheyer. Copyright: Samaya Foundation; 35, *Monks praying on beach at Santa Monica Bay.* Photo: Don Farber. Copyright: Samaya Foundation; 37, *Kalachakra Fire Offering Mandala with John Denver.* Photo: Gregory Durgin. Copyright: Samaya Foundation/Namgyal Monastery.

The Life of The Buddha

Pages 38–39, *Maya's Dream.* Courtesy/copyright: Asian Art Museum of San Francisco, Avery Brundage Collection; 40, *Birth of Buddha.* Courtesy/copyright: Newark Museum, gift Heerameneck

Galleries, 1965; 41, *Infant Buddha (detail)*. Photo: Joseph Szaszfai. Courtesy/copyright: Yale University Art Gallery, gift Paul F. Walter; 42, *Education of Prince Siddhartha*. Courtesy/copyright: R.M.N.–Musée National des Arts Asiatiques–Guimet, Paris; 43, *The Four Encounters of Prince Siddhartha*. Courtesy/copyright: R.M.N.–Musée National des Arts Asiatiques–Guimet, Paris; 44, *Palace Scenes: Prince Siddhartha and Yasodhara Enthroned*. Courtesy/copyright: Seattle Art Museum, Eugene Fuller Memorial Collection, 39.34; 45, (top) *Scenes From the Life of the Buddha*. Courtesy/copyright: Los Angeles County Museum of Art, gift Ahmanson Foundation; 45, (bottom) *The Departure and Buddha's Temptation by Mara and His Daughters*. Courtesy/copyright: Metropolitan Museum of Art, Fletcher Fund, 1928; 46, *Ascetic Shakyamuni*. Courtesy/copyright: Mr. and Mrs. James W. Alsdorf, Chicago; 47, *Buddha Attacked by the Evil Forces of Mara*. Courtesy/copyright: Cleveland Museum of Art, purchase from the J.H. Wade Fund, 71.18; 48, *Shakyamuni Buddha*. Photo/copyright: John Bigelow Taylor/Tibet Center. Courtesy Zimmerman Family Collection; 51, *Buddha Teaching*. Photo: Blakeslee-Lane. Courtesy/copyright: Berthe and John Ford Collection; 52, *Stupa at Sarnath*. Photo: Barry Bryant. Copyright: Samaya Foundation; 57, *Paranirvana*. Photo: Otto E. Nelson. Courtesy/copyright: Mary and Jackson Burke Collection.

The Early History of Kalachakra

Pages 58–59, *3-D Palace of Kalachakra*. Photo/copyright: Robin Bath; 60, *King of Shambala*. Courtesy/copyright: Newark Museum, bequest Elizabeth P. Martin, 1976; 61, *Miniature stupa*. Courtesy/copyright: Newark Museum, Crane Collection, 1911; 62, (left) *Cosmic Mt. Meru*. Courtesy/copyright: Zimmerman Family Collection; 62, (right) *Cosmic Mt. Meru schema*. Drawing: Barry Bryant. Copyright: Samaya Foundation; 64, *Vajrapani*. Courtesy/copyright: Newark Museum, purchase 1977 Mr. C. Suydam Cutting Bequest Fund; 66, *Mandala of Shambala, Tibet*. Courtesy/copyright: R.M.N.–Musée National des Arts Asiatiques–Guimet, Paris, 92EN3902 (MA1041); 70, *The Kingdom of Shambala (detail)*. Courtesy/copyright: R.M.N.–Musée National des Arts Asiatiques–Guimet, Paris; 73, *Mahasiddha.* Courtesy/copyright: Robert Hatfield Elsworth Private Collection; 74, *Virupa, Naropa, Saraha and Dombi Heruka (detail).* Courtesy/copyright: Museum of Fine Arts, Boston, gift John Goelet, C46-316; 75, *Nalanda University.* Photo/copyright: Sean Jones. Courtesy Tibet Image Bank, London.

Kalachakra Comes to Tibet

Pages 76–77, *Padma Sambhava (detail).* Photo: Logan, neg. no. 333391. Courtesy/copyright: Department of Library Services, American Museum of Natural History; 78, *Tara with Throne and Prabhamandala.* Courtesy/copyright: Newark Museum, Sheldon Collection, 1920; 79, *King Songsten Gampo and two wives.* Photo/copyright: Samaya Foundation. Courtesy Mokotoff Asian Arts Gallery, New York; 80, (left) *Jowo Buddha.* Photo/copyright: Tamara W. Hill, 82:20.2; 80, (right) *Jokhang Temple roof.* Photo/copyright: Valrae Reynolds. Courtesy Newark Museum; 81, *Map of Tibet, 1872.* Photo/copyright: Samaya Foundation. Courtesy Office of Tibet, New York; 82, *Samye Monastery.* Courtesy/copyright: Newark Museum, Sheldon Collection, 1920, 20.271; 83, *Three great religious kings of Tibet.* Photo: Barry Bryant. Copyright: Samaya Foundation, 84, *Milarepa.* Photo: Armen. Courtesy/copyright: Newark Museum, purchase 1975 Anderson Bequest Fund, 75.94; 85, (both) *Kalachakra.* Photo: Armen. Courtesy/copyright: Newark Museum, purchase 1976 Members, Membership Endowment, Bedminster, Inc., Samuel C. Miller and Andrew Sponer Funds, Mary Livingston Griggs and Mary Griggs Burk Foundation; 86, *Buton.* Courtesy/copyright: Asian Art Museum of San Francisco, Avery Brundage Collection; 87, *Tsong Khapa.* Courtesy/copyright: Newark Museum, purchase 1920 Sheldon Collection, 20.270; 88, *Ganden Monastery, 1932.* Photo/copyright: Hugh Richardson. Courtesy British Museum, Tibet Image Bank, London; 89, *Ganden Monastery, 1981.* Photo/copyright: Stone Roots. Courtesy Tibet Image Bank, London.

The Dalai Lamas and Namgyal Monastery

Pages 90–91, *Lhamo Lhatso.* Photo/copyright: Philippe Goldin; 92, *Shadakshari Avalokiteshvara.* Photo/copyright: Moke Mokotoff. Courtesy Mokotoff Asian Arts Gallery, New York; 94, *Dalai Lama (Third, Gyalwa Sonam Gyatso).* Courtesy/copyright: Robert Hatfield Elsworth Private Collection; 96, *Namgyalma.* Photo: Barry Bryant. Copyright: Samaya Foundation; 97, *Dalai Lama (Fifth, Gyalwa Ngawang Lobsang Gyatso).* Photo/copyright: John Taylor. Courtesy Rose Art Museum, Brandeis University, Waltham, Massachusetts, gift N. and L. Horch to the Riverside Museum Collection; 98, *Panchen Lama (First).* Courtesy/copyright: Newark Museum; 99, *Potala Palace.* Courtesy/copyright: Newark Museum; 100, *Penden Lhamo.* Photo/copyright: Moke Mokotoff. Courtesy Mokotoff Asian Arts Gallery, New York; 101, *Dalai Lama (Seventh, Gyalwa Kalsang Gyatso).* Courtesy/copyright: Newark Museum, purchase 1920 Sheldon Collection; 103, *Dalai Lama (Thirteenth, Gyalwa Thubten Gyatso).* Photo: Th. Paar Studio. Courtesy/copyright: Newark Museum, gift C. Suydam Cutting, 1935; 104, *Kalachakra Temple, St. Petersburg.* Photo: Mikhail Khusidman. Copyright: Samaya Foundation; 105, *Norbulingka.* Photo: Cutting. Courtesy/copyright: Newark Museum; 106, *Dalai Lama (Fourteenth, Tenzin Gyatso), 1940.* Painting: Kanwal Krishna. Photo: Armen. Courtesy/copyright: Newark Museum, gift Mrs. C. Suydam Cutting; 107, *Dalai Lama (Fourteenth, Tenzin Gyatso), 1950.* Photo: AP/Wide World Photos; 108, (top) *Dalai Lama and Mao Tse-tung, 1954.* Photo: AP/Wide World Photos; 108, (bottom) *Ling Rinpoche.* Photo/copyright: Ernst Haas. Courtesy Ernst Haas Studio; 109, *Dalai Lama journey to exile in India.* Photo: AP/Wide World Photos; 111, *Thekchen Choling.* Photo/copyright: Namgyal Monastery; 113, *Kalu Rinpoche.* Photo: Barry Bryant. Copyright: Samaya Foundation; 115, *Dalai Lama with children.* Photo: Gregory Durgin. Copyright: Samaya Foundation; 116, *Namgyal monks debating.* Photo/copyright: Bill Warren; 117, *Dalai Lama, Noble Peace Prize.* Photo: Gregory Durgin. Copyright: Samaya Foundation.

Tibetan Buddhist Philosophy

Pages 118–119, *Teaching mudra.* Photo/copyright: Ernst Haas. Courtesy Ernst Haas Studio; 120, *Avalokiteshvara (1000 arms).* Courtesy/copyright: Zimmerman Family Collection; 122, *Shakyamuni Buddha teaching.* Courtesy/copyright: Mr. and Mrs. James W. Alsdorf, Chicago; 126, *Wheel of Transmigration.* Photo: A. Rota, neg. no. 323100. Courtesy/copyright: Department of Library Services, American Museum of Natural History; 129, *Monks at bodhi tree, 1973.* Photo/copyright: John C. Smart; 130, *Dalai Lama teaching, 1985.* Photo: Barry Bryant. Copyright: Samaya Foundation.

The Kalachakra Initiation

Pages 132–133, *Monks performing a celebratory dance, 1991.* Photo/copyright: John Bigelow Taylor/Tibet Center; 134, *Kalachakra dance, 1981.* Photo/copyright: Marcia Keegan; 135, *Torma.* Photo: Gregory Durgin. Copyright: Samaya Foundation; 136, (left) *Tooth stick.* Photo/copyright: Kim Yeshi. Courtesy Department of Religions and Culture, Central Tibetan Administration of H.H. Dalai Lama, previously published in *Cho-Yang;* 136, (right) *Requesting initiation.* Photo/copyright: Lawrence Lauterborn; 137, (left) *Six energy centers.* Drawing/copyright: Phuntsok Dorje; 137, (right) *Purbas.* Photo: Gregory Durgin. Copyright: Samaya Foundation; 138, (top) *Vase consecration.* Photo/copyright: John Bigelow Taylor/Tibet Center; 138, (center) *Chalk string consecration.* Photo/copyright: John Bigelow Taylor/Tibet Center; 138, (bottom) *Vajra and bell consecration.* Photo/copyright: John Bigelow Taylor/Tibet Center; 139, (top) *Snapping chalk strings.* Photo/copyright: John Bigelow Taylor/Tibet Center; 139, (bottom) *Monks drawing Kalachakra Mandala.* Photo/copyright: Carlos Gonzalez/Thubten Dhargye Ling; 140, (left) *Vajra Vega.* Photo/copyright: Ernst Haas. Courtesy Ernst Haas Studio; 140, (right) *Dalai Lama as vajra master dancing.* Photo/copyright: John Bigelow Taylor/Tibet Center; 141, *Grains of wheat on mandala drawing.* Photo/copyright: John Bigelow Taylor/Tibet Center; 142, (top) *Dalai Lama holding five wisdom strings.* Photo/copyright: John Bigelow Taylor/Tibet Center; 142, (center) *Monks holding wisdom strings.* Photo/copyright: John Bigelow Taylor/Tibet Center; 142, (bottom) *Dalai Lama applies first sand.* Photo/copyright: John Bigelow Taylor/Tibet Center; 143, *Dalai Lama string at heart center.* Photo/copyright: John Bigelow Taylor/Tibet Center; 144, (top) *Monks seated painting mandala.* Photo: Gregory Durgin. Copyright: Samaya Foundation/Namgyal Monastery; 144, (bottom) *Monks standing painting mandala.* Photo/copyright: John Bigelow Taylor/Tibet Center; 145 and 147, *Offering mandala mudra.* Photo: Gregory Durgin. Copyright: Samaya Foundation; 146, *Dalai Lama (Fourteenth, Tenzin Gyatso) as vajra master, 1973.* Photo/copyright: John C. Smart; 149, *Kusha grass.* Photo/copyright: Moke Mokotoff. Courtesy Mokotoff Asian Arts Gallery, New York; 150, *Students wearing costumes of Kalachakra.* Photo/copyright: Lawrence Lauterborn; 151, *Students with blindfolds.* Photo/copyright: John Bigelow Taylor/Tibet Center; 152, *Students with flowers on foreheads.* Photo/copyright: Ernst Haas. Courtesy Ernst Haas Studio; 155, *Kalachakra/Vishvamata (implements).* Drawing/copyright: Sidney Piburn; 158, 160 (both), 161, 162, 163, and 164, *Initiation substances.* Drawings/copyright: Phuntsok Dorje; 165, *Wheel of the Law.* Courtesy/copyright: Newark Museum, Crane Collection, 1911; 166, *Vajrasattva.* Courtesy/copyright: Newark Museum, purchase 1984 Willard W. Kelsey Bequest Fund; 167, *Rice offering mandala.* Photo/copyright: Ernst Haas. Courtesy Ernst Haas Studio; 168, *Students on line at Leh, Ladakh for blessings.* Photo/copyright: Moke Mokotoff. Courtesy Mokotoff Asian Arts Gallery, New York; 169, *Dalai Lama meditates, 1973.* Photo/copyright: Ernst Haas. Courtesy Ernst Haas Studio; 170, (top) *Dalai Lama removes deities from Kalachakra Sand Mandala.* Photo/copyright: John Bigelow Taylor/Tibet Center; 170, (bottom) *Dalai Lama cuts mandala's energy.* Photo/copyright: Don Farber/Thubten Dhargye Ling; 171, (both) *Sweeping up the mandala.* Photo/copyright: John Bigelow Taylor/Tibet Center; 172, *Dalai Lama prays at Hudson River.* Photo/copyright: Lawrence Lauterborn/Tibet Center; 173, (top) *Dalai Lama pours sand into river, Switzerland.* Photo: Barry Bryant. Copyright: Samaya Foundation; 173, (bottom) *Dalai Lama pours sand into Santa Monica Bay.* Photo/copyright: Don Farber/Thubten Dhargye

Ling; 174, *Dalai Lama pours water on mandala base.* Photo/copyright: Lawrence Lauterborn/Tibet Center; 175, (right) *Monks scrub off mandala lines.* Photo/copyright: John Bigelow Taylor/Tibet Center; 175, (left) *Dalai Lama sitting on mandala base.* Photo/copyright: John Bigelow Taylor/Tibet Center.

The Kalachakra Sand Mandala

Pages 176–177, *Monk applying sand/chakpu.* Photo: Barry Bryant. Copyright: Samaya Foundation/Namgyal Monastery; 178, *Deities represented by dots and syllables.* Photo: Barry Bryant. Copyright: Samaya Foundation/Namgyal Monastery; 179, *Elevation 3-D Kalachakra palace.* Auto-cad drawing: Daniel Maciejczyk/Barry Bryant under direction of Christian Lischewski, Associate Professor Pratt School of Architecture. Computer facility courtesy Perkins + Will. Copyright: Samaya Foundation; 180, *Six circles of mandala.* Photo: Gregory Durgin. Copyright: Samaya Foundation/Namgyal Monastery; 182, *Prajnaparamita text.* Newark Museum, Sheldon Collection, 1920. 183, 184, 185, 186, 187, 188, 189, 190, and 191, *Step-by-step drawings of the Kalachakra Mandala.* Auto-cad drawings: Daniel Maciejczyk/Barry Bryant under the direction of Christian Lischewski, Associate Professor Pratt School of Architecture. Computer facility courtesy Perkins + Will; 192, *Mandala gate.* Drawing: Stanley C. Bryant. Copyright: Samaya Foundation; 193, *Monks painting Mandala of Enlightened Mind.* Photo/copyright: John Bigelow Taylor/Tibet Center; 195, *Monk demonstrating chakpu.* Photo/copyright: Natural History Museum of Los Angeles County; 196, (left) *Monk demonstrating shinga.* Photo: Gregory Durgin. Copyright: Samaya Foundation/Namgyal Monastery; 196, (right) *Mandala class.* Photo: Gregory Durgin. Copyright: Samaya Foundation/Namgyal Monastery; 198, *Monk painting central lotus.* Photo/copyright: John Bigelow Taylor/Tibet Center; 199, *Cross section of center of lotus.* Drawing: Barry Bryant. Copyright: Samaya Foundation. 200, 201, 203, 205, 207, 209, 212, 213, 215, 216, 217, 219, 220, 221, 222, 223, 225, 226, and 227 *Details of Kalachakra Sand Mandala.* Photos: Gregory Durgin. Copyright: Samaya Foundation/Namgyal Monastery;

218, 3-D *Kalachakra Palace (detail)*. Photo/copyright: Robin Bath; 228 and 229, (top) *Dismantling, monks praying and removing deities*. Photo: Gregory Durgin. Copyright: Samaya Foundation/Namgyal Monastery; 229, *Sweeping up sand*. Photo: Warner Bryant Scheyer. Copyright: Samaya Foundation/Namgyal Monastery; 230, *Procession to river*. Photo: Warner Bryant Scheyer. Copyright: Samaya Foundation/Namgyal Monastery; 231, (both) *Monks praying at Hudson River and pouring sand into river*. Photos: Warner Bryant Scheyer. Copyright: Samaya Foundation/Namgyal Monastery.

World View According to Kalachakra

Pages 232–233, *Astrological calculations*. Photo: Rani Gill. Courtesy/copyright: Department of Religions and Culture, Central Tibetan Administration of H.H. Dalai Lama, previously printed in *Cho-Yan;*. 235, *Personal horoscope*. Photo/copyright: Samaya Foundation; 236 and 237, *Tibetan calendar*. Photo: Stephen Germany. Courtesy/copyright: Newark Museum, gift Carter D. Holton Collection, 1936; 238, *Steer (detail Kalachakra Mandala)*. Photo: Gregory Durgin. Copyright: Samaya Foundation/Namgyal Monastery; 239, *Cosmic Mt. Meru/astrological animals*. Photo: Barry Bryant. Copyright: Samaya Foundation; 240, *Sun and moon*. Photo: Gregory Durgin. Copyright: Samaya Foundation/Namgyal Monastery; 242, *Channels*. Drawings/copyright: Phuntsok Dorje.

Transformation of Consciousness

Pages 245–246, *Child painting with sand*. Photo: Barry Bryant. Copyright: Samaya Foundation/Namgyal Monastery; 246, *Monk contemplating*. Photo/copyright: John Bigelow Taylor/Tibet Center; 247, *Monk making torma*. Photo/copyright: Moke Mokotoff. Courtesy Mokotoff Asian Arts Gallery, New York; 248, *Greg Louganis*. Photo/copyright: Lonnie Majors; 249, *Laura Dean Musicians and Dancers*. Photo/copyright: Johan Elbers. Courtesy Laura Dean; 250, *Dismantling mandala at IBM Gallery*. Photo/copyright: John Bigelow Taylor/Tibet Center; 251, *Pouring sand into Santa Monica Bay*. Photo: Don Farber. Copyright: Samaya Foundation/Namgyal Monastery;

254, *Monks practicing the Kalachakra ritual dance.* Photo/copyright: Robyn Brenano.

Afterword

Page 256, *Bodhgaya stupa.* Photo: Barry Bryant. Copyright: Samaya Foundation.

Book Cover

Kalachakra Sand Mandala. Photo: Samaya Foundation. Copyright: Samaya Foundation/Namgyal Monastery. Back flap. *Dalai Lama and Barry Bryant, Los Angeles, 1989.* Photo/copyright: Natural History Museum of Los Angeles County.

Selected Bibliography

Avedon, John. *In Exile from the Land of Snows.* New York: Alfred A. Knopf, 1984.

Bechert, Heintz and Gombrich, Richard, (eds). *The World of Buddhism.* New York: Facts on File, 1984.

Bernbaum, Edwin Marshall. "The Mythic Journey and Its Symbolism: A Study of the Development of Buddhist Guidebooks to Shambhala in Relation to their Antecedents." Ph.D. dissertation, University of California, Berkeley, 1985.

————. *The Way to Shambhala.* Los Angeles: Jeremy P. Tarcher, Inc., 1980.

Bryant, Barry, and Yignyen, Tenzin. *Process of Initiation: The Indo-Tibetan Rite of Passage into Shambala: The Kalachakra Initiation.* New York: Samaya Foundation and Namgyal Monastery, 1990.

Cho Yog Thubten Jamyang. *Kalachakra Initiation, Los Angeles, 1989,* translated by Sharpa Tulku with David Patt, 2nd rev. ed. by Thubten Dhargye Ling. Oregon, Wisconsin: Deer Park Books, 1989.

Council for Religious and Cultural Affairs. *Cho-Yang.* Issues 1, 2, 3, and "Year of Tibet" edition (1986, 1987, 1991). Dharamsala, India.

Cozort, Daniel. *Highest Yoga Tantra.* Ithaca, NY: Snow Lion Publications, 1986.

Dhargyey, Geshe Ngawang. *A Commentary on the Kalachakra Tantra.* Dharamsala, India: Library of Tibetan Works and Archives, 1985.

Dhondup, K. *Songs of the Sixth Dalai Lama.* Dharamsala, India: Library of Tibetan Works and Archives, 1981.

Gyatso, Tenzin (the Fourteenth Dalai Lama). *The Kalachakra Tantra.* Edited by Jeffrey Hopkins. London: Wisdom Publications, 1985.

————. *Kindness, Clarity and Insight.* Ithaca, NY: Snow Lion Publications, 1984.

————. *My Land and My People.* New York: Potala Publications, 1977.

————. *The Union of Bliss and Emptiness.* Ithaca, NY: Snow Lion Publications, 1988.

————. *Universal Responsibility and the Good Heart.* Dharamsala, India: Library of Tibetan Works and Archives, 1977.

Gyatso, Tenzin (the Fourteenth Dalai Lama), Khapa, Tsong, and Hopkins, Jeffrey. *Tantra in Tibet.* Ithaca, NY: Snow Lion Publications, 1977.

Hopkins, Jeffrey. *The Tantric Distinction, An Introduction to Tibetan Buddhism.* London: Wisdom Publications, 1984.

Kalu Rinpoche. *The Kalachakra Empowerment: Taught by the Venerable Kalu Rinpoche.* Vancouver, B.C.: Kagyu Kunkhyab Chuling, 1986.

Kalupahana, David and Indrani. *The Way of Siddhartha, A Life of the Buddha.* Boston: Shambhala Publications, 1982.

Kyabje Dorje Chang. *The Dharma That Illuminates All Beings Like the Light of the Sun and the Moon.* Albany: State University of New York Press, 1986.

Minke, Gisela. "The Kalachakra Initiation." *Tibet Journal,* vol. 2, nos. 3–4. Dharamsala, India: Library of Tibetan Works and Archives, 1972.

Mitchell, Robert Allen. *The Buddha: His Life Retold.* New York: Paragon House, 1989.

Mullin, Glenn H. *Selected Works of the Dalai Lama I.* Ithaca, NY: Snow Lion Publications, 1985.

————. *Selected Works of the Dalai Lama II.* Ithaca, NY: Snow Lion Publications, 1985.

————. *Selected Works of the Dalai Lama VII.* Ithaca, NY: Snow Lion Publications, 1985.

Newman, John Ronald. *The Outer Wheel of Time.* Ph. D. dissertation, 1987. UMI Dissertation Information Service, 1989.

Niwano, Nikkyo. *Shakyamuni Buddha: A Narrative Biography.* Tokyo: Kosei Publishing Co., 1969.

Olischak, Blanch Christine, with Wangyal, Geshe Thupten. *Mystic Art of Ancient Tibet.* New York: McGraw-Hill Publishing Company, 1973.

Pal, Pratapaditya. *Art of the Himalayas.* New York: Hudson Hill Press; American Federation of Arts, 1991.

———. *Art of Tibet.* Berkeley: Los Angeles County Museum of Art; University of California Press, 1988.

———. *Indian Sculpture Vols. 1–2.* Los Angeles: Los Angeles County Museum of Art; Berkeley: University of California Press, 1986.

———. *Light of Asia: Buddha Sakyamuni in Asian Art.* Los Angeles: Los Angeles County Museum of Art, 1984.

Reigle, David. "The Lost Kalachakra Mula Tantra on the Kings of Shambhala." *Kalachakra Research Publications,* no. 1. Talent, OR: Eastern School Press, 1986.

Reynolds, Valrae. *Tibet: A Lost World.* New York: American Federation of Arts, 1978.

Reynolds, Valrae, and Heller, Amy. *Introduction.* Vol. 1, 2nd ed., *The Newark Museum Tibetan Collection.* Newark, NJ: Newark Museum, 1983.

Reynolds, Valrae, Heller, Amy, and Gyatso, Janet. *Sculpture and Painting.* Vol. 3, 2nd ed., *The Newark Museum Tibetan Collection.* Newark, NJ: Newark Museum, 1986.

Rhie, Marylin, M., and Thurman, Robert A. F. *Wisdom and Compassion, The Sacred Art of Tibet.* San Francisco: Asian Art Museum of San Francisco; New York: Tibet House; New York: Harry N. Abrams, 1991.

Shakabpa, Tsepon W.D. *Tibet: A Political History.* New York: Potala Publications, 1984.

Smith, Huston. *The Religions of Man.* New York: Harper & Row, 1958.

Snellgrove, David. *Indo-Tibetan Buddhism.* Vols 1–2. Boston: Shambhala Publications, 1987.

Snellgrove, David, and Richardson, Hugh. *A Cultural History of Tibet.* Boston: Shambhala Publications, 1986.

Sopa, Geshe Lhundub, Jackson, Roger, and Newman, John. *The Wheel of Time: The Kalachakra in Context.* Oregon, WI: Deer Park Books, 1985.

Tharchin, Geshe Lobsang. *Offering of the Mandala.* Washington, D.C.: Mahayana Sutra and Tantric Center, 1981.

Thondup, Tulku. *Buddhist Civilization in Tibet.* Cambridge, MA: Maha Siddha Nyingmapa Center, 1982.

Trungpa, Chogyam. *Shambhala: The Sacred Path of the Warrior.* Boston: Shambhala Publications, 1988.

————. *The Rain of Wisdom.* Boston: Shambhala Publications, 1980.

Videotapes

The Kalachakra Initiation, Bodhgaya, India, Meridian Trust, 1974.

The Kalachakra Initiation, Bodhgaya, India, Samaya Foundation, 1985.

The Kalachakra Initiation, Los Angeles, California, Thubten Dhargye Ling, 1989.

The Kalachakra Initiation, Madison, Wisconsin, Educational Communications, 1981.

The Kalachakra Initiation, Vancouver, Canada, Samaya Foundation, 1986.